Kennedy's
New Latin Primer

SECOND EDITION

US VERSION

D1269557

ALSO FROM TIGER XENOPHON & TIGER OF THE STRIPE

From Latin to Italian
Charles H. Grandgent

**An Introduction to Greek and
Latin Palæography**
Sir Edward Maunde Thompson

A Greek Grammar
William W. Goodwin

Vulgar Latin
Charles H. Grandgent

**An Outline of the Phonology & Morphology
of Old Provençal**
Charles H. Grandgent

Grammaire Élémentaire de l'Ancien Français
Joseph Anglade

Grammar of the Gothic Language
Joseph Wright

A Middle High German Grammar
Joseph Wright

An Anglo-Saxon Primer
Henry Sweet

An Anglo-Saxon Reader
Henry Sweet

A Comparative Germanic Grammar
Eduard Prokosch

The Student's Dictionary of Anglo-Saxon
Henry Sweet

**The History of English Handwriting
A.D. 700–1400**
Sir Edward Maunde Thompson

KENNEDY'S NEW LATIN PRIMER

A SECOND EDITION EDITED BY

GERRISH GRAY

US VERSION

TIGER ☰ XENOPHON
APVD TIGRIDEM A.D. MMXIX
AB VRBE CONDITA MMDCCLXXII

TIGER XENOPHON
is an imprint of
TIGER OF THE STRIPE
50 Albert Road
Richmond
Surrey TW10 6DP
United Kingdom

First edition in this form published in
2008 by Tiger of the Stripe
Reissued with minor revisions 2009
Second edition 2019

ISBN 978-1-904799-71-9

https://www.tigerxenophon.com

https://tigerofthestripe.co.uk

Typeset in the United Kingdom by
Tiger of the Stripe

Table of Contents

Publisher's Foreword

THE BOOK USUALLY known as *Kennedy's Revised Latin Primer* has remained, with good reason, the pre-eminent Latin reference grammar in British schools for many decades. *Kennedy's New Latin Primer* from Tiger Xenophon was the first entirely new edition in two generations. This second edition builds on and refines the first edition. One glaring omission from the first edition was any discussion of why we should be learning Latin in the twenty-first century. I shall attempt to answer that question later in this foreword.

The sections on pronunciation were revised in the first Tiger Xenophon edition to reflect modern scholarship. Readers wishing to learn more about this subject – and particularly the fascinating detective work which allows us to know with reasonable accuracy how Latin was pronounced in the Classical period – are encouraged to consult W. Sidney Allen's *Vox Latina* (2nd edn, Cambridge University Press, 1978).

One of the most vexed questions facing the editors and publishers of modern Latin grammars is whether to spell consonantal **u** as **u** or **v**. James Morwood in his excellent *Latin Grammar* (Oxford University Press, 1999) rejoiced in producing 'the first Latin grammar in English to have banished the letter "v" from the Latin alphabet. It was never there.' It might be more accurate to say that Latin **u** was never there, but that **v** represented both the English vowel **u** and consonant **w**, *never* the sound of English **v**. Because there is a distinction in pronunciation, albeit a subtle one, we use **v** for the consonant in this edition. The only disadvantage is the danger that English-speaking students will be tempted to pronounce the consonant **v** in the English manner, as earlier generations learnt to do. All we can say is *don't!* A UK edition of this book is also available. It differs only in a few spellings and, more importantly, the order in which substantives, pronouns and adjectives are declined. It was Kennedy himself who popularized the order now used in the UK (nom., voc., acc., gen., dat., abl.). Anyone who was brought up with this order is likely to find it natural; unfortunately, anyone who was *not* is likely to find it very *un*natural. The result is another example of 'two nations divided by a common language,' which must be regretted, not least by publishers who have to cater for both preferences!

As well as thoroughly revising this second edition, we have reset the book in a different typeface – Juan Pablo del Peral's excellent Alegreya Sans. We have also taken the opportunity to delete the memorial lines on the gender of Latin substantives which are outmoded and unhelpful.

WHY LEARN LATIN? When I was at school a very long time ago, I was told that Latin would teach me to think logically. Even then this seemed an absurd claim. Natural languages (and even artificial languages) are not particularly logical; what logic natural languages appear to possess is often the result of grammarians (or native speakers/writers) trying to impose some order on natural linguistic chaos. To make matters worse, Roman grammarians based their ideas on the work of Greek grammarians, who quite naturally studied Greek rather than Latin. It is true, however, that the exercise of analyzing the syntax of sentences, i.e. 'parsing,' *does* require the application of some logic, tempered with an awareness that even the most highly-regarded authors often broke what we perceive to be the rules.

There are many other reason to learn Latin, not least so that we may read the great works of Roman literature and history. It is said that the great administrators of the British Empire learnt to govern from reading the Classics. While we may nowadays doubt that empire-building is a 'good thing,' this does show that we can learn from ancient civilizations.

If we wish to know more about European history, Latin is an essential tool, not only for the period of the Roman Empire, but also for the medieval period and beyond. Even after Latin had largely disappeared as an administrative language in western Europe, it remained important in the Roman Catholic church. For a long time it was also the *lingua franca* of science. For instance, Sir Isaac Newton's great work on the laws of motion, *Philosophiæ Naturalis Principia Mathematica*, was first published in Latin in 1687, while an English translation did not appear until 1729. The binomial classification of plants and animals invented by Carl Linnæus also relies on Latin. Even if the pronunciation is sometimes very post-Classical, a basic knowledge of Latin unlocks the jargon of these important disciplines.

English law (and thus also the law of former colonies) has many Latin terms (e.g. *subpœna, nolle prosequi, prima facie, amicus curiæ,* etc.). Equally, Western medicine relies heavily on Latin and Greek vocabulary. It almost goes without saying that no serious study of Romance languages (that is, the languages derived from Latin) is complete without a knowledge of Latin itself.

There are many good reasons to study Latin. It can be interesting and useful; with the help of this Primer, we hope that you will also find it enjoyable.

'Tiger'
Richmond upon Thames, May 2019

The Latin Language

1   Latin was the dialect of the Latini, or people of Latium in Italy. It was spoken by the ancient Romans, and, as their poets and prose-writers all used this dialect, the language was called Latin, not Roman.

Latin belongs to the family of languages known as Indo-European; among the many languages in this group are Sanskrit, Hindi, Urdu, Bengali, the Germanic languages (such as German, English, Swedish, etc.), Russian, Polish, Greek, Farsi, Welsh and Irish. The imperial power of Rome made Latin the general speech of much of Western Europe, and from it are derived modern Italian, French, Spanish, Portuguese, Romansch and Romanian, which are therefore called Romance languages.

Note: In England, after its conquest by the Angles and Saxons, a Germanic language, called Old English or Anglo-Saxon, was spoken. After the Norman Conquest (A.D.1066), English became mixed with Norman French, a dialect of the Romance language, French. After the revival of Classical learning in the sixteenth century, a large number of words were brought into English directly from Latin, and more have been added since, so that to understand the English language thoroughly it is necessary to have a knowledge of Latin.

The influence of Greek civilization on Latin was very great; it was chiefly exerted at two distinct eras. The first of these began about 550 BC, through the commerce of the Romans with the Greek colonies in Southern Italy. The second may be dated from the third century BC, when literary activity began at Rome. This influence was further developed through the conquest of Greece by Rome, which was completed in 146 BC.

Nearly all Latin literature, except the satiric writings of Horace, Persius, and Juvenal, is formed on Greek models. The earliest specimens of Latin we possess are inscriptions, laws, annals, and fragments of songs.

The credit of authorship is first ascribed to Livius Andronicus, who is said to have exhibited plays at Rome 240 BC. The works of the poets who followed soon after this date have mostly perished, except the comedies of Plautus and Terence, about 200 to 140 BC, and a prose fragment of the elder Cato.

The ages regarded as classical may be said to begin about 80 BC, lasting about 200 years.

The so-called Golden Age ended with the death of Augustus, AD 14, when the Silver Age began, ending about AD 120. The authors most studied are, in prose, Cicero, Cæsar, Livy, Tacitus; in poetry, Lucretius, Virgil, Horace, Ovid, and Juvenal.

LETTERS AND LAWS OF SOUND

2   **The Latin Alphabet** contains twenty-three letters, with the following signs:-

A B C D E F G H I K L M N O P Q R S T V X Y Z

a b c d e f g h i k l m n o p q r s t u x y z

Note: In early times C was written to represent the sounds of both C and G, which were probably not clearly distinguished in speaking. Afterwards G, a modified C, was introduced for the voiced consonant; K, becoming superfluous and went out of use. Y and Z were added in Cicero's time, being borrowed directly from the Greek alphabet, but they are only found in words taken from the Greek.

Although the Romans had cursive scripts, as well as the monumental capitals for which they are well known, small letters of a similar form to those we use today were only introduced in medieval times.

The letters are divided into:
1. **Vowels** (sounding by themselves);
2. **Consonants** (sounding with a vowel).

VOWELS

3   The vowels are **a**, **e**, **i**, **o**, **u** and **y**. **i** and **u** were also used as consonant (see below). The most open sound is **a**; the closest sharp sound is **i** ; and the closest flat sound is **u**; **e** is intermediate between **a** and **i**, and **o** is intermediate between **a** and **u**.

$$a$$
$$e \quad o$$
$$i \quad u$$

Y was always a vowel, as in *lyra*, and was sounded as French *u*.

4   QUANTITY OF VOWELS

Each of the six vowels, except y, which is nearly always short, can be either short or long: short when pronounced quickly, like English *a* in *man*; long when the voice dwells on the sound, as in *far*. A short vowel is sometimes distinguished by the *breve* sign ˘, a long one by the *macron* sign −: ămō. A vowel which can be either short or long is indicated in this book by a superscript question mark, e.g. å. However, we will rarely mark short or doubtful vowels (an unmarked vowel being understood to be short). Thus the six vowels stand for eleven different sounds:

$$a \ \bar{a} \ e \ \bar{e} \ i \ \bar{i} \ o \ \bar{o} \ u \ \bar{u} \ y$$

There were, no doubt, many finer shades of sound for each vowel, which cannot be exactly ascertained, but the following ten English words may give an approximate idea of their pronunciation.

a	ā	e	ē	i	ī	o	ō	u	ū
cut	cart	met	mate	kill	keel	cop	cope	foot	boot

5   DIPHTHONGS

A diphthong (double sound) is formed by two vowels meeting in one syllable. The diphthongs commonly found in Latin are **æ** (pronounced like the **y** in English *my*), **au** (like the **ow** in *cow*), **ei** (approximating to the **a** in *race*), **eu** (a short **e** sound gliding into a **u**), **œ** (probably like the **oy** in *boy*), **ui** (like the french word *oui*).

> **Note:** In the oldest Latin there were six diphthongs: **ai, au, ei, eo, ai, au**. Of these, **ai** passes in classical Latin into **æ**, *mensæ* for *mensai*; **au** remains unchanged; **ei** is found in old inscriptions, but in the literary language its place is taken by **ē** or by **ī**, as in *dīco*, except in the exclamation *ei*; **eu** is found in *ceu, heu, neu, seu*, and in many words of Greek origin; **oi** passes into **œ**, and sometimes into later **u**: *poena, punio*; ou becomes **ū**, as in **dūco**.

The diphthongs are always long (see § 474 ff.).

CONSONANTS

6   (i)   velar stops, **c, k, qu** and **g**.

(ii)   dental stops (teeth sounds) **t, d**.

(iii) labial stops (lip sounds) **p, b**.

(iv) the unvoiced alveolar fricative, **s**.

(v) the unvoiced labio-dental fricative, **f**.

(vi) consonant **u**, (written **v** in this book).

(vii) the glottal fricative, **h**.

(viii) consonant **i** (sometimes written **j**), the palatal approximant, like English **y** in yes.

(ix) nasals, **n, m**.

(x) iquids, **l, r**.

Note: **x** is really a double letter, standing for **cs, gs**. The letters **y** and **z** and the three Greek aspirates, **ch, ph, th**, are only found in Greek words, as *zōna, chlamys, phalanx, theātrum*.

Table of Latin Consonants

	STOPS (plosives)		FRICATIVES		LIQUIDS	NASALS	APPROXIMANTS
	unvoiced	voiced	unvoiced	voiced	voiced	voiced	voiced
LABIAL	p	b				m	
LABIO-DENTAL			f				
DENTAL	t	d			l, r	n	
ALVEOLAR			s	z			
LABIO-VELAR							u (v)
VELAR	c, k, q	g				[ng]	
PALATAL							i (j)
GLOTTAL			h				

7 PRONUNCIATION OF CONSONANTS

b was pronounced much as it is in English, except before **t** or **s**, when it became unvoiced, sounding like **p**.

c was similar to English **c** in *cat* but never like English **c** in *cite* or Italian **c** as in *cello*. Originally, Latin had no separate letter for the voiced sound, **g**, hence the abbreviation **C.** for *Gaius*.

d was usually similar to English **d**. However, it is clear from such spellings as *afferō* for *adferō*, that it was often assimilated into a following consonant.

f   was like English **f** in off.

g   was pronounced like English **g** in *goat*, never like **g** in *gin*. The combination **gn** appears to have been pronounced like **gn-n** in the English *wing-nut*.

h   was like English **h**, though it was very lightly pronounced and sometimes disappeared, as happens in some English dialects (e.g., Cockney), witness *Adria* for *Hadria*, Adriatic. Also as in Cockney, those who were prone to drop **h**, often added it to words which had no call for it. Between two vowels, **h** often failed to prevent the vowels eliding.

i   as a consonant is sometimes written **j** and was pronounced like English **y** is *yes* and German **j** as in *ja*. In classical times, it was never pronounced as the English **j** as in *judge* or the French **j** in *juge*, although both words derive from Latin *iūdex*.

k   was rarely used, except for *Kalendæ* and a few other words. It was pronounced as Latin **c**, English **k**.

l   was similar to English **l** in all positions.

m   was similar to English **m**. At the end of words, it tended to be reduced to simply nasalizing the preceding vowel.

n   was like English **n**. It is possible that it was more generally dental (created by contact between the tongue and teeth) rather than alveolar (contact between the tongue and gum ridge) as is more common in English. In some positions, such as before **s**, it was usually only pronounced as a nasalization of the preceding vowel.

p   was similar to English **p** but less aspirated, like Greek **π**.

qu   is thought to have been pronounced as a **k** with rounded lips rather than the English **qu** in *quick*.

r   may have been pronounced in Latin rather as in modern Italian. It was certainly more than a vowel-modifier as it is in some modern English pronunciations.

s   is always unvoiced in classical Latin, as in English *sip*, not English *wise*.

Note: As W. Sidney Allen rather charmingly puts it in *Vox Latina, causæ* should be pronounced *cow-sigh*, not *cow's eye*.

---

t is generally believed to have been created by touching the tongue to the back of the top teeth, although it may also have been articulated in the same way as in most English dialects, with the tongue touching the gum ridge.

v (**consonant u**) was pronounced as English **w** in *water.*

x was simply a sign for **cs**, pronounced as English **x** in tax.

z is a late borrowing from the Greek ζ and is used to represent a voiced fricative, like the English **z** in *zoo*, in foreign words.

8a **Syllables:** A syllable consists of one or more letters which can be sounded with a single accent or tone of the voice: *īlex* is thus two syllables, *ī* and *lex.*

When a consonant comes between two vowels, it belongs to the same syllable as the vowel which follows it: *pa-ter.*

When two or more consonants come between two vowels, at least one of them belongs to the preceding syllable: *mēn-sa, vic-trix,* with the exception that a plosive (**b, c, d, g, p, t**) followed by a liquid (**l, r**) can belong to the following syllable: *pa-trēs.* However, they are sometimes split between the two syllables: *pat-rēs.*

8b The quantity of syllables (that is their weight) is the basis of Latin metre (see § 474 ff.). This is unlike English verse which relies on stress.

A syllable is **heavy** if:

1. it contains a long vowel or diphthong;

2. it ends in two consonants (including **x**, which is really **cs**);

3. it ends in a consonant and the next syllable begins with a consonant.

It can be seen from the above simple rules that the first syllable of *victor* is heavy, although the vowel is short, because the syllable ends in a consonant and the next begins with one: *vic-tor.*

Note 1: The last syllable of a word is called **ultimate**; the last but one **penultimate**; the last but two **antepenultimate**.

Note 2: A syllable ending in a vowel is called **open**. One ending in a consonant is called **closed**.

---

9   **Accent:** The accent or tone falls on some one syllable in every word. The accented syllable was pronounced with greater force and also in a higher key than the other syllables. In Latin the rule is to throw the accent back; therefore in words of two or more syllables, the last syllable is never accented.

In words of more than two syllables the accent always falls on the last but one (penultimate), if it is long.

If the penultimate is short, the accent falls on the last but two (antepenultimate).

The accents are not usually printed in Latin.

VOWEL CHANGE

10   ### I. CHANGE IN ACCENTED SYLLABLES

1. Original **e** may become **i**: *simul* (cf. *semel*), *venia* (cf. *vindex*).
2. **e** becomes **o** before **l**: *solvō* (*se-luō*).
3 **ou** becomes **ū**: *doucō* (later *dūcō*).
4. **i** becomes **e** before **r**: *serō* (for *sisō*).
5. **o** sometimes becomes **u**: *huc* (for *ho-ce*).

11   ### II. CHANGE IN UNACCENTED SYLLABLES

(A) In final syllables

1. **o** becomes **u**: *corpus* (stem *corpos-*).
2. **i** becomes **e**: *mare* (stem *mari-*), or is lost altogether: *animal* (for *animale*, stem *animali-*).

(B) In medial syllables the vowel is commonly affected by the next consonant

1. **e** appears before **r**: *cinis, cineris*.
2. **o** becomes **u** before **l** or a labial: as in *cultus* (*colō*), *epistula* (earlier *epistola*). But when **i** or **e** precedes, the vowel remains **o**: as *filiolus, alveolus*.

3. **i** appears before any other single consonant: as in *meritus, monitus* (*moneō*). (For exception see § 13.)

12 (C) In Compounds

Here the principle is the same, and generally the rules are the same as in (B), but the examples are much more numerous.

a to **e** in closed syllables and before **r**: *cōnsecrō* from *sacer; dēscendō* from *scandō; trādere from dare.*

a to **i** in most open syllables and before **ng**: *difficilis* from *facilis; attingō* from *tangō.*

a to **u** or **i** before labials: *occupō* and *accipiō* from *capiō;* and before **l**: *īnsultō, īnsiliō,* from *saltō, saliō.*

e to **i** often in open syllables, but never before **r**: *diligō* from *legō;* but *ferō, auferō.*

æ to **ī**: *collīdō* from *lædō.*

au to **ū** or **ō**: *inclūdō* from *claudō; explōdō* from *plaudō.*

o and **u** are generally unchanged in compounds.

Note: There is a vowel variation often seen in Latin inflection which is not due to change in the Latin language itself, but came down to it from the Indo-European language. Thus the same noun can have two or more stems, as *homo;* older stem *homon-,* later weak stem, *homin-; agmen-, agmln-; pater, patr-; genus* (orig. *genos*), *gener-.* In these words the vowel of the strong stem is preserved in the nom. sing., while the weak stem appears in the other cases.

13   **Vowel Assimilation and Dissimilation:** The vowels of two following syllables tend to become alike in sound: *vegeō, vegetus* (*vigeō*), *pupugī* (for *pepugī*), *nihil* (for *nē-hil*), *mihi, tibi.*

On the other hand, two vowels coming together are sometimes dissimilated: **ii** becomes **ie** in *pietās, societās, abietis.*

14   **Vowel Contraction:** When two similar vowels are separated by consonant **i** or **u**, or by **h**, they commonly throw out the letter between them, and unite in a long vowel: *rēs* is contracted from *re-i-es*, *nēmō* from *nē-h-emō*, *nīl* from *ni-h-il*, *audīsse* from *audīvisse*.

Two dissimilar vowels sometimes unite in the same manner: *amāre* from *ama-i-ere*; *āmō* from *ama-i-ō*; *amāstī* from *amā-v-istī*.

Two vowels placed next each other often contract: *dēgō* from *dē-agō*; *nullus* from *nē-ullus*; *prōmō* from *prō-emō*.

15   **Syncope:** Dropping of an unaccented vowel between two consonants: *dextra* for *dextera*; *valdē* for *validē*. It often takes place in compounds: *calfaciō* for *calefaciō*. The vowel of the reduplicating syllable sometimes drops; *reppulī* for *repepulī*.

> **Note:** Sometimes when any one of the letters **l, r, m,** or **n** follows a consonant, a vowel not found in the stem springs up before it because of the semi-vocalic character of the sound; *ager*, stem *agro-*; *populus*, original stem *poplo-*; *asinus* (*asno-*); *volumus* (contrast *vul-tis*).

16   **Apocope:** Dropping of a final vowel: **e** is dropped in *quīn* for *quī-nē*; *dīc* for *dīce*; **i** falls off in *ut* for *uti*, *quot*, *tot* (*totidem*).

17   **Changes of Quantity:** A vowel generally shortens before another vowel: thus *rēī* became *rĕī*. A long vowel often becomes short through effect of the accent on the preceding or following syllable: *iūrō* becomes *periŭrō*, afterwards weakening to *pēierō*; *lŭcerna* from *lūceō*. In flectional endings, a vowel originally final is sometimes shortened. But when a final consonant is lost (as final **d** in the ablative), the length of the vowel seems to be preserved: *Gnæō* (earlier *Gnaivōd*).

Vowel lengthening is often due to **compensation**. When two consonants follow an accented vowel the first of the two is often dropped, and the vowel lengthened, so that the syllable keeps its length: *nīdus* for *nisdus* (English *nest* retains the **s**).

CONSONANT CHANGE

18   **Consonants at the beginning of a word:** Two unvoiced consonants at the beginning of a word were avoided. Thus we find *locus* for original *stlocus*, *tīlia* for *ptīlia*. Sometimes a fricative preceding a stop is dropped: *caveō* for *scaveō*, but generally it is retained: *scandō*, *sternō*, *spērō*. A stop followed by a liquid is generally unchanged: as *crescō*, *trēs*, *plaudō*; but **g** before **n** is lost in *nōtus* for *gnōtus* (cf. *ignōtus*), and in

nōdus, knot. The unvoiced fricative **f** remains before a liquid *flos, frons*; but **sm** becomes **m**, as in *mīrus, memor*; **sn** becomes **n** in *nix* (snow), *nurus* (Old English *snoru*), daughter-in-law.

19   **Consonants in the middle of a word:** In the middle of a word, if two consonants come next each other which cannot be easily sounded together, either one drops out, *quālus* for *quas-lus*, basket, or one is assimilated to the other, as in *sella* for *sedla*, a seat. A stop often drops out before a nasal or liquid, with lengthening of the preceding vowel, as in *exāmen* for *exagmen*.

Other cases in which a letter is dropped are *quīntus* for older *quīnctus*; *ascrībō* for *ad-scrībō*; *asportō* for *abs-portō*; *bimēstris* from stem *bi-menstri-*; *iūdex* from *iūs-dic-*.

20   **Consonant assimilation** is of two kinds:

(a) **Complete assimilation**, when the first letter becomes the same as the following one: *alloquor* for *ad-loquor*; *arrogō* for *ad-rogō*; *summus* for *supmus* (*suprēmus*); *assentiō* for *ad-sentiō*, *offerō* for *ob-ferō*; *suggerō* for *sub-gerō*; *accido* for *ad-cadō*; *succumbō* for *sub-cumbō*; *differō* for *dis-ferō*.

(b) **Partial assimilation**, when the first letter changes to one which combines more easily with the following one: *rēxī* (*rēc-sī*), *rēctum* from *regō*; *scrīpsī*, *scrīptum*, from *scrībō*.

m becomes **n** (**ng**) before a guttural and **n** before a dental: *congruō* (sounded *cong-gruō*), *condūcō, constō*. **n** becomes **m** before a labial: *impotēns, imbibō*. An unvoiced stop becomes voiced between vowels or between a vowel and a semi-vowel: *trīgintā* for *trīcentā*; *pūblicus*, stem *poplico-*.

Note: **tt** and **dt** change to **ss**: hence the supines in -*sum* and past partciples in -*sus* are formed: *dēfend-to-* becomes *dēfensso-*, *dēfensum*; *claudto-*, *clausso-*, *clausum*, *pat-to-* becomes *passo-, passus*.
Occasionally a following consonant is assimilated to the preceding one: *collum* for *colsum*; *ferre* for *ferse*.

20a   **Dissimlilation** is seen in *cæruleus* from *cælum*, *merīdiēs* for *medīdiēs*; and in adjectives in -*āris* and -*ālis*, *familiāris*, *nātūrālis*. **s** between two vowels usually changes to **r**: *flōrēs, honōrēs,* from *flōs, honōs; quæsō* becomes *quærō.*

21 **Metathesis:** Interchange of position between a vowel and liquid in the same syllable. This is chiefly seen in the case of **r**: *ter, trēs; spernō, sprēvī; terō, trīvī.*

> **Note:** When the vowel becomes the last letter of the stem by this change of position, it is always lengthened.

22 **Consonants at the end of a word:** A Latin word never ends in a double consonant: *mell-, farr-,* become *mel, far.*

A dental drops off after a guttural: *lac,* from stem *lact-.* The only exceptions are a labial stop or nasal followed by **s**: *urbs, stirps, dēns, hiems* (usually written *hiemps*).

c or **g** followed by **s** is written **x**: *dux, rēx.*

d falls off in *cor,* stem *cord-,* and in the ablative singular *extrā(d), intrā(d).*

n regularly falls off in the nominative of the n-stems : *leo.*

> **Note:** Both **m** and **n** were very lightly sounded at the end of a word, and a syllable ending in **m** is sometimes elided before a vowel: *animum advertere.* This elision takes place regularly in poetry. Final **d** and **t** were also lightly sounded and are sometimes interchanged: *haud, haut.*

23 **Dropping of syllables:** When two syllables beginning with the same letter come together in the middle of a word, the first one is sometimes dropped. Thus *venēnī-ficium* becomes *venēficium, cōnsuētitūdō, cōnsuētūdō.*

INFLECTION

24   Inflection is a change made in the form of a word to show differences of meaning and use.

The **stem** is the simplest form of a word in any language before it undergoes changes of inflection. The **stem character** is the final letter of the stem. The **root** is the primitive element which the word has in common with kindred words in the same or in other languages. Every word has a stem and a root. They may be the same, but more often the stem is formed from the root. Thus in *agitāre, agita-* is the stem and **a** the stem character, but *ag-* is the root, as shown by other words, *agere, agmen, agilis*.

> **Note 1:** A language which expresses changes of meaning chiefly by inflection, and makes little use of help-words, is called synthetic. Latin is a synthetic language. A language which has little inflection and uses many help-words is called analytic. English as now spoken is an analytic language. In analytic languages the place of the inflectional endings is often supplied by prepositions used with nouns: *Cæsaris*, of Cæsar; by auxiliaries used with verbs: *agitur*, it is being done. Analytic languages also use the article: *rēx* can be translated in English as *a* king or *the* king; and they use pronouns with verbs: *agō*, I do.
>
> **Note 2:** Inflection sometimes takes place by letter-change in the root-syllable, *agi-mus, ēgi-mus*, or by an addition before it, which is called a **prefix**, as *ce-cin-ī* from *canō*. Most frequently, however, it consists in an addition made after the stem, which is called a **suffix**, In *agitāre, -re* is a suffix, and is also the ending; in *agitārēmus*, a second suffix, *-mus*, is added and becomes the ending. Some verbs have *-n-* inserted in the stem of some or all tenses; this is called the **nasal infix** (§149).

PARTS OF SPEECH

25   Words are divided into:

Nouns (substantives): names of persons, places, or things:

Cæsar, Cæsar; *Rōma*, Rome; *sōl*, sun; *virtus*, virtue.

Adjectives, which express the qualities of substantives:

Roma antiqua, **ancient** Rome; *sōl clarus*, the **bright** sun.

Pronouns, which stand for substantives:

ego, I; *ille,* that, he.

Verbs, which express actions or states:

Sōl dat lūcem, the sun **gives** light; *Rōma* **manet**, Rome **remains**.

Adverbs, which qualify and limit verbs, adjectives, and sometimes other adverbs:

Rōma **diū** *flōruit; nunc* **minus** *potēns est.* Rome flourished **long**; now it is **less** powerful.

Prepositions, which denote the relation of nouns to other words in the sentence:

Per *Rōmam errō.* I wander **through** Rome.

Conjunctions, which connect words, phrases, and sentences:

Cælum suspiciō **ut** *lūnam* **et** *sīdera videam.*
I look up to the sky **that** I may see the moon **and** stars.

Interjections: words of exclamation: *heu, ēheu,* alas!

Nouns, adjectives, pronouns and **verbs** are inflected (see §24).

26   There is no **article** in Latin. *Lūx* may be translated as *a light,* *the light,* or simply *light.*

27   **Nouns** are:

(a) **Concrete:** *vir,* man; *mēnsa,* table. The names of persons or places are called **proper names** (or **proper nouns**): *Cæsar, Rōma.*

(b) **Abstract:** *virtūs,* virtue.

(c) **Collective:** a word expressing a group or collection of persons or things of the same kind: *turba,* crowd.

DECLENSION DEFINED

28 **Declension** describes the change of form which nouns, adjectives and pronouns undergo to show changes of **number** and **case**.

29 There are **two numbers**:

Singular for one person or thing: *mēnsa*, a table; *gēns*, a nation.

Plural for more than one: *mēnsæ*, tables; *gentēs*, nations.

30 **Case** is the form which a noun takes to show its relation to other words in the sentence.

There are **six cases**:

Nominative, used for the the subject of the sentence, and also the complement.

Genitive, usually expressing possession.

Dative, the case of the indirect object.

Accusative, used for the direct object of the sentence.

Vocative, the case of one addressed.

Ablative, often expressing *from*.

EXAMPLES OF THE CASES

Nominative: ***Dominus** dūcit*, **the lord** leads.
Genitive: *Lūx **sōlis**,* **the sun's** light.
Dative: ***Dominō** librum dō*, I give **the lord** a book.
Accusative: ***Dominum** videō*, I see **the lord**.
Vocative: *Ō **domine***, O **lord**.
Ablative: ***Sōle** lūx ēditur*, light issues **from the sun**.

Note 1: The dative is also rendered *for* in English: *Senātus **urbī** cōnsulit*, the Senate consults **for the city**.

Note 2: The ablative is rendered by many English prepositions besides from: *in, by, with*. To express the person by whom an action is done, the ablative is used with the preposition *ā, ab*: *Remus ā Rōmulō interfectus est*, Remus was slain by Romulus. To express the instrument with which an action is done, the ablative is used alone: *Remus gladiō interfectus est*, Remus was slain with (or by) a sword.

Note 3: In ancient Latin there were two more cases, the **instrumental** answering the question With what? and the **locative** answering the question Where? The use of the instrumental passed entirely to the ablative, but the locative is often found in classical literature: *humī*, on the ground; *Rōmœ*, at Rome; *Athēnīs*, at Athens.

RULES OF GENDER

31   There are **three genders**:
1, **masculine**; 2, **feminine**; 3, **neuter** (*neutrum*, neither of the two).
Gender is shown by the form of a word and by its meaning.

(A) FORM

(a) Masculine are most substantives in **-us** of the second and fourth declensions, and those in **-er** of the second declension.

(b) Feminine are nearly all nouns in **-a**, of the first declension and in **-es** of the fifth declension.

(c) Neuter are nouns in **-um** of the second declension, in **-ū** of the fourth declension, and indeclinable nouns, including the infinitive verb-noun (see §107).

For the third declension no general rule can be given.

(B) MEANING

(a) Masculine are all names of men, gods, months, and winds; also of most rivers and mountains: *Rōmulus, Mars, Octōber, Boreās*, north wind, *Tiberis, Olympus*.

Exceptions: Some mountains and a few rivers ending in **-a** or **-e** are feminine: *Allia, Lēthē, Ætna, Rhodopē, Alpēs* (plur,); neuter, *Pēlion, Sōracte*.

(b) Feminine are all names of women, goddesses, islands; and of most countries, cities, and trees: *Cornēlia, Iūnō, Lesbos, Asia, Rōma, pīnus*.

Exceptions: Countries ending in **-um**, neuter: *Latium; Pontus* is masculine. Cities with plur. form in **-ī** are masculine: *Coriolī, Delphī*; those in **-um, -on, -a** (plur.) are neuter: *Tarentum, Īlion, Arbēla*.

Note 1: In the early ages people imagined natural objects as living beings, and made them masculine or feminine, according to their notions of their qualities: *ventus,* wind, *fluvius,* river, *mōns,* mountain, masculine ; *regiō,* country, *urbs,* city, *arbor,* tree, feminine; and words belonging to these classes took the same genders.

Note 2: Many o- stems masc. (called **mobilia**) have a corresponding form in -**a** feminine:

filius, son	*deus,* god	*arbiter* ⎫
filia, daughter.	*dea,* goddess	*arbitra,* ⎬ umpire.

Other corresponding forms are used: *rēx,* king, *rēgīna,* queen; *victor, victrīx,* conqueror; *nepōs,* grandson, *neptis,* granddaughter; *socer, socrus,* father-, mother-in-law.

Note 3: Nouns which include both masculine and feminine are said to be of **common gender:** *sacerdōs,* priest or priestess; *vātēs,* seer, *parēns,* parent; *dux,* leader; *comes,* companion; *cīvis,* citizen; *custōs,* guardian; *iūdex,* judge; *hērēs,* heir; *āles,* bird; *canis,* dog; *serpēns,* serpent; *tigris,* tiger.

Many names of animals, though used of both sexes, have (in grammar) only one gender; they are called **epicene:** *aquila,* eagle, fem.; *lepus,* hare, masc.; *passer,* sparrow, masc.

DECLENSION OF SUBSTANTIVES

32   Substantives are grouped in declensions according to the character or final letter of the stem as follows:

(1) First declension: **a-** stems, **-æ** genitive singular.

(2) Second declension: **o-** stems, **-ī** genitive singular.

(3) Third declension: consonant stems and **i-** stems, **-is** genitive singular.

(4) Fourth declension: **u-** stems, **ūs** genitive singular

(5) Fifth declension: **e-** stems, **-eī** or **-ēī** genitive singular.

TABLE OF CASE-ENDINGS

Decl.	1	2		3			4	5
stem char	a-	ō-		consonant	i-		u-	ē-
				SINGULAR				
	f. (m.)	m.	n.	m. f. n.	f. m.	n.	m (f) n	f
Nom.	a	us, er	um	various	is, ēs	e, l, r	us ū	ēs
Gen.	æ		ī	is	is		ūs	eī (ēī)
Dat.	æ		ō	ī	ī		uī (ū)	eī (ēī)
Acc.	am	um	um	em var.	em, em	e, l, r	um ū	em
Voc.	a	e, er	um	various	is, ēs	e, l, r	us ū	ēs
Abl.	ā		ō	e	ī or e		ū	ē
				PLURAL				
Nom.	æ	ī	a	ēs a	ēs	ia	ūs ua	ēs
Gen.	ārum	ōrum		um	ium		uum	ērum
Dat.	īs	īs		ibus	ibus		ibus	ēbus
Acc.	ās	ōs	a	ēs a	ēs, īs	ia	ūs ua	ēs
Voc.	æ	ī	a	ēs a	ēs	ia	ūs ua	ēs
Abl.	īs	īs		ibus	ibus		ibus	ēbus

33   The character of the stem is most clearly seen before the ending **-um** or **-rum** of the genitive plural.

The nominative, masculine and feminine, takes **-s**, except in **a-** stems, some stems in **ro-** of the second declension, and stems in **s**, **l**, **r**, **n**, of the third. The vocative is like the nominative, except in the singular of nouns in **-us** of the second declension.

The accusative of neuter nouns is always the same as the the nominative in both singular and plural; the nominative and accusative plural always end in **a**.

FIRST DECLENSION

34   A- Stems

The nominative singular is the same as the stem, except that the final **a** of the nominative is short.

Stem mēnsā-, *table*, f.

	SINGULAR	PLURAL
Nom.	mēnsa, a table	mēnsæ, tables
Gen.	mēnsæ, of a table	mēnsārum, of tables
Dat.	mēnsæ, to a table	mēnsīs, to tables
Acc.	mēnsam, a table	mēnsās, tables
Voc.	mēnsa, o table	mēnsæ, o tables
Abl.	mēnsā, from a table	mēnsīs, from tables

Decline like mensa: **aquila**, *eagle*; **luna**, *moon*; **rēgǐna**, *queen*; **stella**, *star*.

First declension nouns are mostly feminine. A few are masculine, as *scrība*, a notary; *Hadria*, the Adriatic sea.

Note 1: An old form of the gen. sing. -āī for -æ is sometimes used by poets, as *aulāī*. Also an old genitive of *familia* remains in compounds: *pater- (māter-) familiās*, father (mother) of a family.

Note 2: The locative (see §30, note 3) sing. ends in -æ; the plur. in -īs; *Rōmæ*, at Rome; *mīlitiæ*, at the war; *Athēnīs*, at Athens.

Note 3: The genitive plural is sometimes formed in **-um** instead of **-ārum**, by compounds with **-cola, -gena**: *agricola*, a farmer; and in some words borrowed from Greek: *amphora, drachma*.

Note 4: *Dea* and *fīlia* have dative and ablative plural **-ābus**, in order to distinguish them from the dative and ablative plural of *deus* and *fīlius*.

SECOND DECLENSION

35   O- Stems

The nominative is formed from the stem by adding **s**; in neuter nouns, **m**; the character **o** being weakened to **u**.

In the greater number of nouns whose stem ends in **-ero**, or in **-ro** preceded by a stop, the **-o** is dropped, and the nominative ends in **-er**.

Stem	anno- year, m.	puero- boy, m.	magistro- master, m.	bello- war, n.
	SINGULAR			
Nom.	annus, a year	puer	magister	bellum
Gen.	annī, year's	puerī	magistrī	bellī
Dat.	annō, to a year	puerō	magistrō	bellō
Acc.	annum, a year	puerum	magistrum	bellum
Voc.	anne, o year	puer	magister	bellum
Abl.	annō, to a year	puerō	magistrō	bellō

PLURAL

Nom.	annī, *years*	puerī	magistrī	bella
Gen.	annōrum, *years'*	puerōrum	magistrōrum	bellōrum
Dat.	annīs, *to years*	puerīs	magistrīs	bellīs
Acc.	annōs, *years*	puerōs	magistrōs	bella
Voc.	annī, *o years*	puerī	magistrī	bella
Abl.	annīs, *from years*	puerīs	magistrīs	bellīs

Decline like *annus*: amīcus, friend; dominus, lord; servus, slave.

Decline like *puer*: gener, son-in-law; socer, father-in-law; līberī (plur.), children; lūcifer, light-bringer; armiger, armor-bearer.

Decline like *magister*: ager, field; cancer, crab; liber, book. Decline like *bellum*: rēgnum, kingdom; verbum, word.

Most nouns in us, er, are masculine; in um neuter.

As well as words feminine by meaning, the following -us words are feminine: alvus, paunch; colus, distaff; humus, ground; vannus, winnowing-fan; also several from the Greek: arctus, the bear constellation; carbasus, linen; plur. carbasa, n., sails.
Neuter in us (and used in the sing. only) are pelagus, sea; virus, venom.

Note: Vulgus, crowd, is generally neuter, rarely masculine.

35a   The following have some exceptional forms:

Stem	filio-	viro-	deo-
	son, m.	man, m.	god, m.

SINGULAR

Nom.	filius	vir	deus
Gen.	filiī or filī	virī	deī
Dat.	filiō	virō	deō
Acc.	filium	virum	deum
Voc.	filī	vir	deus
Abl.	filiō	virō	deō

PLURAL

Nom.	filiī	virī	dī (deī)
Gen.	filiōrum	virōrum or virum	deōrum or deum
Dat.	filiīs	virīs	dīs (deīs)
Acc.	filiōs	virōs	deōs
Abl.	filiīs	virīs	dīs (deīs)

Note 1: Like *filius* are declined *genius*, guardian spirit, and many proper names in -ius: *Claudius, Virgilius*; like *vir*, its compounds, *decemvir, triumvir*, &c. The contracted gen. sing. in -ī, as *filī, ingenī*, is used by writers of the best age, especially poets.

Note 2: The **locative** singular ends in ī; the plural in īs: *humī*, on the ground; *bellī*, at, the war; *Mīlētī*, at Miletus; *Philippīs*, at Philippi,

Note 3: The genitive plural in -um is often found; especially in words denoting coins, sums, weights, and measures: *nummus*, coin; *talentum*, talent. Some nouns have genitive plural in -um or -ōrum: *socius*, ally; *faber*, smith; *līberī*, children. Also *superī*, the gods, from adj. *superus* (§ 304),

THIRD DECLENSION

36 Consonant and I- Stems

The Third Declension contains:

A. Consonant Stems

Stops (plosives)

	(1) Palatals,	c, g
	(2) Dentals,	t, d
	(3) Labials,	p, b
Fricative,		s
Nasals,		n, m
Liquids,		l, r

B. i- Stems

37 Syllabus of consonant-stem nouns

Stem-end	Nom. Sing.	Genitive Sing.	English
Stems in palatals with **x** in nom. for **cs** or **gs**			
ac-	fax, f.	facis	torch
āc-	pāx, f.	pācis	peace
ec-	nex, f.	necis	death
ec-, ic-	apex, m.	apicis	peak
ēc-	vervēx, m.	vervēcis	wether
ic-	fornix, m.	fornicis	arch
ic-	iūdex, c.	iūdicis	judge
īc-	rādīx, f.	rādīcis	root

ōc-	vōx, f.	vōcis	voice
uc-	dux, c.	ducis	leader
ūc-	lūx, f.	lūcis	light
eg-	grex, m.	gregis	flock
ēg-	rēx, m.	rēgis	king
eg-, ig-	rēmex, m.	rēmigis	rower
ig-	strix, f.	strigis	screech-owl
ug-	coniunx, c.	coniugis	spouse
ūg-	wanting	frūgis, f.	fruit

Stems in dentals drop **t**, **d**, before **s** in the nom.

at-	anas, f.	anatis	duck
āt-	ætās, f.	ætātis	age
et-	seges, f.	segetis	corn-crop
et-	pariēs, m.	parietis	room-wall
ēt-	quiēs, f.	quiētis	rest
et- (it-)	mīles, c.	mīlitis	soldier
it-	caput, n.	capitis	head
ōt-	nepōs, m.	nepōtis	grandson
ūt.	virtūs, f.	virtūtis	virtue, courage
ct-	lac, n.	lactis	milk
ad-	vas, m.	vadis	surety
ed-	pēs, m.	pedis	foot
ēd-	mercēs, f.	mercēdis	hire
æd-	præs, m.	prædis	bondsman
ed- (id-)	obses, c.	obsidis	hostage
id-	lapis, m.	lapidis	stone
ōd-	custōs, c.	custōdis	guardian
ud-	pecus, f.	pecudis	beast
ūd-	incūs, f.	incūdis	anvil
aud-	laus, f.	laudis	praise
rd-	cor. n.	cordis	heart

Stems in labials form nom. regularly with **s**

ap-	wanting	dapis, f.	banquet
ep- (ip-)	prīnceps, c.	prīncipis	chief
ip-	wanting	stipis, f.	dole (a coin)
op-	wanting	opis, f.	help
ep- (up-)	auceps, m.	aucupis	fowler

Stems in the frivative **s**, which, except in **vās**, becomes **r**

ās-	vās, n.	vāsis	vessel
æs- ær-	æs, n.	æris	copper, bronze

es- er-	Cerēs, f.	Cereris	Ceres
is- er-	cinis, m.	cineris	cinder
ōs- ōr-	honōs, m.	honōris	honor
os- or-	tempus, n.	temporis	time
us- er-	opus, n.	operis	work
ūs- ūr-	crūs, n.	crūris	leg

Stems in liquids

al-	sāl, m.	salis	salt
ell-	mel, n.	mellis	honey
il-	mūgil, m.	mūgilis	mullet
ōl-	sōl, m.	sōlis	sun
ul-	cōnsul, m.	cōnsulis	consul
ar-	iubar, n.	iubaris	sunbeam
arr-	fār, n.	farris	flour
er-	ānser, m.	ānseris	goose, gander
ēr-	vēr, n.	vēris	spring
ter- (tr-)	māter, f.	mātris	mother
or-	æquor, n.	æquoris	sea
or-	ebur, n.	eboris	ivory
ōr-	soror, f.	sorōris	sister
ur-	vultur, m.	vulturis	vulture
ūr-	fūr, m.	fūris	thief

Stems in nasals

en- in-	nōmen, n.	nōminis	name
on- in-	homō, m.	hominis	man
ōn-	leō, m.	leōnis	lion
iōn-	ratiō, f.	ratiōnis	reason
rn-	carō, f.	carnis	flesh
an-	canis, c.	canis	dog
en-	iuvenis, c.	iuvenis	young person
em-	hiem(p)s, f.	hiemis	winter

A. CONSONANT STEMS

38 **(1) Stems in palatals: c, g**

Stem	iūdic- judge, c.		rādīc- root, f.	rēg- king, m.
SINGULAR				
Nom.	iūdex,	a judge	rādīx	rēx
Gen.	iūdicis,	of a judge	rādīcis	rēgis
Dat.	iūdicī,	to a judge	rādīcī	rēgī
Acc.	iūdicem,	a judge	rādīcem	rēgem
Abl.	iūdice,	from a judge	rādīce	rēge
PLURAL				
Nom.	iūdicēs,	judges	rādīcēs	rēgēs
Gen.	iūdicum,	of judges	rādīcum	rēgum
Dat.	iūdicibus,	to judges	rādīcibus	rēgibus
Acc.	iūdicēs,	judges	rādīcēs	rēgēs
Abl.	iūdicibus,	from judges	rādīcibus	rēgibus

Decline also: f. vōx, vōc-, voice; c. dux, duc-, leader; m. grex, greg-, flock.

Note: The vocative is the same form as the nominative in the third declension.

---

39 **(2) Stems in dentals: t, d**

Stem	mīlit- soldier, c.	ped- foot, m.	capit- head, n.
SINGULAR			
Nom.	mīles	pēs	caput
Gen.	mīlitis	pedis	capitis
Dat.	mīlitī	pedī	capitī
Acc.	mīlitem	pedem	caput
Abl.	mīlite	pede	capite
PLURAL			
Nom.	mīlitēs	pedēs	capita
Gen.	mīlitum	pedum	capitum
Dat.	mīlitibus	pedibus	capitibus
Acc.	mīlitēs	pedēs	capita
Abl.	mīlitibus	pedibus	capitibus

Decline also: f. virtūs, virtūt- virtue; c. seges, seget-, corn; m. lapis, lapid-, stone;
c. sacerdōs, sacerdōt-, priest.

40   (3) Stems in labials: *p*, *b*

Stem	princep-, princip- *chief,* c.	
	SINGULAR	PLURAL
Nom	princeps	principēs
Gen.	principis	principum
Dat.	principī	principibus
Acc.	principem	principēs
Abl.	principe	principibus

Decline also: c. *forceps, forcip-* , tongs; m. *auceps, aucup-*, fowler; f. *trabs, trab-*, beam.

41   (4) Stems in the fricative *s*

Stems in **s** do not add **s** in the nominative singular, and generally they change **s** into **r** in the other cases.

Stem	**flōs-**	**opus-**	**crūs-**
	flōr-	**oper-**	**crūr-**
	flower, m.	*work,* n.	*leg,* n.

SINGULAR

Nom.	**flōs**	opus	crūs
Gen.	**flōris**	operls	crūris
Dat.	**flōrī**	operī	crūrī
Acc.	**flōrem**	opus	crūs
Abl.	**flōre**	opere	crūre

PLURAL

Nom.	**flōrēs**	opera	crūra
Gen.	**flōrum**	operum	crūrum
Dat.	**flōribus**	operibus	crūribus
Acc.	**flōrēs**	opera	crūra
Abl.	**flōribus**	operlbus	crūribus

Decline also: m. *honōs, honor-*, honor; n. *tempus, tempor-*, time ; *corpus, corpor-*, body; *genus, gener-*, race; *iūs, iūr-*, law.

Note 1: Vās, vasis, n., a vessel, keeps **s** in all the cases, and has plural vāsa, vāsōrum, vāsīs. Os, oss-, n., bone; ās, ass-, m., a coin, keep **s** in all the cases, and have gen. plur. ossium, assium.

Note 2: Honōs, honor, colōs, color, and other words changed in later classical Latin to honor, color, &c., in the nom. sing., with gen. -ōris. Arbōs, f., changed to arbor, arboris, tree.

42   **(5) Stems in liquids: l, r**

Stems in **l, r,** do not take **s** in the nominative singular.

Stem	cōnsul- consul, m.	amōr- love, m.	pater-, patr- father, m.	æquor- sea, n.
SINGULAR				
Nom.	cōnsul	amōr	pater	æquor
Gen.	cōnsulis	amōrls	patrls	æquoris
Dat.	cōnsulī	amōrī	patrī	æquorī
Acc.	cōnsulem	amōrem	patrem	æquor
Abl.	cōnsule	amōre	patre	æquore
PLURAL				
Nom.	cōnsulēs	amōrēs	patrēs	æquora
Acc.	cōnsulēs	amōrēs	patrēs	æquora
Gen.	cōnsulum	amōrum	patrum	æquorum
Dat.	cōnsulibus	amōribus	patribus	æquoribus
Abl.	cōnsulibus	amōribus	patribus	æquoribus

Decline also: m. sōl, sōl-, sun; ōrātor, ōrātōr-, speaker; carcer, carcer-, prison; frāter, frātr-, brother; n. ebur, ebor-, ivory.

43   **(6) Stems in Nasals: n, m**

Stems ending in **n** do not take **s** in the nominative singular. Stems in **ōn, on,** drop the **n.**

Stem	leōn- lion, m.	virgōn-, virgin- virgin, f.	nōmen-, nōmin- name, n.
SINGULAR			
Nom	leō	virgō	nōmen
Gen.	leōnis	virginis	nōminis
Dat.	leōnī	virginī	nōminī
Acc.	leōnem	virginem	nōmen
Abl.	leōne	virgine	nōmine

PLURAL

Nom.	leōnēs	virginēs	nōmina
Gen.	leōnum	virginum	nōminum
Dat.	leōnibus	virginibus	nōminibus
Acc.	leōnēs	virginēs	nōmina
Abl.	leōnibus	virginibus	nōminibus

Decline also: m. *latrō, latrōn-*, robber; f. *ratiō, ratiōn-*, reason; m. *ōrdō, ōrdin-*, order; *homō, homin-*, man; n. *carmen, carmin-*, song.

There is only one stem in **m**: *hiem(p)s*, winter; gen. *hiemis*, f.

B. I-STEMS.

44   **(1) Stems with nom. sing. in *-is*, and in *-er* from stem *ri-***

Stem	cīvi-	imbri-
	citizen, c.	*shower*, m.
SINGULAR		
Nom.	cīvis	imber
Gen.	cīvis	imbris
Dat.	cīvī	imbrī
Acc.	cīvem	imbrem
Abl.	cīve, -ī	imbre, -ī
PLURAL		
Nom.	cīvēs	imbrēs
Gen.	cīvium	imbrium
Dat.	civibus	imbribus
Acc.	cīvēs, īs	imbrēs, -īs
Abl.	cīvibus	imbribus

Decline like **cīvis**: m. *amnis*, river; *ignis*, fire; f. *avis*, bird.

Decline like **imber**: f. *linter*, boat; m. *ūter*, leather bottle.

Note 1: Some words have acc. **-im**, abl. **ī**: f. *tussis*, cough; *sitis*, thirst; most rivers and towns, m. *Tiberis*, Tiber; f. *Neāpolis*, Naples. Sometimes f. *febris*, fever; *puppis*, stern; *turris*, tower; *clāvis*, key; *nāvis*, ship; *restis*, rope; *secūris*, axe; *sēmentis*, sowing. *Ignis* has usually abl. *ignī*. The acc. plur. is sometimes written **-īs**, which is the older form.

Note 2: **Vīs**, force, is the only long ī-stem. It has acc. sing. *vīm*, abl. sing. *vī*, plur. *vīrēs*, *vīrium*, *vīribus*.

Note 3: Some nominatives in **-is** form their genitive plurals in **-um**.

45   **(2) Stems with nom. sing. in -ēs:**

	Stem	nūbi-	*cloud,* f.
		SING.	PLUR.
Nom.		nūbēs	nūbēs
Gen.		nūbis	nūbium
Dat.		nūbī	nūbibus
Acc.		nūbem	nūbēs, -īs
Abl.		nūbe	nūbibus

Decline also: *cautēs,* rock; *mōlēs,* pile; *rūpēs,* crag.

Note: Some have nom. sing. *-ēs* or *-is: vallēs* or *vallis,* valley; *vulpēs* or *vulpis,* fox. *Trabs,* beam, *plebs,* the common people, are often found for *trabēs, plebēs. Famēs,* hunger, and *tābēs,* corruption, have abl. sing. *-ē* (not *-ĕ*).

---

46   **(3) Stems with two consonants before *i***

These generally drop **i** before the **s** in the nom. sing.

	Stem	monti-	urbi-
		mountain, m.	*city,* f.
SINGULAR			
Nom.		mōns	urbs
Gen.		montis	urbis
Dat.		montī	urbī
Acc.		montem	urbem
Abl.		monte	urbe
PLURAL			
Nom.		montēs	urbēs
Gen.		montium	urbium
Dat.		montlbus	urbibus
Acc.		montēs, -īs	urbēs, īs
Abl.		montibus	urbibus

Decline also: f. *arx, arci-,* citadel; *ars, arti-,* art; *stirps, stirpi-,* stem; *frons, fronti-,* forehead; *frōns, frondi-,* leaf; m. *dēns, denti-,* tooth.

47 **(4) Neuter stems with nom. sing. in -e, -al, -ar**

These either change **i** into **e** in the nom. sing. or drop the vowel and shorten the final syllable.

Stem	cubīli *couch*	animāli- *animal*	calcāri- *spur*
SINGULAR			
Nom.	cubīle	animal	calcar
Gen.	cubīlis	animālis	calcāris
Dat.	cubīlī	animālī	calcārī
Acc.	cubīle	animal	calcar
Abl.	cubīlī	animālī	calcārī
PLURAL			
Nom.	cubīlia	animālia	calcāria
Gen.	cubīlium	animālium	calcārium
Dat.	cubīlibus	animālibus	calcāribus
Acc.	cubīlia	animālia	calcāria
Abl.	cubīlibus	animālibus	calcāribus

Decline also: *conclāve*, room; *sedīle*, seat; *rēte*, net (abl. sing. -e); *tribūnal*, tribunal; *exemplar*, pattern.

Note: *Mare*, sea, has abl. sing. *marī*, or more rarely *mare*; the gen. plur. is only found once: *marum*. *Baccar*, an aromatic root, *fār*, flour, *iubar*, a sunbeam, *nectar*, nectar, have abl. sing. -e.

48 **Consonant Stems and i-Stems**

Consonant stems and i-stems are placed in one declension because of the difficulty of distinguishing their forms. i-stems are very rare in early Latin; they were being developed in the Classical period, and their forms are liable to uncertainty. The genitive plural (by which in other declension the stem is determined) often varies in the third declension between **-um** and **-ium**. In classing words as consonant or i-stems, the genitive plural must be considered, together with the accusative singular **-im** (not **-em**), ablative singular **-ī**; accusative plural **-īs** (not **-ēs**) and in neuters the nominative plural **-ia**; but often the classification remains doubtful, and rests chiefly on analogy with other Latin words, or on comparison with cognate words in other languages.

49 The following rule with regard to the form of the genitive plural may be given for practical convenience:

Nouns with a syllable more in the genitive singular than the nominative (**imparisyllabic nouns**) have genitive plural in -**um**.

Nouns with the same number of syllables in the nominative singular and genitive singular (**parisyllabic nouns**) have genitive plural in -**ium**. The chief exceptions to this rule are the following:

(a) Imparisyllabic nouns which have genitive plural in -**ium** are: *glīs, līs, mās, mūs, nox*, and nouns of one syllable of which the nominative singular ends in -**ns, -rs, -ps, -bs, -rx, -lx;**[*] and neuters in -**al, -ar**.

Often also *rēn, lār, dōs, fraus*, nouns of two syllables with nominative singular ending -**ns, -rs,** and most nouns in -**ās** (genitive -**ātis**). These last and nouns in -**ns** are especially variable. Horace writes both *parentum* and *parentium*, but the latter is rare. Livy writes always *cīvitātium*.

(b) Parisyllabic nouns which have genitive plural in -**um** are: *canis, iuvenis, senex, sēdēs, pater, māter, frāter, accipiter.*[†]

50 **Nouns with exceptional forms**

(1) **Iuppiter** (originally *Dieu + piter* for *pater*) and **bōs**, ox.

		SING.	PLUR.
Nom.	Iuppiter	bōs	bovēs
Acc.	Iovem	bovem	bovēs
Gen.	Iovis	bovis	boum
Dat.	Iovī	bovī	bōbus or būbus
Acc.	Iovem	bovem	bovēs
Abl.	Iove	bove	bōbus or būbus

---

[*] Nouns of one syllable of which the stem has two consonants before i-, are apparently only imparisyllabic because the nom. sing. originally ended in -**is** (§ 46), and some are recorded with both forms, e.g. *orbs* and *orbis*. Similarly, neuters in -**al, -ar** originally ended -**āle, -āre**.

[†] *Pater, māter, frāter, accipiter* are only apparently parisyllabic because the **e** of the nom. sing. has fallen out in the other cases.

(2) Two stems in **-u**, declined like consonant nouns: **grūs**, crane, **sūs**, pig. These are the only uncontracted **u-** nouns.

	SING.	PLUR.	SING.	PLUR.
Nom.	grūs	gruēs	sūs	suēs
Gen.	gruis	gruum	suis	suum
Dat.	gruī	gruibus	suī	suibus or subus
Acc.	gruem	gruēs	suem	suēs
Abl.	grue	gruibus	sue	suibus or subus

Iter, n., journey, has gen. sing. *itineris* (and rarely *iteris*); *iecur*, n., liver, *iecoris, and iecinoris.*

Senex, n., old man, has sing. acc. *senem*; gen. *senis*; dat. *senī*; abl. *sene*; plur., n., acc. *senēs*; gen. *senum*; dat., abl. *senibus.*

Supellex, f., furniture, forms the other cases from stem **supellectil-** with abl. in ī or **e**.

Iūsiūrandum, n., oath, is declined in both parts: n., v., acc. *iūsiūrandum*; gen. *iūrisiūrandī*; dat. *iūriiūrandō*; abl. *iūreiūrandō*. No plural.

Paterfamiliās, māterfamiliās, father, mother of a family, have *pater, māter* fully declined in the sing. cases, but *familiās* remains unaltered. The plur. *patrēsfamiliārum* is sometimes found.

Note: The locative sing. of the third declension ends in **-ī** or **-e**; the plural in **-ibus**: *rurī, rure*, in the country; *vesperī, vespere*, in the evening ; *Carthāginī, Carthāgine*, at Carthage; *Gādibus*, at *Gādes* (Cadiz).

GENDER IN THE THIRD DECLENSION

51   Consonant Stems

Nouns which end in **-ōs, -ō** (except **-dō, -gō, -iō**), **-or, -er**, and **imparisyllabic** nouns in **-is es, ēs** are masculine.

Exceptions:
cōs, whetstone; *dōs*, dowry, f.; *os, ossis*, bone; *ōs, ōris*, mouth, n.; *ēchō*, echo; *carō*, flesh, f.
arbor, tree, f.; *æquor*, sea; *marmor*, marble; *cor*, heart, n.
vēr, spring; *cadāver*, corpse; *iter*, journey; *tūber*, hump; *ūber*, udder; *verber*, lash, n.; *linter*, skiff, f.; also some names of plants, as *papāver*, poppy, n.
compēs, fetter; *mercēs*, hire; *merges*, sheaf; *quiēs*, rest, *requiēs*; rest, *seges*, corn; *tēges*, mat, f.

52 Nouns which end in **-x, -ās, -ps, -dō, -gō, -iō,** and nouns in **-ūs** of more than one syllable are feminine.

Exceptions:

Nouns in **-ex, ēx** are masculine or common, but *lēx*, law; *nex*, death; *forfex*, shears; *supellex*, furniture; *īlex*, oak, f.; *calix*, cup; *fornix*, arch, m.; *dux*, leader, c.;

ās, coin; *fās*, right; *nefās*, wrong; *vās*, vessel, n.; *manceps*, buyer, m.;

mūniceps, burgess, c.; *prīnceps*, chief, c.;

cardō, hinge; *ōrdō*, order; *harpagō*, grappling hook, m.;

ligō, hoe, m.; *margō*, brink, c.

Concrete nouns in **-iō** are masculine: *pūgiō*, dagger; *pāpiliō*, butterfly.

Abstract nouns in **-iō** are feminine: *ratiō*, reason; *regiō*, region.

53 Nouns ending in **-us, -ūs** (in words of one syllable), **-en, ēn, -l, -ar, -ur** are neuter.

Exceptions:

lepus, hare, m.; *pecus, pecudis*, single head of cattle, f.;

mūs, mouse, m.; *grūs*, crane; *sūs*, pig, c.;

pecten, comb; *rēn*, kidney; *splēn*, spleen; *tībīcen*, flute-player, m.;

mūgil, mullet; *sāl*, salt; *sōl*, sun, m.;

lār, god of the hearth, m.;

furfur, bran; *lemur*, goblin; *turtur*, turtle dove; *vultur*, vulture, m.;

præs, bondsman, is masc; *laus*, praise; *fraus*, deceit, are fem.

54 **I- Stems**

Most parisyllabic nouns in **-is** and **-ēs** are feminine.

Exceptions: the following nouns in **-is** are masculine: *acīnacēs*, scimitar; *amnis*, river; *axis*, axle;, *canālis*, canal; *caulis*, cabbage; *clūnis*, buttock; *collis*, hill; *crīnis*, hair; *ēnsis*, sword; *fascis*, bundle; *follis*, bag; *fūstis*, cudgel; *ignis*, fire; *mēnsis*, month; *orbis*, circle; *pānis*, bread; *piscis*, fish; *postis*, post; *torris*, firebrand; *unguis*, nail; *vectis*, lever; *vermis*, worm; *verrēs*, boar.

Words which are usually masculine are: *callis*, path; *fīnis*, end; *fūnis*, rope; *sentis*, thorn; *torquis*, necklace.

Nouns in **-al, -ar,** and **-e** are neuter.

Nouns in **-x, -bs, -ls, -ns, -rs** are feminine.

Exceptions:

fōns, fountain; *mōns*, mountain; *dēns*, tooth; *bidēns*, fork; *rudēns*, rope; *torrēns*, torrent; *oriēns*; east; *occidēns*, west, are masculine.

Infāns, infant; parēns, *parent*, common.

FOURTH DECLENSION

55   U- Stems (contracted)

The nominative of masculine and feminine nouns is formed by adding **s**; neuters have the plain stem with **ū**.

Stem	**gradu-** *step,* m.		**genū** *knee,* n.
SINGULAR			
Nom.	**gradus**	*a step*	**genū**
Gen.	**gradūs**	*of a step*	**genūs**
Dat.	**graduī**	*to a step*	**genū**
Acc.	**gradum**	*a step*	**genū**
Voc.	**gradus**	*o step*	**genū**
Abl.	**gradū**	*from a step*	**genū**
PLURAL			
Nom.	**gradūs**	*steps*	**genua**
Gen.	**graduum**	*of steps*	**genuum**
Dat.	**gradibus**	*to steps*	**genibus**
Acc.	**gradūs**	*steps*	**genua**
Voc.	**gradūs**	*o steps*	**genua**
Abl.	**gradibus**	*from steps*	**genibus**

Decline like *gradus*: m. *frūctus,* fruit; *senātus,* senate; f. *manus,* hand. Decline like *genū*: *cornū,* horn; *verū,* spit (dat. abl. plur.,**-ibus** or **-ubus**).

Feminine nouns of this declension, besides *manus,* are: *acus,* needle; *porticus,* porch; *tribus,* tribe; *Īdūs,* Ides, and words feminine by meaning. Neuters are: *genū, cornū, verū.*

Note 1: The dat. sing. **-uī** is sometimes contracted into **-ū**. The dat. and abl. plur. **-ubus** is generally changed into **-ibus**; but *acus, tribus, arcus,* bow, *lacus,* lake, *partus,* birth, and *artūs* (plur.), limbs, have always **-ubus**; *portus,* harbor, has **-ibus** or **-ubus**.

Note 2: Some nouns have forms of both **u**- and **o**- stems, especially names of trees: *laurus,* bay; *myrtus,* myrtle. *Colus,* distaff, has gen. **-ī** and **ūs**, abl.**-ō** and **-ū**, acc. pl. **-ōs** and **ūs**. See § 56.

Note 3: The vocative is identical in form to the nominative in all fourth declension nouns.

56   *Domus, f.*, is declined thus:

	SINGULAR	PLURAL
Nom.	domus	domūs
Gen.	domūs or domī	domōrum or domuum
Dat.	domuī or domō	domibus
Acc.	domum	domūs or domōs
Abl.	domō	domibus

The locative **domī**, at home, is often used.

FIFTH DECLENSION

57   **Ē- Stems**

The nominative singular is formed by adding **s** to the stem.

Stem rē- *thing*

SINGULAR.			PLURAL.		
Nom.	rēs	a thing	rēs	things
Gen.	reī	of a thing	rērum	of things
Dat.	reī	to a thing	rēbus	to things
Acc.	rem	a thing	rēs	things
Voc.	rēs	o thing	rēs	o things
Abl.	rē	from a thing	rēbus	from things

Decline like *rēs*: *diēs*, day (gen. dat., *diēī*); *aciēs*, line of battle; *faciēs*, face; *seriēs*, series; *speciēs*, form; *spēs*, hope; *fidēs*, faith; *glaciēs*, ice; *meridiēs*, noon.

Rēs and *diēs* are the only of these nouns which occur in the gen., dat., and abl. plural. *Fidēs, meridiēs*, are singular only.

All nouns of this declension are feminine except *diēs* and *meridiēs*. *Diēs* also is feminine when it means 'an appointed day' or 'a period of time.'

Note 1: The greater number of nouns of this declension were originally **ia**-stems, and have forms both of **e**- and **a**- stems. They are declined like *māteriēs*, matter, singular only:

Stem	māteriā-	māteriē-
Nom.	māteriā	māteriēs
Gen.	māteriæ	māteriēī
Dat.	māteriæ	māteriēī
Acc.	māteriam	māteriem
Abl.	māteriā	māteriē

Note 2: The contracted gen. and dat. sing. in -ē, as *fidē* for *fideī*, is found in Virgil and Horace. An old gen. in -ī occurs in *tribūnus plēbī*, tribune of the people. The locative ends in -ē.

58 **Note 3:** Rēspūblica, the public interest, the republic, the state, is declined in both its parts:

	SINGULAR	PLURAL
Nom.	rēspūblica	rēspūblicæ
Gen.	reīpūblicæ	rērumpūblicārum
Dat.	reīpūblicæ	rēbuspūblicīs
Acc.	rempūblicam	rēspūblicās
Abl.	rēpūblicā	rēbuspūblicīs

DEFECTIVE AND VARIABLE SUBSTANTIVES

59 Many nouns are found only in the singular; these are chiefly proper names and words of general meaning:

humus, ground.	*ævum*, an age	*iūstitia*, justice	*aurum*, gold
lætitia, joy	*argentum*, silver	*vēr*, spring	*cælum*, heaven
vesper, evening	*lētum*, death		

Note: In poetry some words take plural form with singular meaning: *mella*, honey, *nivēs*, snow; *silentia*, silence; *rūra*, country.

60 **Many nouns are used only in the plural**

arma, arms	*artūs*, limbs	*cūnæ*, cradle
dīvitiæ, riches	*fāstī*, annals	*fēriæ*, holidays
indūtiæ, truce	*īnsidiæ*, ambush	*līberi*, children
mānēs, departed spirits	*mœnia*, town walls	*nūgæ*, trifles
penātēs, household gods	*tenebræ*, darkness	

And names of towns, days, festivals: *Athēnæ; Delphī; Kalendæ*, Calends; *Bacchanālia*, festival of Bacchus.

61   Some words have a different meaning in singular and plural

SINGULAR	PLURAL
ædēs, temple	*ædēs*, house
auxilium, help	*auxilia*, allied forces
castrum, fort	*castra*, camp
cēra, wax	*cērœ*, waxen tablet
cōpia, plenty	*cōpiœ*, forces
fīnis, end	*fīnēs*, boundaries
grātia, favor	*grātiœ*, thanks
impedīmentum, hindrance	*impedīmenta*, baggage
littera, letter of the alphabet	*litterœ*, epistle, literature
lūdus, play	*lūdī*, public games
opem (acc), help	*opēs*, wealth
sāl, salt	*salēs*, wit

62   Some nouns have two or more forms of declension

NOM.	GEN.		NOM.	GEN.	
tergum,	-ī, n.	} back	**pecus**	-oris, n.	} cattle,
tergus,	-oris, n.		**pecus**	-udis, f.	head of cattle
ēventum,	-ī, n.	} event	**plēbs,**	-is, f.	} the common people
ēventus,	-ūs, m.		**plēbēs,**	-eī, f.	

NOM.	GEN.		NOM.	GEN.	ABL.	
iūgerum,	-ī, n.	} acre	**vespera,**	-æ	-ā, f.	
[iūger],	-is, n.		**vesper,**	-ī,	-ō, m.	} evening
			vesper,	—	-e, m.	

Quiēs, f., rest, *-ētis*, is a **t-** stem only; but its compound *requiēs* takes also the **e-** forms (5th declension): *requiem, requiē*.

63   Some o- stems vary between masc. and neut. in sing. and plur.
e.g.: *baculus*, m., *baculum*, n., a stick; *pileus*, m., *pileum*, n., a hat.

Some other **o-** stems have masculine and neuter forms in the plural only: *frēnum*, bit, plur. *frēnī, frēna*; *iocus*, jest, plur. *iocī, ioca*; *rāstrum*, harrow, plur. *rāstrī, rāstra*.

Locus, place, has plurals *loca*, meaning places or district and *locī*, usually meaning passages in a text.

64   In many nouns some of the cases are wanting; thus:

	feast, f.	fruit, f.	help, f.	prayer, f.	change, f.
Nom.	—	—	—	—	—
Gen.	dapis	frūgis	opis	—	vicis
Dat.	dapī	frūgī	—	precī	—
Acc.	dapem	frūgem	opem	precem	vicem
Voc.	—	—	—	—	—
Abl.	dape	frūge	ope	prece	vice

These have full plural -ēs, -um, -ibus, except gen. *vicium.*

65   Many are used in the ablative singular only

coāctū,	by force	nātū,	by birth
concessū,	by permission	noctū,	by night
(diū) interdiū,	by day	rogātū,	by request
iussū,	by command	sponte,	by choice
iniussū	without command		

66   Some nouns have only nominative and accusative singular

E.g.: *fās*, right, *nefās*, wrong, *īnstar*, likeness, size, *nihil*, nothing.

DECLENSION OF GREEK NOUNS

67   First declension, a- stems

At an early time many Greek nouns were used in Latin, in an almost or entirely Latin form. Masculine nouns ending in **-as, -es,** and feminine nouns in **-a, -e,** all alike took the ending **-a** in the nominative, and were declined throughout like *mēnsa.* Such words are *nauta,* sailor, *poēta,* poet.

Afterwards the Greek forms, especially of proper names, were brought in by the poets, and thus in many instances both Greek and Latin forms of the same words are found, while of some words, used chiefly in poetry, the Greek forms alone occur.

Note 1: Early borrowings were from the Doric dialect, e.g. ναυτάς, μαχανά, rather than from the Attic, ναύτης, μηχανή.

Note 2: Patronymics (family names) are usually in the Greek form, as *Atrīdēs* (son of Atreus), *Pēlīdēs* (son of Peleus); and though they sometimes have **-a** for **-ēs** in the nom. They always retain the Greek acc. in **-ēn**. Names of people ending in **-ātes**, **-ītēs**, or **-ōtes**, as *Eleātēs* (inhabitant of Elea), generally have **-em** or **-am** in acc., being nearer to Latin words. All these usually follow the Latin declension in the plural, even when they have the Greek form in the singular.

Masculine nouns in -ās, -ēs, and feminine nouns in -ē

SINGULAR

Nom.	Ænēās	Atrīdēs, -a	Cybelē, a
Gen.	Ænēæ	Atrīdæ	Cybelēs, -æ
Dat.	Ænēæ	Atrīdæ	Cybelæ
Acc.	Ænēān	Atrīdēn	Cybelēn, -am
Voc.	Ænēā	Atrīdē, -a, -ā	Cybelē, -a,
Abl.	Ænēā	Atrīdē, -ā	Cybelē, -ā,

Plural in all cases like that of *mēnsa*.

Decline also: *Boreās*, the north wind, *Persa* (*-ēs*), a Persian, *Ēpiretēs* (*-ōta*), native of Epirus, *Helenē*, f.

68   Second declension, o- stems

Greek nouns of the second declension, especially names of persons and places, often keep their Greek forms in the nom. and acc., but the other cases generally take the Latin forms.

SINGULAR

Nom.	Dēlos, f.	Athos, m.	Pēlion, n.
Gen.	Dēlī	Athō	Pēliī
Dat.	Dēlō	Athō	Pēliō
Acc.	Dēlon, -um	Athōn	Pēlion
Voc.	(Dēle)	(Athōs)	(Pēlion)
Abl.	Dēlō	Athō	Pēliō

Note 1: The feminine words of this declension are chiefly names of towns, islands, plants, and precious stones.

Note 2: Nouns ending in **-ros** sometimes take the Latin ending **-er** in the nom., as *Euander* (or *-dros*).

Note 3: Decline also: *scorpios*, m., scorpion; *lōtos*, f., lotus; *Samos*; *Īlion*.

Note 4: The Greek plural forms are rare, but plural nom. in **-œ**, as *Canēphorœ*, and plur. gen. in **-ōn**, as *Būcolicōn*, are sometimes found.

69   Third declension

These nouns are very numerous, having many different endings in the nominative singular.

	SINGULAR	PLURAL	SINGULAR.	PLURAL.
Nom.	hērōs, m., *hero*	hērōes	lynx, c., *lynx*	lynces
Gen.	hērōis	hērōum	lyncis	lyncum
Dat.	hērōī	hērōibus	lyncī	lyncibus
Acc.	hērō-a, -em	hērōas	lync-em, -a	lync-as, -ēs
Voc.	hērōs,	hērōes	lynx,	lynces
Abl.	hērōe	hērōibus	lynce	lyncibus

Note 1: Decline also: f. *lampas*, gen. *lampadis*, torch; m. *gigās, gigantis*, giant; *āēr, āēris*, air; *æthēr, ætheris*, the upper air.

Note 2: Names of this class are found in different forms, from the tendency to latinize Greek words. Thus Perseus is called *Persēūs* by Livy, but by Cicero latinized to *Persēs* in the nom., with the other cases like Greek names of the first declension, as *Atrīdēs*.

Note 3: Greek nouns in **-ōn** often drop the **n** in the nom., as *Platō, Platōnis*; but sometimes it is kept, as in *Cīmōn*. Some nouns have a second form, as *elephās*, elephant, which is usually declined like *gigās*, but sometimes latinized to *elephantus, elephantī*.
Dīdō also has two forms of declension, (1) as an **-ōn** stem, gen. *Didōnis*, (2) as a **u-** stem, gen. *Dīdūs*.

Note 4: *Poēma, poēmatis*, n., poem, is regularly declined, but Cicero has dat, and abl. plur. *poēmatīs*. *Poēsis*, f., poetry, is an **i-** noun, acc. *poēsin* or *poēsim*, abl. *poēsī*.

Note 5: The accusative singular endings in **-em** and in **-a** are both frequent. Gen. sing. usually in **-is**, but the Greek ending **-os** is often found in poetry. The abl. sing. is always in **-e**, and dat, sing. in **-ī**, but the latter is often short (Ĭ) as in Greek. The nom. plur. is always in **-es**, often short. In acc. plur. the Greek **-as** is usual. The Greek ending of the abl. plur. in **-si (-sin)** is occasionally used by the poets.

Note 6: Many names in **-ēs**, **-eus**, and in **-is** have cases from two forms. **i-** forms and consonant forms appear in

Nom.	Gen.	Dat.	Acc.	Voc.	Abl.
Thalēs	-is, -ētis	-ī, ētī	-em, ēn, ēta	-ēs, -e	-ē, ēte m.
Paris	-idis, -idos	-idi	-idem, -ida	-is, -i	-ide f., m.
Iris			-in, -im		

Forms of both the second and third declension appear in:

Nom.	Gen.	Dat.	Acc.	Voc.	Abl.
Orphēus	-eī, -eos	-ēī	-eum, -ea	-eu	-eō, ēō m.
Achillēus	-eī, -eos	-ī	-ea	-eu	-e, -ē m.
Achillēs	īs, -ī	-ī	-em, ēn	-ē	-e, -ē m.

Note 7 *Tigris*, tiger, is declined throughout as an **i-** noun, like *cīvis*; but also as a consonant stem in **d**, like *Paris*; forming plur. *tigrides, tigridum, tigridas*, without dat. and abl. Decline *Ulixēus (Ulixēs)* like *Achillēus (Achillēs)*.

70   DECLENSION OF ADJECTIVES

Adjectives are declined by gender, number and case.

71   A. Adjectives declined like 2nd and 1st declension nouns

Adjectives of three endings in *-us, -a, -um* or *-er, -a, -um* are declined like nouns of the second and first declension, **o-** and **a-** stems.

Stem	bono-	bonā-	bono-
		good	
SING.	M.	F.	N.
Nom.	bonus	bona	bonum
Gen.	bonī	bonæ	bonī
Dat.	bonō	bonæ	bonō
Acc.	bonum	bonam	bonum
Voc.	bone	bona	bonum
Abl.	bonō	bonā	bonō
PLURAL			
Nom.	bonī	bonæ	bona
Gen.	bonōrum	bonārum	bonōrum
Dat.,Abl.	bonīs	bonīs	bonīs
Acc.	bonōs	bonās	bona

Note 1: Decline also: *cārus*, dear; *dūrus*, hard; *malus*, bad; *magnus*, great; *parvus*, small; *dubius*, doubtful.

Note 2: Adjectives in **-ius, -ia, -ium** as *eximus*, excellent, have m. voc. sing in **-ie**; m. and n. gen. sing. in **-iī**, unlike similar nouns.

Stem	tenero-	tenera-	tenero
	tender		
SING.	M.	F.	N.
Nom.	tener	tenera	tenerum
Gen.	tenerī	teneræ	tenerī
Dat.	tenerō	teneræ	tenerō
Acc.	tenerum	teneram	tenerum
Voc.	tener	tenera	tenerum
Abl.	tenerō	tenerā	tenerō

PLURAL.

Nom.	tenerī	teneræ	tenera
Gen.	tenerōrum	tenerārum	tenerōrum
Dat.	tenerīs	tenerīs	tenerīs
Acc.	tenerōs	tenerās	tenera
Voc.	tenerī	teneræ	tenera
Abl.	tenerīs	tenerīs	tenerīs

Note: Also declined thus are: *asper*, rough; *lacer*, torn; *līber*, free; *miser*, wretched; *prōsper*, prosperous; *frūgifer*, fruit-bearing, *plūmiger*, feathered, and other compounds of *fero* and *gero*; also *satur*, full, *satura*, f, *saturum*, n.

Stem	nigro-	nigrā- black	nigro
SING.	M.	F.	N.
Nom.	niger	nigra	nigrum
Gen.	nigrī	nigræ	nigrī
Dat.	nigrō	nigræ	nigrō
Acc.	nigrum	nigram	nigrum
Voc.	niger	nigra	nigrum
Abl.	nigrō	nigrā	nigrō
PLURAL			
Nom.	nigrī	nigræ	nigra
Gen.	nigrōrum	nigrārum	nigrōrum
Dat.	nigrīs	nigrīs	nigrīs
Acc.	nigrōs	nigrās	nigra
Voc.	nigrī	nigræ	nigra
Abl.	nigrīs	nigrīs	nigrīs

Note 1: Decline also: *æger*, sick; *āter*, jet-black; *pulcher*, beautiful; *ruber*, red; *sacer*, sacred.

Note 2: *Dexter*, on the right hand, may be declined like *tener* or like *niger*.

72 B. Adjectives of 2 endings and 1 ending in nom. sing.

Adjectives of two endings and of one ending in the nominative singular are declined like substantives of the third declension.

73   **(1) Adjectives with nom. sing. in -is, masc. and fem.; in -e neuter: i- stems**

Stem		**tristi-,** sad	
	SINGULAR		PLURAL
	M. F.	N.	M. F.	N.

	M. F.	N.	M. F.	N.
Nom.	trĭstis	trĭste	trĭstēs	trĭstia
Gen.	trĭstis	trĭstis	trĭstium	trĭstium
Dat..	trĭstī	trĭstī	trĭstibus	trĭstibus
Acc.	trĭstem	trĭste	trĭstēs, -īs	trĭstia
Voc.	trĭstis	trĭste	trĭstēs	trĭstia
Abl.	trĭstī	trĭstī	trĭstibus	trĭstibus

Note: Decline also: *brevis*, short; *omnis*, all; *æquālis*, equal; *hostīlis*, hostile; *facilis*, easy; *illūstris*, illustrious; *lūgubris*, mournful.

Some stems in **ri-** form the masc. nom. sing. in **-er**:

Stem		**ācri-,** keen	
SINGULAR	M.	F.	N.
Nom.	ācer	ācris	ācre
Gen.	ācris	ācris	ācris
Dat.	ācrī	ācrī	ācrī
Acc.	ācrem	ācrem	ācre
Voc.	ācer	ācris	ācre
Abl.	ācrī	ācrī	ācrī
PLURAL			
Nom.	ācrēs	ācrēs	ācria
Gen.	ācrium	ācrium	ācrium
Dat.	ācribus	ācribus	ācribus
Acc.	ācrēs, -īs	ācrēs, -īs	ācria
Voc.	ācrēs	ācrēs	ācria
Abl.	ācribus	ācribus	ācribus

Note 1: Decline like ācer: *celeber*, famous; *salūber*, healthy; *alacer*, brisk; *volucer*, winged; *campester*, level; *equester*, equestrian; *pedester*, pedestrian; *palūster*, marshy; *puter*, crumbling; names of months are adjectives agreeing with *mēnsis* (m), *Kalendæ* (f) and *Nōnnæ* (f). *Aprīlis* declines like *trĭstis*. *September, Octōber, November, December* are masculine only and decline like *ācer*.

Note 2: In *celer, celeris, celere*, swift, the stem ends in **-eri-** and the **e** is kept throughout.

74   (2) Adjectives with nom. sing. the same for all genders

(a) i- Stems

Stem **fēlīci-**, happy

	SINGULAR		PLURAL	
	M. F.	N.	M. F.	N.
Nom.	fēlīx	fēlīx	fēlīces	fēlīcia
Gen.	fēlīcis	fēlīcis	fēlīcium	fēlīcium
Dat.	fēlīcī	fēlīcī	fēlīcibus	fēlīcibus
Acc.	fēlīcem	fēlīx	fēlīces, -īs	fēlīcia
Voc.	fēlīx	fēlīx	fēlīces	fēlīcia
Abl.	fēlīcī	fēlīcī	fēlīcibus	fēlīcibus

Stem **ingenti-**, huge.

	SINGULAR		PLURAL	
	M. F.	N.	M. F.	N.
Nom.	ingēns	ingēns	ingentēs	ingentia
Gen.	ingentis	ingentis	ingentium	ingentium
Dat.	ingentī	ingentī	ingentibus	ingentibus
Acc.	ingentem	ingēns	ingentēs, -īs	ingentia
Voc.	ingēns	ingēns	ingentēs	ingentia
Abl.	ingentī	ingentī	ingentibus	ingentibus

Decline also: *audāx, audāci-*, bold; *simplex, simplici-*, simple; *duplex, duplici-*, double; *vēlōx, vēlōci-*, swift; *amāns, amanti-*, loving; *sapiens, sapienti-*, wise; *concors, concordi-*, agreeing; *pār, pari-*, like.

Note 1: Some adjectives with stems in **ti** have genitive plural in **-um** as well as **-ium**: *recēns, recentum* or *recentium; cōnsors, cōnsortum* or *cōnsortium*. In participles, however, the gen. plur. is almost always in **-ium**.

Note 2: It is to be remarked that when either in a noun or an adjective a long vowel comes before the stem character, the genitive plural generally ends in **-ium**; when a short vowel comes before the stem character, it ends in **-um**; but this cannot be laid down as an invariable rule.

Note 3: The abl. sing. generally ends in **-ī** when an adjective is used with a substantive: *ā mīlite vigilī*, by a watchful soldier; and in **-e** when an adjective stands for a substantive: *ā vigile*, by a watchman, but a few have abl. sing. always in **-ī**. The same rule applies to present participles; but in the ablative absolute construction the ablative always ends in **-e**: *viridantī quercū cīnctus*, wreathed with green oak; *viridante quercū*, when the oak is green.

75   (b) Consonant stems
            Stem **veter-**, old

	Sing.		Plur.	
	M. F.	N.	M. F.	N.
Nom.	vetus	vetus	veterēs	vetera
Gen.	veteris	veteris	veterum	veterum
Dat.	veterī	veterī	veteribus	veteribus
Acc.	veterem	vetus	veterēs	vetera
Abl.	vetere	vetere	veteribus	veteribus

Stem **dīvet-, dīvit-**, rich.

	SING.	PLUR.
Nom.	dīves	dīvitēs
Gen.	dīvitis	dīvitum
Dat.	dīvitī	dīvitibus
Acc.	dīvitem	dīvitēs
Abl.	dīvite	dīvitibus

Note 1: Decline like *veter* and *dives*: *pauper, paupeis,* poor; *dēgener, dēgeneris,* degenerate; *sōspes, sōspitis,* safe; *superstes, superstitis,* surviving; *dēses, dēsidis,* slothful; *compos, compotis,* possessing; *cælebs, cælibis,* unmarried.

Note 2: *Dives* has a contracted form *dīs,* nom., *dītem,* acc. &c., with abl. sing. *dītī* and neut. plur. *dītia,* gen. plur. *dītium.*

Note 3: *Inops, memor* have abl. sing. in -ī.

COMPARISON OF ADJECTIVES

76   Adjectives are compared in three degrees.
      (1) Positive: **dūrus,** hard, **trīstis,** sad.
      (2) Comparative: **dūrior,** harder, rather hard, too hard; **trīstior,** sadder, rather hard, too hard (§ 310).
      (3) Superlative: **dūrissimus,** hardest, very hard; **trīstissimus,** saddest, very sad (§ 309).

The **positive** is the adjective itself expressing the quality; the **comparative** expresses a greater degree; the **superlative** expresses a very great, or the greatest, degree of the quality. The comparative is formed from the positive by adding the suffix **-ior** (or **-ius** in neut.)

to the last consonant of the stem; the superlative generally by adding
-issimus to the last consonant of the stem.

Stem	Positive	Comparative	Superlative
dūr-o-	dūrus	dūr-ior	dūr-issimus
trīst-i-	trīstis	trīst-ior	trīst-issimus
audāc-i-	audāx	audāc-ior	audāc-issimus

77   The Comparative is declined as follows:

	SING.		PLUR.	
	M.F.	N.	M.F.	N.
Nom.	trīstior	trīstius	trīstiōres	trīstiōra
Gen.	trīstiōris	trīstiōris	trīstiōrum	trīstiōrum
Dat.	trīstiōrī	trīstiōrī	trīstiōribus	trīstiōribus
Acc.	trīstiōrem	trīstius	trīstiōres	trīstiōra
Voc.	trīstior	trīstius	trīstiōres	trīstiōra
Abl.	trīstiōr-e, -ī*	trīstiōr-e, -ī*	trīstiōribus	trīstiōribus

* The ablative in -ī of the comparative is rare, and only used by late writers.

78   The superlative is declined from o- and a- stems, like *bonus.*

Adjectives with stems in **ro-**, **ri-**, form the superlative by doubling the
last consonant of the stem and adding **-imus**. Words like **niger** insert
e before **r** in the Superlative.

Stem	Positive	Comparative	Superlative
tenero-	tener	tenerior	tenerrimus
nigro-	niger	nigrior	nigerrimus
celeri-	celer	celerior	celerrimus

Six adjectives with stems in **-ili-** also form the superlative by doubling
the last consonant of the stem and adding **-imus**:

facilis, easy	**similis**, like	**gracilis**, slender
difficilis, difficult	**dissimilis**, unlike.	**humilis**, lowly

e.g.   root *facili-*, positive *facilis*, comparative *facilior*, superlative *facillimus*

79   Many participles are compared like adjectives:

amāns, loving   amantior   amantissimus
parātus, ready   parātior   parātissimus

Irregular Comparison

80   (1) Some comparatives and superlatives are formed from stems distinct from that of the positive:

Positive	Comparative	Superlative
bonus, good	melior, better	optimus, best
malus, bad	peior,[†] worse	pessimus, worst
parvus, small	minor, less	minimus, least
multus, much	plūs, more	plūrimus, most
magnus, great	maior[†]	maximus
nēquam*, wicked	nēquior	nēquissimus
frūgī*, honest	frūgālior	frūgālissimus
senex, old	{ senior / nātū maior	nātū maximus
iuvenis, young	{ iūnior / nātū minor	nātū minimus

* Indeclinable. † The consonant i was pronounced as a double vowel; therefore the first syllable is heavy even though the preceding vowel is short.

Note 1: *Senior, iūnior* are not used as true comparatives of *senex, iūvenis*, but with the meaning old rather than young, and young rather than old.

Note 2: *Dīves* has both uncontracted and contracted forms:

dīves,	} rich	dīvitior	dīvitissimus
(dīs)		dītior	dītissimus
vetus,	} old has	{ vetustior	veterrimus
(veter)		{ (veterior)	

Following its meaning, *plūs* as an adjective is always *more* than one, that is, plural, although it exists in the singular as a neuter noun:

	SING. (noun)	PLURAL	
	Neuter	M. F.	N.
Nom.	plūs	plūres	plūra
Gen.	plūris	plūrium	plūrium
Dat.	plūrī	plūribus	plūribus
Acc.	plūs	plūres	plūra
Abl.	plūre	plūribus	plūribus

81 (2) Adjectives compounded with **-dicus, -ficus, -volus** (from *dīcō, faciō, volō*), form the comparative and superlative as if from participles in *-ēns.*

Positive	Comparative	Superlative:
maledicus, scurrilous	**maledīcentior**	**maledīcentissimus**
beneficus, generous	**beneficentior**	**beneficentissimus**
benevolus, well-wishing	**benevolentior**	**benevolentissimus**
also:		
egēnus, needy	**egentior**	**egentissimus**
prōvidus, provident	**prōvidentior**	**prōvidentissimus**

82 (3) Adjectives in **-eus, -ius, -uus** are generally compared with the adverbs *magis, maximē: dubius*, doubtful, *magis dubius*, more doubtful; *maximē dubius*, most doubtful.

> **Note:** Adjectives in **-quus** are compared regularly, the first **u** being consonantal: *æquus*, level, *æquior, æquissimus*; so *antīquus*, ancient. *Ēgregius*, excellent, has comparative *ēgregior; strēnuus*, vigorous, sometimes has *strēnuior.*

83 (4) Some adjectives have no comparative forms; some no superlative; of some the comparative and superlative are found without the positive: *ōcior*, swifter, *ōcissimus*, swiftest.

84 Some comparatives denoting relations of place have no positive, but correspond to adverbs from the same stem.

Adverb	Comparative Adj	Superlative Adj.
extrā,* outside	**exterior**	**extrēmus, extimus**
intrā, within	**interior**	**intimus**
suprā,* above	**superior**	**suprēmus, summus**
īnfrā,* below	**īnferior**	**īnfimus, īmus**
citrā, on this side	**citerior**	**citimus**
ultrā, beyond	**ulterior**	**ultimus**
præ, before	**prior**	**prīmus**, first
post,* after	**posterior**	**postrēmus**, last
prope, near	**propior**	**proximus**

> *****Note:** The adjectives *exterus, superus, īnferus, posterus*, are, however, sometimes found. Also: *dexter* (adj.), on the right, *dexterior dexterrimus* or *dextimus; sinister* (adj.), on the left, *sinisterior; dēter*, down [obs. adj. from prep *dē*], *deterior*, worse, *deterrimus*, worst.

Comparison of Adverbs

85 Adverbs derived from adjectives and ending in **-ē, -ō, -ter**, and rarely **-e**, form comparative in **-ius**, superlative in **-issimē**.

Note: These forms are the neut. acc. sing. of the comparative adjective and an old neut. abl. sing. of the superlative adjective.

Adjective	Adverb	Comparative	Superlative
dignus, worthy	**dignē**, worthily	**dignius**	**dignissimē**
tūtus, safe	**tūtō**, safely.	**tūtius**	**tūtissimē**
fortis, brave	**fortiter**, bravely	**fortius**	**fortissimē**
cōnstāns, firm	**cōnstanter**, firmly	**cōnstantius**	**cōnstantissimē**
audāx, bold	**audācter**, boldly	**audācius**	**audācissimē**
facilis, easy	**facile**, easily	**facilius**	**facillimē**

86 Irregular comparison has corresponding forms in adverbs.

Adverb	Comparative	Superlative
bene, well	**melius**	**optimē**
male, badly	**peius** (see §80)	**pessimē**
paulum, little	**minus**	**minimē**
multum, much	**plūs**	**plūrimum**
magnopere, greatly	**magis**	**maximē**
—	**ōcius**, more quickly	**ōcissimē**
nēquiter, wickedly.	**nēquius**	**nēquissimē**

Note: *Magis*, more (in degree); *plūs*, more (in quantity).

---

87 In like manner are compared:

diū, long	**diūtius**	**diūtissimē**
intus, within	**interius**	**intimē**
(**præ**, before)	**prius**	**prīmō, prīmum**
post, after	**posterius**	**postrēmō**
prope, near	**propius**	**proximē**
sæpe, often	**sæpius**	**sæpissimē**
nūper, lately	—	**nūperrimē**
—	**potius**, rather	**potissimum**, especially

88   Numerals (see also § 311)

Numeral adjectives are of three kinds:

1. **Cardinals**, answering the question, *How many?*
2. **Ordinals**, answering the question, *Which in order of number?*
3. **Distributives**, answering the question, *How many each?*

88a   Numeral adverbs answer the question, *How many times?*

89   Ūnus, one, from **o-** and **ā-** stems, is declined as follows:

	SINGULAR			PLURAL		
Nom.	ūnus	ūna	ūnum	ūnī	ūnæ	ūna
Gen.	ūnīus	ūnīus	ūnīus	ūnōrum	ūnārum	ūnōrum
Dat.	ūnī	ūnī	ūnī	ūnīs	ūnīs	ūnīs
Acc.	ūnum	ūnam	ūnum	ūnōs	ūnās	ūna
Abl.	ūnō	ūnā	ūnō	ūnīs	ūnīs	ūnīs

Duo, two, is an **o-** stem, and **tres**, three, an **i-** stem:

	M.	F.	N.	M. and F.	N.
Nom.	duo	duæ	duo	trēs	tria
Gen.	duōrum	duārum	duōrum	trium	trium
Dat.	duōbus	duābus	duōbus	tribus	tribus
Acc.	duōs, duo	duās	duo	trēs (trī)	tria
Abl.	duōbus	duābus	duōbus	tribus	tribus

Note 1: The **i** of gen. sing. *ūnīus* is sometimes short. Some pronominal adjectives are declined like *ūnus* (§ 101).

Note 2: *Duum* is sometimes used for *duōrum, duārum.*

The **cardinals** from *quattuor* to *centum* are indeclinable. Hundreds from two to nine hundred are **o-** and **ā-** stems: *ducentī, ducentæ, ducenta. Mīlle* (a thousand) is an indeclinable adjective; but *mīlia* (thousands) is a neuter noun declined like *animālia. Mīlle passus,* a mile.

In **compound numbers** between twenty-one and ninety-nine, either the smaller number with **et** comes first (as was common in English until quite recently), or the larger without **et** (as in current English usage): *septem et trīgintā,* seven and thirty; or *trīgintā septem,* thirty-seven. *Ūnus* usually stands first: *ūnus et vīgintī,* twenty-one. In numbers above a hundred the larger comes first, with or without *et.*

Thousands are expressed by putting (1) the numeral adverbs **bis**, **ter**, &c., before *mīlle: bis mīlle*; or (2) cardinal numbers before *mīlia: duo milia. Mīlia* is followed by a genitive: *duo mīlia hominum*, two thousand men.

90   LIST OF NUMBERS

Arabic	Roman	Cardinals	Ordinals	Distrubutives	Adverbs
			-us, f. -a, -um	m. -i, f. -æ, n.. -a	
1	I	ūnus	primus (prior), first	singulī, one each	semel, once
2	II	duo	secundus (alter), second	bīnī, two each, etc.	bis, twice
3	III	trēs	tertius, third, &c.	ternī, or trīnī,	ter, thrice, &c.
4	IIII or IV	quattuor	quārtus	quaternī	quater
5	V	quīnque	quīntus	quīnī	quīnquiēns
6	VI	sex	sextus	sēnī	sexiēns
7	VII	septem	septimus	septēnī	septiēns
8	VIII or IIX	octō	octāvus	octōnī	octiēns
9	VIIII or IX	novem	nōnus	novēnī	noviēns
10	X	decem	decimus	dēnī	deciēns
11	XI	ūndecim	ūndecimus	ūndēnī	ūndeciēns
12	XII	duodecim	duodecimus	duodēnī	duodeciēns
13	XIII	tredecim	tertius decimus	ternī dēnī	tredeciēns
14	XIIII or XIV	quattuordecim	quārtus decimus	quaternī dēnī	quattuor-deciēns
15	XV	quīndecim	quīntus decimus	quīnī dēnī	quīndeciēns
16	XVI	sēdecim	sextus decimus	sēnī dēnī	sēdeciēns
17	XVII	septendecim	septimus decimus	septēnī dēnī	septies decēns
18	XVIII or XIIX	duodēvigintī or octōdecim	duodēvicēnsimus	duodēvīcēnī	duodēvīciēns
19	XVIIII or XIX	ūndēvigintī or novendecim	ūndēvicēnsimus	ūndēvīcēnī	ūndēvīciēns
20	XX	vigintī	vicēnsimus	vīcēnī	vīciēns
21	XXI	ūnus at vigintī	ūnus et vicēnsimus	vīcēnī singulī	semel et vīciēns
22	XXII	duo et vigintī	alter et vicēnsimus	vīcēnī bīnī	bis et vīciēns
28	XXVIII or XXIIX	duodētrigintā	duodētricēnsimus	duodētrīcēnī	duodētrīciēns
29	XXVIIII or XXIX	ūndētrigintā	ūndētricēnsimus	ūndētrīcēnī	ūndētrīciēns
30	XXX	trigintā	tricēnsimus	trīcēnī	trīciēns
40	XXXX or XL	quadrāgintā	quadrāgēnsimus	quadrāgēnī	quadrāgiēns
50	L	quīnquāgintā	quīnquāgēnsimus	quīnquāgēnī	quīnquāgiēns
60	LX	sexāgintā	sexāgēnsimus	sexāgēnī	sexāgiēns
70	LXX	septuāgintā	septuāgēnsimus	septuāgēnī	septuāgiēns

Arabic	Roman	Cardinals	Ordinals	Distrubutives	Adverbs
			-us, f. -a, -um	m. -i, f. -æ, n.. -a	
80	LXXX or XXC	octōgintā	octōgēnsimus	octōgēnī	octōgiēns
90	LXXXX or XC	nōnāgintā	nōnāgēnsimus	nōnāgēnī	nōnāgiēns
98	XCIIX or IIC	octō et nōnāgintā	duodēcentēnsimus	duodēcentēnī	duodēcentiēns
99	XCIX or IC	ūndēcentum	ūndēcentēnsimus	ūndēcentēnī	ūndēcentiēns
100	C	centum	centēnsimus	centēnī	centiēns
101	CI	centum et ūnus	centēnsimus primus	centēnī singulī	centiēns semel
126	CXXVI	centum vīgintī sex	centēnsimus vīcēnsimus sextus	centēnī vīcēnī sēnī	centiēns vīciēns sexiēns
200	CC	ducenti, æ, a	ducentēnsimus	ducēnī	ducentiēns
300	CCC	trecentī	trecentēnsimus	trecēnī	trecentiēns
400	CCCC	quadringentī	quadringentēnsimus	quadringēnī	quadringentiēns
500	Ɔ or D	quīngentī	quīngentēnsimus	quīngēnī	quīngentiēns
600	DC	sescentī	sescentēnsimus	sescēnī	sescentiēns
700	DCC	septingentī	septingentēnsimus	septingēnī	septingentiēns
800	DCCC	octingentī	octingentēnsimus	octingēnī	octingentiēns
900	DCCCC	nōngentī,	nōngentēnsimus	nōngēnī	nōngentiēns
1,000	CIƆ or M	mīlle	millēnsimus	singula mīlia	mīliēns
2,000	CIƆCIƆ or MM	duo mīlia	bis millēnsimus	bīna mīlia	bis mīliēns
5,000	IƆƆ	quīnque mīlia	quīnquiēns millēnsimus	quīna mīlia	quīnquiēns mīliēns
10,000	CCIƆƆ	decem mīlia	deciēns millēnsimus	dēna mīlia	deciēns mīliēns
50,000	IƆƆƆ	quīnquāgintā mīlia	quīnquāgiēns millēnsimus	quīnquāgēna mīlia	quīnquāgiēns mīliēns
100,000	CCCIƆƆƆ	centum mīlia	centiēns millēnsimus	centēna mīlia	centiēns mīliēns
500,000	IƆƆƆƆ	quīngenta mīlia	quīngentiēns millēnsimus	quīngēna mīlia	quīngentiēns mīliēns
1,000,000	CCCCI ƆƆƆƆ	deciēns centena mīlia	deciēns centiēns millēnsimus	deciēns centēna mīlia	deciēns centiēns mīliēns

Note 1: Multiplicatives answering the question, *how many fold?* are: *simplex, duplex, triplex, &c., centuplex,* a hundredfold (formed with stem *plic-*, fold).

Note 2: Proportionals, answering the question, *how many times as great?* are: *simplus; duplus,* double; *triplus,* treble; *quadruplus,* quadruple.

PRONOUNS AND POSSESSIVE ADJECTIVES

91 Pronouns stand in the place of nouns.

There are three persons:

First: The person speaking: I or we.

Second: The person spoken to: you (singular), you (plural).

Third: The person or thing spoken of: he, she, it, they.

Personal pronouns stand only in place of nouns.

Possessive pronominal adjectives (such as *meus*, my) modify nouns. Unlike English, Latin does not have distinct **possessive pronouns** (*mine, yours, hers, ours, theirs*); instead the pronouns have identical forms to those of the possessive adjectives.

92a Personal Pronouns

SINGULAR

	1st Person		2nd Person	
Nom.	**ego** I		**tū**	you (so also vocative)
Gen.	**meī** of me		**tuī**	of you
Dat.	**mihi** or **mihī** to me		**tibi** or **tibī** to you	
Acc.	**mē** me		**tē**	you
Abl.	**mē** from me		**tē**	from you

PLURAL

	1st Person		2nd Person	
Nom.	**nōs**	we	**vōs**	you (so also vocative)
Gen.	**nostrī** / **nostrum**	of us	**vestrī** / **vestrum**	of you
Dat.	**nōbīs**	to us	**vōbīs**	to you
Acc.	**nōs**	us	**vōs**	you
Abl.	**nōbīs**	from us	**vōbīs**	from you

Note 1: Nostrī, vestrī, are called **objective genitives**: *memor nostrī*, mindful of us (§ 264). Nostrum, vestrum, are called **partitive genitives**, because they are used after words which express a part: *ūnus nostrum*, one of us (§ 259). Note that possessive adjectives, not genitives of pronouns, are not used to express possession.

Note 2: For the personal pronoun of the 3rd person, he, she, it, the demonstrative **is, ea, id**, is used (see § 94).

92b Reflexive Pronouns

SINGULAR and PLURAL

Nom.	—	
Gen.	suī	of himself, etc.
Dat.	sibi or sibī	to himself, etc.
Acc.	sē or sēsē	himself, herself, itself, or themselves
Abl.	sē or sēsē	from himself, etc.

Note: **Suus, sua, suum**, his, her, its, their, is the possessive pronoun of the reflexive.

93 Possessive Pronominal Adjectives

SINGULAR	M.	F.	N.	
1st person:	meus	mea	meum	my
2nd person:	tuus	tua	tuum	your

PLURAL	M.	F.	N.	
1st person:	noster	nostra	nostrum	our
2nd person:	vester	vestra	vestrum	your

Note: **Meus, tuus, suus** are declined like *bonus*; **noster, vester**, like *niger*. **Meus** has voc. sing. masc. **mī**. The other possessives, except **noster**, have no vocative.

94 Demonstrative Pronouns

Is, that, *or* he, she, it

	SINGULAR			PLURAL		
	M.	F.	N.	M.	F.	N.
Nom.	is	ea	id	eī, iī, ī	eæ	ea
Gen.	eius*	eius*	eius*	eōrum	eārum	eōrum
Dat.	eī	eī	eī	eīs, iīs	eīs, iīs	eīs, iīs
Acc.	eum	eam	id	eōs	eās	ea
Abl.	eō	eā	eō	eīs, iīs	eīs, iīs	eīs, iīs

Hic, this (near me), *or* he, she, it.

	SINGULAR.			PLURAL.		
	M.	F.	N.	M.	F.	N.
Nom.	hic*	hæc	hoc*	hī	hæ	hæc
Gen.	huius†	huius†	huius†	hōrum	hārum	hōrum
Dat.	huic	huic	huic	hīs	hīs	hīs
Acc.	hunc	hanc	hoc*	hōs	hās	hæc
Abl.	hōc	hāc	hōc	hīs	hīs	hīs

* **Hic** and **hoc** are generally pronounced *hicc, hocc,* so the syllables are heavy.

† Although the first vowel of **eius, huius** is short, the i was pronounced as a double consonant, so the syllable is heavy.

Ille, that (over there), *or* he, she, it.

	SINGULAR.			PLURAL.		
	M.	F.	N.	M.	F.	N.
Nom.	ille	illa	illud	illī	illæ	illa
Gen.	illīus	illīus	illīus	illōrum	illārum	illōrum
Dat.	illī, illi	illī, illi	illī, illi	illīs	illīs	illīs
Acc.	illum	illam	illud	illōs	illās	illa
Abl.	illō	illā	illō	illīs	illīs	illīs

Iste, that (near you)

	SINGULAR.			PLURAL.		
	M.	F.	N.	M.	F.	N.
Nom.	iste	ista	istud	istī	istæ	ista
Gen.	istīus	istīus	istīus	istōrum	istārum	istōrum
Dat.	istī, isiti	istī, isti	istī, isti	istīs	istīs	istīs
Acc.	istum	istam	istud	istōs	istās	ista
Abl.	istō	istā	istō	istīs	istīs	istīs

95 Definitive Pronoun

Īdem, same

	SINGULAR		
	M.	F.	N.
Nom.	īdem	eadem	idem
Gen.	eiusdem	eiusdem	eiusdem
Dat.	eīdem	eīdem	eīdem
Acc.	eundem	eandem	idem
Abl.	eōdem	eādem	eōdem

	PLURAL		
Nom.	eīdem or īdem	eædem	eadem
Gen.	eōrundem	eārundem	eōrundem
Dat.	eīsdem or īsdem	eīsdem or īsdem	eīsdem or īsdem
Acc.	eōsdem	eāsdem	eadem
Abl.	eīsdem or īsdem	eīsdem or īsdem	eīsdem or īsdem

96 Intensive Pronoun

Ipse, self

	SINGULAR			PLURAL		
	M.	F.	N.	M.	F.	N.
Nom.	ipse	ipsa	ipsum	ipsī	ipsæ	ipsa
Gen.	ipsīus	ipsīus	ipsīus	ipsōrum	ipsārum	ipsōrum
Dat.	ipsī	ipsī	ipsī	ipsīs	ipsīs	ipsīs
Acc.	ipsum	ipsam	ipsum	ipsōs	ipsās	ipsa
Abl.	ipsō	ipsā	ipsō	ipsīs	ipsīs	ipsīs

Note: The suffixes -met, -te, -pte or -pse, -ce are added to some cases of pronouns for emphasis: (a) -met may be joined (1) to *ego* and its cases, except gen. plur.: *egomet*, I myself; (2) to the cases of *tū*, except nom. sing.: *vōsmet*, you yourselves; (3) to *sē* and its cases, except *suī*: *sibimet*; (4) to the cases of *suus*: *suamet facta*; (b) -te is joined to *tū*: *tūte*; also *tūtemet*, you youself; (c) -pte is joined especially to the abl. sing. of the possessive pronouns: *meōpte cōnsiliō*, by my advice. (d) -ce or -c is joined to the demonstrative: *hunce, huiusce; istece, illece,* are written *istīc, illīc*:

	SING.	M.	F.	N.
	Nom.	istīc	istæc	istuc
	Gen.	istīusce	istīusce	istīusce
	Acc.	istunc	istanc	istuc
	Abl.	istoc	istac	istoc

Īdem (for *is-dem*), and **ipse** (for *is-pse*) are emphatic forms of *is*.

97 Relative Pronoun

Quī, who, which

	SINGULAR.			PLURAL.		
	M.	F.	N.	M.	F.	N.
Nom.	quī	quæ	quod	quī	quæ	quæ
Gen.	cuius*	cuius*	cuius*	quōrum	quārum	quōrum
Dat.	cui	cui	cui	quibus or quīs		
Acc.	quem	quam	quod	quōs	quās	quæ
Abl.	quō	quā	quō	quibus or quīs		

---

* The **i** in *cuius* is pronounced as a double consonant, so the first syllable is heavy.

---

98 Interrogative Pronoun

Quis, who? what?

	M	F	N
Nom.	**quis** or **quī**	(**quis**) or **quæ**	**quid**
Acc.	**quem**	**quam**	**quid** or **quod**

Note: In all other cases singular and plural *qui* interrogative is like the relative pronoun.

---

99 Indefinite Pronoun

Quis, anyone or anything

	M	F	N
Nom.	**quis** or **quī**	**qua** or **quæ**	**quid** or **quod**
Acc.	**quem**	**quam**	**quid** or **quod**

Note: In the other cases singular and plural the indefinite is like the relative, except that *qua* or *quæ* may be used in neut. nom. and acc. plural.

Quis, both interrogative and indefinite, and its compounds, are used chiefly as substantives; **quī** and its compounds chiefly as adjectives.

Quid and its compounds are used only as substantives; **quod** and its compounds only as adjectives.

EXAMPLES:

Is quī venit. The man who comes. (*quī* relative)

Quis venit? Who comes? (*quis* interrogative)

Quī homō venit? What man comes? (*quī* interrogative)

Aliquid amārī. Some bitterness.

Aliquod verbum. Some word.

100   Compound Pronouns

MASC.	FEM.	NEUT.	
quīcumque	quæcumque	quodcumque	whosoever or
quisquis	quisquis	quidquid or quicquid	whatsoever
quīdam	quædam	quiddam (quoddam)	a certain person or thing
aliquis	aliqua	aliquid	someone or
aliquī	aliqua	aliquod	something
quispiam	quæpiam	quippiam (quodpiam)	someone
quīvīs	quævīs	quidvīs (quodvīs)	anyone
quīlibet	quælibet	quidlibet (quodlibet)	you like
quisquam	—	quidquam or quicquam	anyone at all
quisque	quæque	quidque (quodque)	each one severally
uterque	utraque	utrumque	each of two
ūnusquisque	ūnaquæque	ūnumquidque (ūnumquodque)	each single one
ecquis	ecqua	ecquid (ecquod)	Is there any who?
quisnam	quænam	quidnam (quodnam)	Who, pray?

Note 1: **Quisquis** is found only in nom., acc. and abl.

Note 2: **Quisquam** is used as a substantive, sing. only, chiefly in negative sentences and the adjective which corresponds to it is *ūllus: haud quisquam*, not anyone.

Note 3: In the **compound pronouns** *quī, quis,* and *uter* follow their own declension in the oblique cases; the prefix or suffix is unaltered: *alicuius, cuiusque, cuivis, utrōque, quamlibet.* But in *ūnusquisque* both *ūnus* and *quisque* are declined.

101   The following pronominal adjectives form the genitive singular in **-ius** or **īus** and the dative singular in **-ī** like *ille*: **alius**, other, another; **ūllus**, any; **nūllus**, none; **sōlus**, sole; **tōtus**, whole; **ūter**, which of two?; **alter**, one of two, the other; **neuter**, neither.

	SINGULAR			PLURAL		
	M.	F.	N.	M.	F.	N.
Nom.	alius	alia	aliud	aliī	aliæ	alia
Gen.	alīus	alīus	alīus	aliōrum	aliārum	aliōrum
Dat.	aliī	aliī	aliī	aliīs	aliīs	aliīs
Acc.	alium	aliam	aliud	aliōs	aliās	alia
Abl.	aliō	aliā	aliō	aliīs	aliīs	aliīs

Note 1: In **alius** the i of the genitive singular is always long. In the genitive of words declined like it the quantity of the i is doubtful; also in the genitive of **uter**, neuter. The genitive singular of **alter** or **aliēnus** is often substituted for **alīus** to avoid confusion with the nominative singular.

Note 2: Like **alius**, but with neuter singular in -um, are declined **ūllus, nūllus, sōlus, tōtus.**

SINGULAR

	M.	F.	N.
Nom.	alter	altera	alterum
Gen.	alterīus, alterĭus	alterīus, alterĭus	alterīus, alterĭus
Dat.	alterī	alterī	alterī
Acc.	alterum	alteram	alterum
Abl.	alterō	alterā	alterō

PLURAL

	M.	F.	N.
Nom.	alterī	alteræ	altera
Gen.	alterōrum	alterārum	alterōrum
Dat.	alterīs	alterīs	alterīs
Acc.	alterōs	alterās	altera
Abl.	alterīs	alterīs	alterīs

Note 1: Like **alter**, but casting out e before r in all cases except the nom. sing. masculine, are declined: **uter, utra, utrum**, which (of two); neuter, **neutra, neutrum**, neither. These are seldom used in the plural.

Note 2: **Uter** forms compounds by taking nearly all the same suffixes as **quis** and **quī**: **utercumque**, whichever of two; **utervīs, uterlibet. Alteruter**, one or the other, is usually declined only as **uter**, but sometimes both parts are declined.

Note 3: The genitive and ablative singular of **nūllus** are used for the genitive and ablative of the substantive **nēmō**, nobody, which are very rarely found.

102 Table of Correlative Pronouns, Adjectives and Adverbs

INTERROGATIVE	DEMONSTRATIVE	RELATIVE	INDEFINITE (1)	INDEFINITE (2)	DISTRIBUTIVE	UNIVERSAL RELATIVE
quis, quī, who which?	is that	quī who, which	(sī) quis (if) anyone	aliquis some one	quisque each	quīcumque whoever, whatever
uter which of two?	alter one of two, other of two			alteruter one or other of two	uterque each of two	utercumque whichever of two
quālis of what kind?	tālis of such kind	quālis as				quāliscumque of whatever kind
quantus how great?	tantus so great	quantus as (great)		aliquantus some (in quantity)		quantuscumque however great
quot how many?	tot so many	quot as (many)		aliquot some (in number)		quotcumque however many
ubi where?	ibi there	ubi where	sīcubi if anywhere	alicubi somewhere	ubique everywhere	ubicumque wheresoever
unde whence?	inde thence	unde whence	sīcunde if from any quarter	alicunde from some quarter	undique from every side	undecumque whencesoever
quō whither?	eō thither	quō whither	(sī) quō (if) to anywhere	aliquō to somewhere		quōcumque withersoever,
quā by what way?	eā by that way	quā by what way	(sī) quā (if) by any way	aliquā by some way		quācumque by whatsoever way
quam how?	tam so	quam as				
quandō when?	tum then	quandō when ubi when cum when	(sī) quandō (if) ever	aliquandō at some time		quandōcumque whensoever
quotiēns how often?	totiēns so often	quotiēns as (often)		aliquotiēns at some (various) times		quotiēnscumque however often

VERBS

103 **The verb has:**

3 **persons:** first, second, third

2 **numbers:** singular and plural

6 **tenses:** (1) present, (2) future simple,
      (3) past imperfect, (4) perfect,   The verb finite
      (5) future perfect, (6) pluperfect

3 **moods:** (1) indicative, (2) imperative,
      (3) subjunctive

The **infinitives** (verbal substantives)

3 **participles** (verbal adjectives)

The **gerund** and **gerundive** (verbal sub-
      stantive and adjective).   The verb infinite

2 **supines** (verbal substantives)

2 **voices:** (1) active, (2) passive

The **verb finite** is so called because it is limited by **mood** and **persons**, while the **verb infinite** is not so limited.

104 **Person and number**

In modern English, **pronouns** are used with **verbs** to express the three persons singular and plural: **I** come, **we** come, with only a vestige of inflection as in **he** come-**s**. But in Latin person and number are expressed by the inflections alone:

su-**m**, I come	su-**mus**, we are
e-**s**, you (sing.) are	es-**tis**, you (pl.) are
es-**t**, he (she, it) is	su-**nt**, they are
am-**ō**, I love	amā-**mus**, we love
amā-**s**, you (sing.) love	amā-**tis**, you (pl.) love
ama-**t**, he (she, it) loves	ama-**nt**, they love

Table of Personal Endings in the Indicative and Subjunctive Moods

	ACTIVE VOICE	PASSIVE VOICE
Singular		
1	**-m** or **-ō**	**-r**
2	**-s**	**-ris** or **-re**
3	**-t**	**-tur**
Plural		
1	**-mus**	**-mur**
2	**-tis**	**-minī**
3	**-nt**	**-ntur**

The **imperative mood** has only the second and third person singular and plural, not the first.

105 Tenses

Tenses express the time of the action or state denoted by the verb, as being: (1) present, past, or future; (2) complete or incomplete; (3) momentary or continuous.

In English, by means of auxiliary verbs, differences of time can be more accurately expressed than in Latin; so that one tense in Latin may correspond to two tenses in English, of which one is momentary, the other continuous. Thus, **rogō**, I ask, has the following tenses:

Present {	**Present**	incomplete	rogō	{ I ask / I am asking
	Perfect	complete	rogāvī	I have asked
Future {	**Fut. Simple**	incomplete	rogābō	{ I shall ask / I shall be asking
	Fut. Perf.	complete	rogāverō	I shall have asked
Past {	**Perfect** } **Imperfect** }	incomplete	rogāvī / rogābam	{ I asked / I was asking
	Pluperfect	complete	rogāveram	I had asked

Note: Latin has no separate tenses corresponding to the Greek aorist and perfect; therefore the perfect has to fill the place of two tenses: the aorist, I loved, and the perfect, I have loved.

The present, the future simple, and the future perfect are called **primary tenses**. The imperfect and the pluperfect are called **historic tenses**. The perfect in the sense of *I have asked* is **primary**; in the sense of *I asked* it is **historic**.

106   Mood

Moods are the forms in which the idea contained in the verb is presented.

The **indicative** states or enquires about a fact: **amō**, I love; **amat?**, does he love?

The **imperative** expresses a command: **amā**, love!

> **Note:** The forms of the Imperative in **-tō, -tōte**, are emphatic, and were used anciently in laws.

The **subjunctive** expresses something desired, conditional or prospective: *ut amem*, that I may love; *si amārem*, if I were to love.

> **Note:** In the paradigms the tenses of the subjunctive are given without any English translation, because their meaning varies so much according to the context that it is impossible to convey it by any one rendering (see also § 351–363).

107   The Verb Infinite

The **infinitive** is a **verb noun** expressing action or state, without limit of person or number: *amāre*, to love, *amāvisse*, to have loved.

The **gerund** is a **verbal noun** declined like neuters of the second declension. It supplies cases to the infinitive: as *amandī*, of loving.

The **gerundive** is a **participle,** or **verbal adjective,** passive in meaning: *amandus, -a, -um*, fit to be loved.

The **supines** are cases of a **verbal substantive**: *amātum*, in order to love; *amātū*, for loving *or* in loving.

The **participles** are so called because they have partly the properties of verbs and partly those of adjectives; there are three besides the gerundive: (a) **active present participle** *amāns*, loving (declined like *ingēns*); (b) **active future participle** *amātūrus*, about to love (declined like *bonus*);(c) **passive perfect participle** *amātus*, loved (declined like *bonus*).

> **Note:** The three participles wanting are: (a) **active perfect**; (b) **passive present**; (c) **passive future**.

108 Voice

The **active voice** expresses what the subject of a verb is or does: *sum*, I am; *valeō*, I am well; *amō*, I love; *regō*, I rule.

The **passive voice** expresses what is done to the subject of the verb: *amor*, I am loved; *regor*, I am ruled.

109 Deponent verbs are verbs which have chiefly the forms of the passive voice with the meaning of the active voice: *loquor*, I speak.

110 Verbs in the active voice and deponent verbs are: (a) **transitive** (*transīre*, to pass over), acting on an object: *eum amō*, I love him, *hortor vōs*, I exhort you; (b) **intransitive**, not acting on a direct object: *stō*, I stand, *loquor*, I speak.

Only transitive verbs have the full passive voice.

111 THE CONJUGATIONS

Verbs are generally arranged according to the character of the present stem in four conjugations.

The **stem character** is most clearly seen before the suffix **-re** (or **-ere**) of the present active infinitive.

Conjugation	Stem	Pres. Act. Inf.
1st	-ā	-āre
2nd	-ē	-ēre
3rd	consonant or -u	-ere
4th	-ī	-īre

Deponent verbs are also divided into four conjugations with the same stem endings.

112 The following forms (the **'principle parts'**) must be known in order to give the full conjugation (see § 147).

stems:	a-	e-	cons. & u-	i-
ACTIVE VOICE				
1 Pers. Pres. Indic.	amō	moneō	regō	audiō
Infin. Pres.	amāre	monēre	regere	audīre
Perfect.	amāvī	monuī	rēxī	audīvī
Supine in -um	amātum	monitum	rēctum	audītum

PASSIVE VOICE (AND DEPONENT VERBS)

1 Pers. Pres. Indic.	amor	moneor	regor	audior
Infin. Pres.	amārī	monērī	regī	audīrī
Partic. Perf.	amātus	monitus	rēctus	audītus
Gerundive	amandus	monendus	regendus	audiendus

113 In the perfects **-āvī**, **-ēvī**, **-ōvī**, **v** sometimes drops out before **-is** or **-er**, and contraction follows: *amāvistī* becomes *amāstī, amāverunt* → *amārunt, amāvissem* → *amāssem*. In **i-** stems, **v** is sometimes dropped in other forms: *audīvī* becomes *audiī, audīvērunt* → *audiērunt* (see § 14).

For **-ērunt** (3rd pers. pl. perfect active), **-ēre** is often written: *amāvēre, implēvēre, audīvēre*.

The 2nd pers. sing. in the passive ends in **-ris** or **-re**: *amābāris, amābāre*; but in pres. indic. the ending in **-re** is rare.

The 2nd pers. sing. and 1st and 2nd pers. pl. endings are **-is**, **-imus**, **-itis**, while in the perf. subj. they are **īs**, **īmus**, **ītis**. However, poets tend to treat *all* these **-i-** as either long or short.

Note 1: An old form in **-ier** of the pres. infin. passive is sometimes found in poetry: *amārier* for *amārī*.

Note 2: Poets sometimes use old forms in the future active and passive of **i-** stems; as *audibo, audibor,* for *audiam, audiar*.

Note 3: In consonant and **i-** stems, gerunds & gerundives sometimes end in **-undum,-undus**.

114 **Periphrastic Conjugation**

The **active future participle** and the **gerundive** may be used with all the tenses of the verb *sum* to create a periphrastic tense (i.e. one created by a combination of words rather than an inflection):

amātūrus (-a) sum (eram), I am (was) about to love
amātūrus (-a) es (erās), you (sing.) are (were) about to love
amātūrus (-a) est (erat), he/she is (was) about to love
amātūrī (-æ) sumus (erāmus), we are (were) about to love
amātūrī (-æ) estis (erātis), you (pl.) are (were) about to love
amātūrī (-æ) sunt (erant), they are (were) about to love

amandus (-a) sum (erām), I am (was) fit to be loved
amandī (-æ) sumus (erāmus), we are (were) fit to be loved

In the same way the participle **futūrus** may be used with the tenses of **sum**: *futurus sum,* I am about to be.

115   The verb sum, I am (sum, fuī, esse, futūrus)

Before the regular verbs it is necessary to conjugate the irregular verb sum, I am, esse, to be, because it is used as an auxiliary in the conjugation of other verbs. This verb is formed from two roots, (es-, to be,

TENSE	INDICATIVE	
Present	sum	I am
	es	you (sing.) are
	est	he is
	sumus	we are
	estis	you (pl.) are
	sunt	they are
Future Simple	erō	I shall be
	eris	you (sing.) will be
	erit	he will be
	erimus	we shall be
	eritis	you (pl.) will be
	erunt	they will be
Imperfect	eram	I was
	erās	you (sing.) were
	erat	he was
	erāmus	we were
	erātis	you (pl.) were
	erant	they were
Perfect	fuī	I have been or I was
	fuistī	you (sing.) have been or you were
	fuit	he has been or he was
	fuimus	we have been or we were
	fuistis	you (pl.) have been or you were
	fuērunt	they have been or they were
Future Perfect	fuerō	I shall have been
	fueris	you (sing.) will have been
	fuerit	he will have been
	fuerimus	we shall have been
	fueritis	you (pl.) will have been
	fuerint	they will have been
Pluperfect	fueram	I had been
	fuerās	you (sing.) had been
	fuerat	he had been
	fuerāmus	we had been
	fuerātis	you (pl.) had been
	fuerant	they had been

and **fu-**, to be or become). The **present stem** is formed from the root **es-**, the perfect and participial stems from the root **fu-**. In the tense forms **es-** sometimes drops **e**: *sum, sumus;* sometimes **s** changes to **r**: *eram.*

SUBJUNCTIVE	IMPERATIVE
sim	
sīs	**es, estō,** be (sing.)
sit	**estō,** let him be
sīmus	**este, estōte** be (pl.)
sītis	**suntō** let them be
sint	

THE VERB INFINITE
Infinitives

Present	**esse** to be
Perfect	**fuisse,** to have been

essem *or* **forem**
esses *or* **forēs**
esset *or* **foret**

Future	$\left\{ \begin{array}{l} \textbf{futūrus esse} \\ \textbf{fore} \end{array} \right\}$ to be about to be

essēmus
essētis
essent *or* **forent**

Participles

Present	*(none)*
Future	**futūrus,** about to be

fuerim
fuerīs
fuerit

Gerunds and Supines
(none)

fuerīmus
fuerītis
fuerint

Note: There is no present participle of *sum*. It is only seen in a few compounds: *absēns, præsēns.*

fuissem
fuissēs
fuisset
fuissēmus
fuissētis
fuissent

Like *sum* are conjugated its compounds: *absum,* I am absent; *adsum,* I am present; *dēsum,* I am wanting; *īnsum,* I am in or among; *intersum,* I am among; *obsum,* I hinder; *præsum,* I am set over; *prōsum,* I am of use; *subsum,* I am under; *supersum,* I survive. In *prōsum,* the final **d** of the old preposition is kept before **e**: *prōdes.*

116   First Conjugation, a- Stems, Active Voice

TENSE	INDICATIVE	
Present	amō	I love or I am loving
	amās	you (sing.) love or you are loving
	amat	he (she, it) loves or he is loving
	amāmus	we love or we are loving
	amātis	you (pl.) love or you are loving
	amant	they love or they are loving
Future Simple	amābō	I shall love
	amābis	you (sing.) will love
	amābit	he (she, it) will love
	amābimus	we shall love
	amābitis	you (pl.) will love
	amābunt	they will love
Imperfect	amābam	I was loving
	amābās	you (sing.) were loving
	amābat	he (she, it) was loving
	amābāmus	we were loving
	amābātis	you (pl.) were loving
	amābant	they were loving
Perfect	amāvī	I have loved or I loved
	amāvistī	you (sing.) have loved or you loved
	amāvit	he (she, it) has loved or he loved
	amāvimus	we have loved or we loved
	amāvistis	you (pl.) have loved or you loved
	amāvērunt	they have loved or they loved
Future Perfect	amāverō	I shall have loved
	amāveris	you (sing.) will have loved
	amāverit	he (she, it) will have loved
	amāverimus	we shall have loved
	amāveritis	you (pl.) will have loved
	amāverint	they will have loved
Pluperfect	amāveram	I had loved
	amāverās	you (sing.) had loved
	amāverat	he (she, it) had loved
	amāverāmus	we had loved
	amāverātis	you (pl.) had loved
	amāverant	they had loved

SUBJUNCTIVE	IMPERATIVE
amem amēs amet amēmus amētis ament	amā, amātō, love (sing.) amātō, let him love amāte, amātōte love (pl.) amantō let them love

THE VERB INFINITE

amārem amārēs	Infinitives
amāret	Present amāre, to love
amārēmus amārētis	Perfect amāvisse, to have loved
amārent	Future amātūrus esse, to be about to love
amāverim amāverīs	
amāverit	Gerund
amāverīmus	Nom. Acc. amandum, the loving
amāverītis	Gen. amandī, of loving
amāverint	Dat. Abl. amandō, for or by loving

Supines
amātum, in order to love
amātū, in or for loving

Participles
Pres. amāns, loving
Fut. amātūrus, about to love

amāvissem
amāvissēs
amāvisset
amāvissēmus
amāvissētis
amāvissent

117 Second Conjugation, e-Stems, Active Voice

TENSE		INDICATIVE
Present	moneō	I advise *or* I am advising
	monēs	you (s.) advise *or* you are advising
	monet	he advises *or* he is advising
	monēmus	we advise *or* we are advising
	monētis	you (pl.) advise *or* you are advising
	monent	they advise *or* they are advising
Future Simple	monēbō	I shall advise
	monēbis	you (sing.) will advise
	monēbit	he (she, it) will advise
	monēbimus	we shall advise
	monēbitis	you (pl.) will advise
	monēbunt	they will advise
Imperfect	monēbam	I was advising,
	monēbās	you (sing.) were advising
	monēbat	he (she, it) was advising
	monēbāmus	we were advising
	monēbātis	you (pl.) were advising
	monēbant	they were advising
Perfect	monuī	I have advised *or* I advised
	monuistī	you (s.) have advised *or* you advised
	monuit	he (she, it) has advised *or* he advised
	monuimus	we have advised *or* we advised
	monuistis	you (pl.) have advised *or* you advised
	monuērunt	they have advised *or* they advised
Future Perfect	monuerō	I shall have advised
	monueris	you (sing.) will have advised
	monuerit	he (she, it) will have advised
	monuerimus	we shall have advised
	monueritis	you (pl.) will have advised
	monuerint	they will have advised
Pluperfect	monueram	I had advised
	monuerās	you (sing.) had advised
	monuerat	he (she, it) had advised
	monuerāmus	we had advised
	monuerātis	you (pl.) had advised
	monuerant	they had advised

SUBJUNCTIVE	IMPERATIVE
moneam	
moneās	monē, monētō, advise (sing.)
moneat	monētō, let him advise
moneāmus	monēte, monētōte advise (pl.)
moneātis	monentō let them advise
moneant	

THE VERB INFINITE

monērem	Infinitives
monērēs	
monēret	Present monēre, to advise
monērēmus	
monērētis	Perfect monuisse, to have advised
monērent	Future monitūrus esse, to be about to advise
monuerim	
monuerīs	Gerund
monuerit	Nom. Acc. monendum, the advising
monuerīmus	Gen. monendī, of advising
monuerītis	Dat. Abl. monendō, for or by advising
monuerint	

Supines
monitum, in order to advise
monitū, in or for advising

Participles
Pres. monēns, advising
Fut. monitūrus, about to advise

monuissem
monuissēs
monuisset
monuissēmus
monuissētis
monuissent

118   Third Conjugation, Consonant and u Stems, Active Voice

TENSE	INDICATIVE	
Present	regō	I rule *or* I am ruling
	regis	you (s.) rule *or* you are ruling
	regit	he (she, it) rules *or* he is ruling
	regimus	we rule *or* we are ruling
	regitis	you (pl.) rule *or* you are ruling
	regunt	they rule *or* they are ruling
Future Simple	regam	I shall rule
	regēs	you (sing.) will rule
	reget	he (she, it) will rule
	regēmus	we shall rule
	regētis	you (pl.) will rule
	regent	they will rule
Imperfect	regēbam	I was ruling
	regēbās	you (sing.) were ruling
	regēbat	he (she, it) was ruling
	regēbāmus	we were ruling
	regēbātis	you (pl.) were ruling
	regēbant	they were ruling
Perfect	rēxī	I have ruled *or* I ruled
	rēxistī	you (s.) have ruled *or* you ruled
	rēxit	he (she, it) has ruled *or* he ruled
	rēximus	we have ruled *or* we ruled
	rēxistis	you (pl.) have ruled *or* you ruled
	rēxērunt	they have ruled *or* they ruled
Future Perfect	rēxerō	I shall have ruled
	rēxeris	you (sing.) will have ruled
	rēxerit	he (she, it) will have ruled
	rēxerimus	we shall have ruled
	rēxeritis	you (pl.) will have ruled
	rēxerint	they will have ruled
Pluperfect	rēxeram	I had ruled
	rēxerās	you (sing.) had ruled
	rēxerat	he (she, it) had ruled
	rēxerāmus	we had ruled
	rēxerātis	you (pl.) had ruled
	rēxerant	they had ruled

SUBJUNCTIVE	IMPERATIVE
regam regās regat regāmus regātis regant	**rege, regitō,** rule (sing.) **regitō,** let him rule **regite, regitōte** rule (pl.) **reguntō** let them rule

THE VERB INFINITE

Infinitives

regerem regerēs regeret regerēmus regerētis regerent	Present **regere,** to rule Perfect **rēxisse,** to have ruled Future **rēctūrus esse,** to be about to rule

Gerund

Nom. Acc. **regendum,** the ruling
Gen. **regendī,** of ruling
Dat. Abl. **regendō,** for *or* by ruling

| rēxerim
rēxerīs
rēxerit
rēxerīmus
rēxerītis
rēxerint | |

Supines
rēctum, in order to rule
rēctū, in *or* for ruling

Participles
Pres. **regēns,** ruling
Fut. **rēctūrus,** about to rule

| rēxissem
rēxissēs
rēxisset
rēxissēmus
rēxissētis
rēxissent | **Note:** *Faciō, dīcō, dūcō,* and the compounds of *dūcō* in the 2nd
person of the present imperative make *fac, dīc, dūc, etc.* |

119   Fourth Conjugation, i- Stems, Active Voice

TENSE	INDICATIVE	
	audiō	I hear *or* I am hearing
	audīs	you (s.) hear *or* you are hearing
Present	audit	he (she, it) hears *or* is hearing
	audīmus	we hear *or* we are hearing
	raudītis	you (pl.) hear or you are hearing
	audiunt	they hear or they are hearing
	audiam	I shall hear
	audiēs	you (sing.) will hear
Future Simple	audiet	he (she, it) will hear
	audiēmus	we shall hear
	audiētis	you (pl.) will hear
	audient	they will hear
	audiēbam	I was hearing
	audiēbās	you (sing.) were hearing
Imperfect	audiēbat	he (she, it) was hearing
	audiēbāmus	we were hearing
	audiēbātis	you (pl.) were hearing
	audiēbant	they were hearing
	audīvī	I have heard *or* I heard
	audīvistī	you (s.) have heard *or* you heard
Perfect	audīvit	he (she, it) has heard *or* he heard
	audīvimus	we have heard *or* we heard
	audīvistis	you (pl.) have heard *or* you heard
	audīvērunt	they have heard *or* they heard
	audīverō	I shall have heard
	audīveris	you (sing.) will have heard
Future Perfect	audīverit	he (she, it) will have heard
	audīverimus	we shall have heard
	audīveritis	you (pl.) will have heard
	audīverint	they will have heard
	audīveram	I had heard
	audīverās	you (sing.) had heard
Pluperfect	audīverat	he (she, it) had heard
	audīverāmus	we had heard
	audīverātis	you (pl.) had heard
	audīverant	they had heard

SUBJUNCTIVE	IMPERATIVE
audiam	
audiās	**audī, audītō,** hear (sing.)
audiat	**audītō,** let him hear
audiāmus	**audīte, audītōte** hear (pl.)
audiātis	**audiuntō** let them hear
audiant	

THE VERB INFINITE

	Infinitives
audīrem	
audīrēs	
audīret	Present **audīre,** to hear
audīrēmus	Perfect **audīvisse,** to have heard
audīrētis	
audīrent	
audīverim	Future **audītūrus esse,** to be about to hear
audīveris	
audīverit	Gerund
audīverīmus	Nom. Acc. **audiendum,** the hearing
audīverītis	Gen. **audiendī,** of hearing
audīverint	Dat. Abl. **audiendō,** for or by hearing

Supines
audītum, in order to hear
audītū, in or for hearing

	Participles
audīvissem	Pres. **audiēns,** hearing
audīvissēs	Fut. **audītūrus,** about to hear
audīvisset	
audīvissēmus	
audīvissētis	
audīvissent	

120 First Conjugation, a- Stems, Passive Voice

TENSE	INDICATIVE	
Present	amor	I am loved *or* I am being loved
	amāris	you (s.) are loved *or* you are being loved
	amātur	he (she, it) is loved *or* he is being loved
	amāmur	we are loved *or* we are being loved
	amāminī	you (pl.) are loved *or* you are being loved
	amantur	they are loved *or* they are being loved
Future Simple	amābor	I shall be loved
	amāberis (-re)	you (sing.) will be loved
	amābitur	he (she, it) will be loved
	amābimur	we shall be loved
	amābiminī	you (pl.) will be loved
	amābuntur	they will be loved
Imperfect	amābar	I was being loved
	amābāris (-re)	you (sing.) were being loved
	amābātur	he (she, it) was being loved
	amābāmur	we were being loved
	amābāminī	you (pl.) were being loved
	amābantur	they were being loved
Perfect	amātus sum	I have been loved *or* I was loved
	amātus es	you (s.) have been loved *or* you were loved
	amātus est	he (she, it) has been loved *or* he was loved
	amātī sumus	we have been loved *or* we were loved
	amātī estis	you (pl.) have been loved *or* you were loved
	amātī sunt	they have been loved *or* they were loved
Future Perfect	amātus erō	I shall have been loved
	amātus eris	you (sing.) will have been loved
	amātus erit	he (she, it) will have been loved
	amātī erimus	we shall have been loved
	amātī eritis	you (pl.) will have been loved
	amātī erunt	they will have been loved
Pluperfect	amātus eram	I had been loved
	amātus erās	you (sing.) had been loved
	amātus erat	he (she, it) had been loved
	amātī erāmus	we had been loved
	amātī erātis	you (pl.) had been loved
	amātī erant	they had been loved

SUBJUNCTIVE	IMPERATIVE
amer amēris (-re) amētur amēmur amēminī amentur	amāre, amātor, be loved (sing.) amātor, let him be loved amāminī, be loved (pl.) amantor, let them be loved

amārer amārēris, amārēre amārētur amārēmur amārēminī amārentur	THE VERB INFINITE

amātus sim   Present   amārī, to be loved

amātus sīs

amātus sit   Perfect   amātus esse, to have been loved

amātī sīmus   Future   amātum īrī, (see § 387)

amātī sītis

amātī sint   Participle

Perf. amātus, loved or having been loved

Gerundive

amandus, fit to be loved

amātus essem

amātus essēs

amātus esset

amātī essēmus

amātī essētis

amātī essent

121   Second Conjugation, e- Stems, Passive Voice

TENSE	INDICATIVE	
Present	moneor	I am advised *or* I am being advised
	monēris	you (s.) are advised *or* are being advised
	monētur	he is advised *or* he is being advised
	monēmur	we are advised *or* we are being advised
	monēminī	you (pl.) are advised *or* are being advised
	monentur	they are advised *or* are being advised
Future Simple	monēbor	I shall be advised
	monēberis (-re)	you (sing.) will be advised
	monēbitur	he (she, it) will be advised
	monēbimur	we shall be advised
	monēbiminī	you (pl.) will be advised
	monēbuntur	they will be advised
Imperfect	monēbar	I was being advised
	monēbāris (-re)	you (sing.) were being advised
	monēbātur	he (she, it) was being advised
	monēbāmur	we were being advised
	monēbāminī	you (pl.) were being advised
	monēbantur	they were being advised
Perfect	monitus sum	I have been advised *or* I was advised
	monitus es	you (s.) have been advised *or* were advised
	monitus est	he has been advised *or* was advised
	monitī sumus	we have been advised *or* we were advised
	monitī estis	you (pl.) have been advised *or* were advised
	monitī sunt	they have been advised *or* were advised
Future Perfect	monitus erō	I shall have been advised
	monitus eris	you (sing.) will have been advised
	monitus erit	he (she, it) will have been advised
	monitī erimus	we shall have been advised
	monitī eritis	you (pl.) will have been advised
	monitī erunt	they will have been advised
Pluperfect	monitus eram	I had been advised
	monitus erās	you (sing.) had been advised
	monitus erat	he (she, it) had been advised
	monitī erāmus	we had been advised
	monitī erātis	you (pl.) had been advised
	monitī erant	they had been advised

SUBJUNCTIVE	IMPERATIVE
monear	
moneāris, moneāre	monēre, monētor, be advised (sing.)
moneātur	monētor, let him be advised
moneāmur	monēminī, be advised (pl.)
moneāminī	monentor, let them be advised
moneantur	

monērer
monērēris, monērēre
monērētur
monērēmur
monērēminī
monērentur
monitus sim
monitus sīs
monitus sit
monitī sīmus
monitī sītis
monitī sint

THE VERB INFINITE

Infinitives

Present   **monērī**, to be advised

Perfect   **monitus esse**, to have been advised

Future   **monitum īrī**, (see § 387)

Participle

Pres. **monitus**, advised *or* having been advised

Gerundive

monendus, fit to be advised

monitus essem
monitus essēs
monitus esset
monitī essēmus
monitī essētis
monitī essent

122 Third Conjugation, Consonant & u- Stems, Passive Voice

TENSE		INDICATIVE
Present	regor	I am ruled *or* I am being ruled
	regeris	you (s.) are ruled *or* you are being ruled
	regitur	he is ruled *or* he is being ruled
	regimur	we are ruled *or* we are being ruled
	regiminī	you (pl.) are ruled *or* you are being ruled
	reguntur	they are ruled *or* they are being ruled
Future Simple	regar	I shall be ruled
	regēris, regēre	you (sing.) will be ruled
	regētur	he (she, it) will be ruled
	regēmur	we shall be ruled
	regēminī	you (pl.) will be ruled
	regentur	they will be ruled
Imperfect	regēbar	I was being ruled
	regēbāris (-re)	you (s.) were being ruled
	regēbātur	he (she, it) was being ruled
	regēbāmur	we were being ruled
	regēbāminī	you (pl.) were being ruled
	regēbantur	they were being ruled
Perfect	rēctus sum	I have been ruled *or* I was ruled
	rēctus es	you (s.) have been ruled *or* you were ruled
	rēctus est	he (she, it) has been ruled *or* he was ruled
	rēctī sumus	we have been ruled *or* we were ruled
	rēctī estis	you (pl.) have been ruled *or* you were ruled
	rēctī sunt	they have been ruled *or* they were ruled
Future Perfect	rēctus erō	I shall have been ruled
	rēctus eris	you (sing.) will have been ruled
	rēctus erit	he (she, it) will have been ruled
	rēctī erimus	we shall have been ruled
	rēctī eritis	you (pl.) will have been ruled
	rēctī erunt	they will have been ruled
Pluperfect	rēctus eram	I had been ruled
	rēctus erās	you (sing.) had been ruled
	rēctus erat	he (she, it) had been ruled
	rēctī erāmus	we had been ruled
	rēctī erātis	you (pl.) had been ruled
	rēctī erant	they had been ruled

SUBJUNCTIVE	IMPERATIVE
regar regāris (-re) regātur regāmur regāminī regantur	regere, regitor, be ruled (sing.) regitor, let him be ruled regiminī, be ruled (pl.) reguntor, let them be ruled

regerer regerēris (-re) regerētur regerēmur regerēminī regerentur	THE VERB INFINITE
rēctus sim rēctus sīs rēctus sit rēctī sīmus rēctī sītis rēctī sint	Infinitives Present regī, to be ruled Perfect rēctus esse, to have been ruled Future rēctum īrī, (see § 387) Participle Perf. rēctus, ruled or having been ruled Gerundive regendus, fit to be ruled

rēctus essem
rēctus essēs
rēctus esset
rēctī essēmus
rēctī essētis
rēctī essent

## 123	Fourth Conjugation, i- Stems, Passive Voice

TENSE		INDICATIVE
Present	audior	I am heard or I am being heard
	audīris	you (s.) are heard or you are being heard
	audītur	he is heard or he is being heard
	audīmur	we are heard or we are being heard
	audīminī	you (pl.) are heard or you are being heard
	audiuntur	they are heard or they are being heard
Future Simple	audiar	I shall be heard
	audiēris (-re)	you (sing.) will be heard
	audiētur	he (she, it) will be heard
	audiēmur	we shall be heard
	audiēminī	you (pl.) will be heard
	audientur	they will be heard
Imperfect	audiēbar	I was being heard
	audiēbāris (-re)	you (sing.) were being heard
	audiēbātur	he (she, it) was being heard
	audiēbāmur	we were being heard
	audiēbāminī	you (pl.) were being heard
	audiēbantur	they were being heard
Perfect	audītus sum	I have been heard or I was heard
	audītus es	you (s.) have been heard or you were heard
	audītus est	he (she, it) has been or he was heard
	audītī sumus	we have been or we were heard
	audītī estis	you (pl.) have been or you were heard
	audītī sunt	they have been or they were heard
Future Perfect	audītus erō	I shall have been heard
	audītus eris	you (sing.) will have been heard
	audītus erit	he (she, it) will have been heard
	audītī erimus	we shall have been heard
	audītī eritis	you (pl.) will have been heard
	audītī erunt	they will have been heard
Pluperfect	audītus eram	I had been heard
	audītus erās	you (sing.) had been heard
	audītus erat	he (she, it) had been heard
	audītī erāmus	we had been heard
	audītī erātis	you (pl.) had been heard
	audītī erant	they had been heard

SUBJUNCTIVE	IMPERATIVE
audiar	
audiāris (-re)	audīre, audītor, be heard (sing.)
audiātur	audītor, let him be heard
audiāmur	audīminī, be heard (pl.)
audāminī	audiuntor, let them be heard
audiantur	

audīrer	
audīrēris (-re)	THE VERB INFINITE
audīrētur	
audīrēmur	
audīrēminī	Infinitives
audīrentur	
audītus sim	Present **audīrī**, to be heard
audītus sīs	Perfect **audītus esse**, to have been heard
audītus sit	
audītī sīmus	Future **audītum īrī**, (see § 387)
audītī sītis	
audītī sint	Participle
	Perf. **audītus**, heard or having been heard
	Gerundive
	audiendus, fit to be heard

audītus essem
audītus essēs
audītus esset
audītī essēmus
audītī essētis
audītī essent

124   Deponent Verb, (3rd Conjugation)

TENSE		INDICATIVE
Present	ūtor	I use or I am using
	ūteris	you (s.) use or are using
	ūtitur	he uses or he is using
	ūtimur	we use or we are using
	ūtiminī	you (pl.) use or you are using
	ūtuntur	they use or they are using
Future Simple	ūtar	I shall use
	ūtēris, ūtēre	you (s.) will use
	ūtētur	he (she, it) will use
	ūtēmur	we shall use
	ūtēminī	you (pl.) will use
	ūtentur	they will use
Imperfect	ūtēbar	I was using
	ūtēbāris (-re)	you (s.) were using
	ūtēbātur	he (she, it) was using
	ūtēbāmur	we were using
	ūtēbāminī	you (pl.) were using
	ūtēbantur	they were using
Perfect	ūsus sum	I have used or I used
	ūsus es	you (s.) have used or you (sing.) used
	ūsus est	he (she, it) has used or he (she, it) used
	ūsī sumus	we have used or we used
	ūsī estis	you (pl.) have used or you used
	ūsī sunt	they have used or they used
Future Perfect	ūsus erō	I shall have used
	ūsus eris	you (s.) will have used
	ūsus erit	he (she, it) will have used
	ūsī erimus	we shall have used
	ūsī eritis	you (pl.) will have used
	ūsī erunt	they will have used
Pluperfect	ūsus eram	I had used
	ūsus erās	you (s.) had used
	ūsus erat	he (she, it) had used
	ūsī erāmus	we had used
	ūsī erātis	you (pl.) had used
	ūsī erant	they had used

SUBJUNCTIVE	IMPERATIVE
ūtar	
ūtāris (-re)	ūtere, ūtitor, use (sing.)
ūtātur	ūtitor, let him use
ūtāmur	ūtiminī, use (pl.)
ūtāminī	ūtuntor, let them use
ūtantur	

THE VERB INFINITE

Infinitives

	Present	ūtī, to use
ūterer	Perfect	ūsus esse, to have used
ūterēris (-re)	Future	ūsūrus esse, to be about to use
ūterētur		
ūterēmur		Gerund
ūterēminī		ūtendum using
ūterentur		
ūsus sim		Supines
ūsus sīs		ūsum to use
ūsus sit		ūsū in *or* for using
ūsī sīmus		
ūsī sītis		Participles
ūsī sint		Pres. ūtēns, using

Future ūsūrus about to use
Perfect ūsus having used

Gerundive
ūtendus, fit to be used

ūsus essem	Note: Deponent verbs are passive in form but active in meaning.
ūsus essēs	
ūsus esset	
ūsī essēmus	
ūsī essētis	
ūsī essent	

125 Deponent Verbs of the Four Conjugations

1	vēnor	vēnātus sum	vēnārī, hunt
2	vereor	veritus sum	verērī, fear
3	ūtor	ūsus sum	ūtī, use
4	partior	partītus sum	partīrī, divide

INDICATIVE

TENSE	1st Conj.	2nd Conj.	3rd Conj.	4th Conj.
Pres.	vēnor	vereor	ūtor	partior
	vēnāris (-re)	verēris (-re)	ūteris (-re)	partīris (-īre) etc.
Fut. S.	vēnābor	verēbor	ūtar	partiar
Imperf.	vēnābar	verēbar	ūtēbar	partiēbar
Perf.	vēnātus sum	veritus sum	ūsus sum	partītus sum
Fut.Perf.	vēnātus erō	veritus erō	ūsus erō	partītus erō
Pluperf.	vēnātus eram	veritus eram	ūsus eram	partītus eram

SUBJUNCTIVE

Pres.	vēner	verear	ūtar	partiar
Imperf.	vēnārer	verērer	ūterer	partīrer
Perf.	vēnātus sim	veritus sim	ūsus sim	partītus sim
Pluperf.	vēnātus essem	veritus essem	ūsus essem	partītus essem

IMPERATIVE

	vēnāre	verēre	ūtere	partīre
	vēnātor	verētor	ūtitor	partītor

THE VERB INFINITE

Infinitives

Pres.	vēnārī	verērī	ūtī	partīrī
Perf.	vēnātus esse	veritus esse	ūsus esse	partītus esse
Fut.	vēnātūrus esse	veritūrus esse	ūsūrus esse	partītūrus esse

Participles

Pres.	vēnāns	verēns	ūtēns	partiēns
Perf.	vēnātus	veritus	ūsus	partītus
Fut.	vēnātūrus	veritūrus	ūsūrus	partītūrus

Gerunds

	vēnandum	verendum	ūtendum	partiendum

Gerundive

	vēnandus	verendus	ūtendus	partiendus

Supines

in -um	vēnātum	veritum	ūsum	partītum
in -ū	vēnātū	veritū	ūsū	partītū

Note: Some deponents also have an active form: *pūnior* and *pūniō*, punish.

126 Many perfect participles of deponent verbs are used passively as well
as actively: as *cōnfessus* from *cōnfiteor,* confess; *imitātus* from *imitor,*
imitate; *meritus* from *mereor,* deserve; *pollicitus* from *polliceor,* promise.

127 Some verbs have a perfect of passive form with a present of active
form; they are called **semi-deponents**:

audeō, I dare	**ausus sum,** I have dared *or* I dared
gaudeō, I rejoice	**gāvīsus sum,** I have rejoiced *or* I rejoiced
soleō, I am wont *or* am accustomed	**solitus sum,** I have been accustomed
fīdō, I trust	**fīsus sum,** I have trusted *or* I trusted

128 Some verbs have an active form with passive meaning; they are called
quasi-passive (see § 303):

exsulō, I am banished	**liceō,** I am put up for sale
vāpulō, I am beaten	**vēneō,** I am on sale
fīō, I am made (see § 141)	

129 Some verbs have perfect participles with active meaning, like the
deponent verbs:

adolēscō, I grow up	**adolēvi,** I grew up	**adultus,** having grown up
cēnō, I dine	**cēnāvi,** I dined	**cēnātus,** having dined
iūrō, I swear	**iūrāvī,** I swore	**iūrātus,** having sworn
pōtō, I drink	**pōtāvi,** I drank	**pōtus,** having drunk
prandeō, I dine	**prandī,** I dined	**prānsus,** having dined

130 **Inceptive verbs,** with present stem in **-scō** (third conjugation), express
beginning of action, and are derived from verb stems or from nouns:

> **pallēscō,** I turn pale, from **palleō**
> **nigrēscō,** I turn black, from **niger**

Note: The vowel before **-sc** is always long.

131 **Frequentative verbs** (first conj.) express repeated or intenser action,
and are formed from supine stems:

> **rogitō,** ask repeatedly (**rogō**); **cantō,** sing with energy (**canō**); **cursō,** run about (**currō**)

132 **Desiderative verbs** (fourth conj.) express desire of action, and are
formed from the supine stem and end in **-uriō**:

> **ēsuriō,** I am hungry (from **edō** – see § 140)

133 Mixed Conjugation

Verbs in **-iō** with pres. infinitive in **-ere**.

Forms from present stem, **cap-i-**, take

PRESENT	ACTIVE VOICE		PASSIVE VOICE	
	INDIC.	SUBJUNC.	INDIC.	SUBJUNC.
	capiō	capiam	capior	capiar
	capis	capiās	caperis	capiāris (-re)
	capit	capiat	capitur	capiātur
	capimus	capiāmus	capimur	capiāmur
	capitis	capiātis	capiminī	capiāminī
	capiunt	capiant	capiuntur	capiantur

FUTURE SIMPLE

capiam	capiar
capiēs	capiēris (-re)
capiet	capiētur
capiēmus	capiēmur
capiētis	capiēminī
capient	capientur

IMPERFECT

capiēbam	caperem	capiēbar	caperer
capiēbās	caperēs	capiēbāris (-re)	caperēris (-re)
capiēbat	caperet	capiēbātur	caperētur
capiēbāmus	caperēmus	capiēbāmur	caperēmur
capiēbātis	caperētis	capiēbāminī	caperēminī
capiēbant	caperent	capiēbantur	caperentur

IMPERATIVE

2 sing.	cape, capitō		2 sing.	capere, capitor
3 sing.	capitō		3 sing.	capitor
2 pl.	capite, capitōte		2 pl.	capiminī
3 pl.	capiuntō		3 pl.	capiuntor

INFINITE

Infin. Pres.	capere,		capī
Gerund	capiendum	Gerundive	capiendus
Pres. Partic.	capiēns		

The verbs in **-iō** are:

capiō, cupiō, faciō	⎫ and their	take, desire, make
fodiō, fugiō, iaciō	⎬ compounds	dig, flee, throw
pariō, rapiō, sapiō, quatiō	⎭	bring forth, seize, know, shake
compounds of speciō & laciō	obsolete verbs	look at, entice
Deponents: **gradior, patior, morior**		step, suffer, die
Semi-deponents (see §161): **potior, orior**		get possession of, arise

134   Irregular Verbs

Verbs are called irregular: (1) because they are formed from more than one root, as **sum**; or (2) because their tense-forms differ from those of regular verbs.

135   Possum, I can, **posse, potuī:** the present indicative, **possum,** is compounded of *sum*, I am, and the adjective *potis*, able.

INDIC.	SUBJUNC.	INDIC.	SUBJUNC.
PRESENT		PERFECT	
possum	possim	potuī	potuerim
potes	possīs	potuistī	potueris
potest	possit	potuit	potuerit
possumus	possīmus	potuimus	potuerīmus
potestis	possītis	potuistis	potuerītis
possunt	possint	potuērunt	potuerint
FUTURE SIMPLE		FUTURE PERFECT	
poterō		potuerō	
poteris		potueris	
poterit		potuerit	
poterimus		potuerimus	
poteritis		potueritis	
poterunt		potuerint	
IMPERFECT		PLUPERFECT	
poteram	possem	potueram	potuissem
poterās	possēs	potuerās	potuissēs
poterat	posset	potuerat	potuisset
poterāmus	possēmus	potuerāmus	potuissēmus
poterātis	possētis	potuerātis	potuissētis
poterant	possent	potuerant	potuissent

Infinitive present **posse** (*pot-esse*), perfect **potuisse**. **Potēns** is used as an adjective, powerful, able, never as a participle.

136   **Fero**, bear, **ferre, tulī, lātum**

ACTIVE VOICE		PASSIVE VOICE	

PRESENT

INDIC.	SUBJUNC.	INDIC.	SUBJUNC.
ferō	feram	feror	ferar
fers	ferās	ferris	ferāris (-re)
fert	ferat	fertur	ferātur
ferimus	ferāmus	ferimur	ferāmur
fertis	ferātis	feriminī	ferāminī
ferunt	ferant	feruntur	ferantur

FUTURE SIMPLE

feram	ferar
ferēs	ferēris (-re)
feret	ferētur
ferēmus	ferēmur
ferētis	ferēminī
ferent	ferentur

IMPERFECT

ferēbam	ferrrem	ferēbar	ferrrer
ferēbās	ferrrēs	ferēbāris (-re)	ferrrēris (-re)
ferēbat	ferrret	ferēbātur	ferrrētur
ferēbāmus	ferrrēmus	ferēbāmur	ferrrēmur
ferēbātis	ferrrētis	ferēbāminī	ferrrēminī
ferēbant	ferrrent	ferēbantur	ferrrentur

IMPERATIVE

2 sing.	fer, fertō	2 sing.	ferre, fertor
3 sing.	fertō	3 sing.	fertor
2 pl.	ferte, fertōte	2 pl.	feriminī
3 pl.	feruntō	3 pl.	feruntor

INFINITE

Infin. Pres.	ferre		ferrī
Gerund	ferendum, -i, -o	Gerundive	ferendus
Pres. Partic.	ferēns		

Perfect stem forms are regular:
tul-ī, -erō, -eram, -erim, -issem   Infin. **tulisse**

The supine stem forms are also regular: **lātum, lātū**; participles **lātus,
lātūrus**; infinitives **lātus esse, lātus īrī**.

137   Eō (for eiō), go, īre, iī (or īvī), itum

INDICATIVE	SUBJUNCTIVE	IMPERATIVE
Present		
eō	eam	
īs	eās	2nd s. ī, ītō
it	eat	3rd s. ītō
īmus	eāmus	
ītis	eātis	2nd pl. īte, ītōte
eunt	eant	3rd pl. euntō

Future Simple
ībō
ībis
ībit
ībimus
ībitis
ībunt

THE VERB INFINITIVE

Infinitives

Imperfect		Present īre
ībam	īrem	Perfect īsse, īvisse
ībās	īrēs	Future itūrus esse
ībat	īret	
ībāmus	īrēmus	Gerund eundum
ībātis	īrētis	
ībant	īrent	Supines itum, itū

Perfect		Participles
iī or īvī	ierim	Pres. iēns (acc. euntem)
īstī or īvīstī	ierīs	Future. itūrus
iit or ivit	ierit	
iimus or ivimus	ierīmus	
īstis or ivistis	ierītis	
iērunt or ivērunt	ierint	

Note: In the perfect tense of eō the forms iī, īstī &c. are more usual than īvī &c.; also in the compounds rediī, rediīstī, redistī.

The impersonal passive, ītur, itum est, is often used.

138   Queō, can, nequeō, cannot, are conjugated like eo in the forms which are found, but the perfect usually ends in īvī; they have no imperative and no gerunds. Ambiō, go round, canvass, is conjugated like audiō.

139 **Volō**, am willing, wish; **nōlō**, am unwilling, do not wish; **mālō**, prefer, wish rather. **Nōlō** is compounded of ne and **volō**. **Mālō** of **magis** and **volō**.

INDICATIVE			IMPERATIVE
Present			nōlī, nōlītō
volō	nōlō	mālō	nōlītō
vīs	nōn vīs	māvīs	
vult	nōn vult	māvult	nōlīte, nōlītōte,
volumus	nōlumus	mālumus	nōluntō
vultis	nōn vultis	māvultis	
volunt	nōlunt	mālunt	volō and mālō have no imperative.
Future Simple			
volam	(nōlam)	(mālam)	
volēs	nōlēs	(mālēs)	
volet	nōlet	mālet	THE VERB INFINITE
volēmus	(nōlēmus)	(mālēmus)	
volētis	(nōlētis)	(mālētis)	Infinitives
volent	(nōlent)	mālent	Present { velle, nōlle, mālle
Imperfect			
volēbam	nōlebam	mālēbam	
volēbās	nōlebās	mālēbās	Gerunds
&c.	&c.	&c.	volendum, -ī, -ō
SUBJUNCTIVE			nōlendum, -ī, -ō
Present			mālendum, -ī, -ō
velim	nōlim	mālim	
velīs	nōlīs	mālīs	Supines
velit	nōlit	mālit	None
velīmus	nōlīmus	mālīmus	
velītis	nōlītis	mālītis	Participles
velint	nōlint	mālint	Present { volēns (nōlēns) _____
Imperfect			
vellem	nōllem	māllem	
vellēs	nōllēs	māllēs	
vellet	nōllet	māllet	
vellēmus	nōllēmus	māllēmus	
vellētis	nōllētis	māllētis	
vellent	nōllent	māllent	

The perfect-stem forms are regular:

volu-ī	-erō	-eram	-erim	-issem		voluisse
nōlu-ī	-erō	-eram	-erim	-issem	Infin. {	nōluisse
mālu-ī	-erō	-eram	-erim	-issem		māluisse

140   Edō, I eat, ēsse, ēdī, ēsum

Pres. ind. act.	edō, ēs, ēst, edimus, ēstis, edunt
Imperf. subj. act.	ēssem, ēssēs, ēsset, etc.
Imperat. pres. act.	ēs, ēste
Imperat. fut. act	ēstō, ēstōte; eduntō
Inf. pres. act.	ēsse
Present ind. passive	ēstur
Present subj. passive	ēssētur

The other forms of this verb are regular; except that **edim, edīs, edit, edint** are often found in the present subjunctive.

141   Fīō, I am made, I become, fierī, factus sum
Fīō is defective, having only present, future and imperfect forms. The perfect is supplied by the perfect passive of **faciō**, make: *factus sum*, I have been made.

INDICATIVE	SUBJUNCTIVE	IMPERATIVE
Present		
fīō	fīam	fī
fīs	fīās	fīte
fit	fīat	
(fīmus)	fīāmus	
(fītis)	fīātis	
fīunt	fīant	THE VERB INFINITE
Future Simple		
fīam		Infinitives
fīēs		Present⎫
fīet		Imperf.⎭ fierī
fīēmus		Perfect ⎫
fīētis		Pluperf.⎭ factus esse
fīent		Future **factum īrī**
Imperfect		
fīēbam	fierem	Gerundive
fīēbās	fierēs	**faciendus**
fīēbat	fieret	
fīēbāmus	fierēmus	
fīēbātis	fierētis	
fīēbant	fierent	

Perfect **factus sum** &c.   Perf. subj. **factus sim, &c.**

142 Defective Verbs

Defective verbs are those of which only some forms are used.

coepī, I begin ⎫ have only perfect-stem forms in the
meminī, I remember ⎬ classical period; meminī and ōdī have
ōdī, I hate ⎭ present meanings despite their forms.

INDICATIVE

Perfect.	coepī, I begin	meminī, I remember	ōdī, I hate.
Fut. Perf.	coeperō, I shall begin	meminerō, I shall remember	ōderō, I shall hate
Pluperf.	coeperam, I began	memineram, I remembered	ōderam, I hated

SUBJUNCTIVE

Perfect.	coeperim	meminerim	ōderim
Pluperf.	coepissem	meminissem	ōdissem

INFINITIVE, PARTICIPLES, IMPERATIVE

Infin.	coepisse, to begin	meminisse	ōdisse
Perf. Part.	coeptus	—	ōsus, hating
Fut. Part.	coeptūrus esse, about to begin	—	ōsūrus esse about to hate
Imperative	—	mementō, mementōte	—

Nōvī (perf. of *nōscō*) is used with present meaning, I have got to know, I know. **Nōverō**, I shall know. **nōveram** or **nōram** (§ 113), I knew. **Nōvisse**, to know, etc.

nōverō {nōveram / nōram} nōverim {nōvissem / nōssem} infin. {nōvisse / nōsse}

Aiō, I say or affirm

Ind. Pres.	aiō, ais, ait, —,—, aiunt
Impf.	aiēbam, aiēbās, aiēbat, aiēbāmus, aiēbātis, aiēbant
Subj. Pres.	—,—, aiat, —,—, aiant
Participle	aiēns

Note: Except in **ais, ait**, -**i**- is consonantal and 1st syllable is heavy.

Inquam, I say

Ind. Pres.	inquam	inquis	inquit	inquimus,	inquitis	inquiunt
Imperfect	—	—	inquiēbat	—	—	inquiēbant
Future S.	—	inquiēs	inquiet	—	—	—
Perf.	—	inquīstī	inquit	—	—	—
Imperative		inque	—	inquitō		

Fārī, to speak

Indic. Pres.	fātur	
Indic. Fut.	fābor, fābitur	
Imperative	fāre, speak!	
Participles:	Pres. Acc. fantem	Perf. fātus
Gerund.	fandī, fandō	Gerundive fandus

Quæsō, entreat (an old form of *quærō*), has first pers. plur. **quæsumus.**

The following imperatives are found:
   apage, be gone!
   avē (havē), avēte, hail!   Infin. **avēre,** to have a desire
   cedo, cedite (cette), give!
   salvē, salvēte hail!   Infin. **salvēre,** to be well.

Note: **Age, agite,** come; **valē, valēte,** farewell, are used with special meaning; but the verbs **agō,** I do, **valeō,** I am well, are fully conjugated.

---

143 **Impersonal Verbs (§ 288–295)**

Impersonal verbs are used only in the forms of the third person singular of each tense, and do not refer to a subject in the nominative. They have also infinitive and gerund.

144 The principal impersonal verbs are the following:

Present	Perfect	Infinitive
miseret, it moves to pity	(**miseruit**)	(**miserēre**)
piget, it vexes	**piguit**	**pigēre**
pænitet, it repents	**pænituit**	**pænitēre**
pudet, it shames	**puduit**	**pudēre**
tædet, it wearies	**tæduit**	**tædēre**

decet, it is becoming	**decuit**	**decēre**
dēdecet, it is unbecoming	**dēdecuit**	**dēdecēre**
libet, it pleases	**libuit**	**libēre**
licet, it is lawful	**licuit**	**licēre**
oportet, it behoves	**oportuit**	**oportēre**
rēfert, it matters, it concerns	**rētulit**	**rēferre**

Note 1: Decet, dēdecet have also 3rd. pers. plur., *decent, dēdecent.*

Note 2: A few passive forms are found: *miseritum est, pigitum est, puditum est, pertœsum est.* Other forms are occasionally found: *pœnitendus, pudendus.*

145 Some impersonal verbs express change of weather and time:

fulgurat, it lightens	**tonat,** it thunders
ningit, it snows	**lūcēscit,** it dawns
pluit, it rains	**vesperāscit,** it grows late

146 Of some verbs which have all the personal forms, the third person singular is used impersonally with special meaning:

accēdit, it is added	**expedit,** it is expedient
accidit, it happens	**fallit, fugit,** it escapes one
appāret, it is evident	**interest,** it concerns
attinet, it belongs	**iuvat,** it delights
cōnstat, it is agreed	**pertinet,** it pertains
contingit, it befalls	**placet,** it seems good
convenit, it suits	**rēfert,** it matters
dēlectat, it charms	**restat,** it remains
ēvenit, it turns out	

Intransitive Verbs are used impersonally in the passive (see § 299).

147 DERIVATION FROM THE THREE TENSE STEMS

1. From the Present-Stem.

Pres. Indic. Act.	am -ō	mone -ō	reg -ō	audi -ō
Pres. Indic. Pass.	-or	e -or	-or	i -or
Pres. Subj. Act.	-em	e-am	-am	i -am
Pres. Subj. Pass.	-er	e -ar	-ar	i -ar
Imperf. Indic. Act.	ā -bam	ē -bam	-ēbam	i -ēbam
Imperf. Indic. Pass.	ā -bar	ē -bar	-ēbar	i -ēbar
Imperf. Subj. Act.	ā -rem	ē -rem	-ērem	ī -rem
Imperf. Subj. Pass.	ā -rer	ē -rer	-erer	ī -rer
Fut. Indic. Act.	ā -bō	ē -bō	-am	i -am
Fut. Indic. Pass.	ā -bor	ē -bor	-ar	i -ar
Imperative Act.	ā	ē	-e	ī
Imperative Pass.	ā -re	ē -re	-ere	ī -re
Infin. Pres. Act.	ā -re	ē -re	-ere	ī -re
Infin. Pres. Pass.	ā -rī	ē -rī	-ī	ī -rī
Partic. Pres. Act.	ā -ns	ē -ns	-ēns	i -ēns
Gerund	a -ndum	e -ndum	-endum	i -endum
Gerundive	a -ndus	e -ndus	-endus	i -endus

2. From the Perfect-Stem

Perfect Indic. Act.	amāv -ī	monu -ī	rēx -ī	audīv -ī
Perfect Subj. Act.	-erim	-erim	-erim	-erim
Future Perf. Ind. Act	-erō	-erō	-erō	-erō
Pluperfect Indic. Act.	-eram	-eram -eram		-eram
Pluperfect Subj. Act.	-issem	-issem -issem		-issem
Infin. Perf. Act.	-isse	-isse	-isse	-isse

3. From the Supine-Stem (see § 151)

Supine I	amāt -um	monit-um	rēct -um	audīt -um
Infin. Fut. Pass.	-um īrī	-um īrī	-um īrī	-um īrī
Supine II	-ū	-ū	-ū	-ū
Partic. Fut. Act.	-ūrus	-ūrus	-ūrus	-ūrus
Partic. Perf. Pass.	-us	-us	-us	-us
Perf. Indic. Pass.	-us sum	-us sum	-us sum	-us sum
Perf. Subj Pass.	-us sim -us sim		-us sim	-us sim
Fut. Perf. Pass.	-us erō	-us erō	-us erō	-us erō
Plup. Ind. Pass	-us eram	-us eram	-us eram	-us eram
Plup. Subj. Pass.	-us essem	-us essem	-us essem	-us essem
Infin. Pass.	-us esse	-us esse	-us esse	-us esse

148 FORMATION OF THE THREE STEMS IN VERBS

The forms of the Latin verb vary in many respects from those of the parent and related languages. Both in the past and in the future tenses Latin has developed new endings of its own, so that the original forms are only seen in the present.

The verbs in the older language were divided into two principal classes:

1. In which the personal endings were joined immediately to the root, the tenses being partly formed by changes in the root vowel.

2. In which the verb-stem was formed by a so-called **thematic vowel** (see § 149) added to the root.

Of the first class there are very few remains in Latin, most of the verbs which belonged to it having gone over into the second class.

The old ending **-m** (for **-mi**) for the first person singular is seen in *sum*, I am, and in other tenses, as *eram*. A few irregular verbs retain part of their old forms side by side with later forms borrowed from the thematic verbs. These are:

sum, Iam; **eō**, I go; **dō**, I give; **stō**, I stand; **fīō**, I become; **edō**, I eat; **volō**, I will; **nōlō**, I will not; **mālō**, I prefer (and compounds of all these except **dō**).

PERSONAL ENDINGS IN ATHEMATIC AND THEMATIC VERBS

	ACTIVE VOICE		PASSIVE VOICE
	Athematic	Thematic	
Singular 1	**-m**	**-ō**	**-r**
2	**-s**	**-s**	**-ris** *or* **-re**
3	**-t**	**-t**	**-tur**
Plural 1	**-mus**	**-mus**	**-mur**
2	**-tis**	**-tis**	**-minī**
3	**-nt**	**-nt**	**-ntur**

Note: The **-r** of the passive probably comes from an old form of a third voice, called the **middle voice**, which is not preserved in Latin.

149   Present-Stem Formation

The thematic verbs are divided into six groups according to the formation of their present stems from the verb root.

1. The present stem is the same as the verb-stem, being formed by the addition of the thematic vowel to the stem-syllable either with or without lengthening of the stem-vowel (originally **-e** or **-o**): **pet-i-t, veh-i-t, cēd-i-t, fend-i-t, dīc-i-t, fīdō, dūc-i-t, claud-i-t**, etc.

> **Note.** This class had originally two divisions: (a) with long root vowel, (b) with short root vowel, but in Latin the distinction between them is not clear.

2. Reduplicated presents. Of this class very few are preserved in Latin: **gignō** for **gi-g(e)nō** (c.f. **genus**, race); sisto for **si-stō**, etc..

3. With suffix **-t** added to the stem-syllable (i.e. with a **t** inserted between the verb-root and the thematic vowel): **plec-t-ō, flec-t-ō, nec-t-ō**.

4. Nasalized stems:
   (a) with addition of the suffix **-n** to the stem-syllable: **cer-n-ō** (for **cri-n-ō**), **ster-n-ō, sper-n-ō, tem-n-ō**, and two roots ending in **-i**: **si-n-ō, li-n-ō**. Verbs in **-llō, fallō, pellō, percellō**, etc., also belong to this class, **-llō** standing for older **-lnō**.
   (b) Verbs in which **-n-** is inserted in the verb root, as **plangō** (verb-stem **plag-**), **iungō, findō, scindō**. This is known as the nasal infix (§24). The **n** becomes **m** before labials, as in **rumpō (rūpi, ruptum)**. In some of these verbs the nasal goes through all the tenses, as in **ungō, unxi, unctum**. In others it appears only in the present stem, as in **frangō, frēgī, frāctum**. A few have the nasal in the perfect, but not in the supine, as in **pingō, pīnxī, pictum**.

5. With suffix **-scō**. This class also has two divisions:
   (a) With the suffix joined immediately to the root-syllable: **nōscō, crēscō, discō, pāscō**.
   (b) Derivative verbs in **-ā-scō, -ē-scō, -ī-scō**, derived from other verbs or from nouns: **congelāscō**, from *gelo*; **calēscō**, from *caleō*; **gemīscō**, from *gemō*; **dūrēscō**, from *dūrus*, etc.

6. With **-i-** between the verb root and the thematic vowel. The verbs in **-iō** of the 3rd Conj. (consonant-stems) belong to this class: **capio, facio**, etc. It included originally the large number of derivative verbs with vowel-stems, as **amō** (for **ama-iō**), **moneō** (**mone-iō**) (see §14).

150 Formation of the Perfect

The perfect first person singular ends in **ī**. When the suffix **-ī** is joined to the stem, with or without change in the stem-syllable, it is called a **strong formation**. When the perfect is formed by adding to the stem one of the suffixes **-sī, -vī, -uī,** the formation is called **weak**.

In some vowel-stems, especially in many **e**-stems, the final or character vowel of the verb-stem is dropped before the perfect suffix, and the stem is then called the **clipped stem**. This is seen in **mon-uī** (stem **mone-**), **mān-sī, cāv-ī, pepend-ī,** and also in some **a-** and **i-** stems, as **dom-uī, sal-uī**.

Strong Formation of the Perfect

1. With **reduplication**. This is the oldest way of forming the perfect, and arose from a doubling of the stem-syllable. In Latin it is formed by a vowel (originally **e**) prefixed to the stem. When the stem begins with a single consonant, this vowel is preceded by the same consonant: **pendō, pependī**. When the stem begins with **s**, followed by another consonant (**sc, sp, st**), the reduplicating syllable begins with the double consonant, but the stem-syllable drops the **s**: **spondeō, spopondī; stō, stetī**. The **e** of the reduplicating syllable is often assimilated to the stem-vowel, **mo-mordī, pupugī, didicī** (§ 13). In compounds it is sometimes partly lost, as in **rettulī** (§ 15). In many reduplicated perfects, the vowel of the stem-syllable is weakened through loss of the accent: **cadō, cecidī**.

2. With **lengthened stem-vowel**. This formation is seen in two **a-** stems: **iūvī, lāvī**; in a few **e-** stems: **sēdī, vīdī, cāvī, fōvī,** etc.; in consonant-stems: **vīcī, fūgī, lēgī, fūdī,** etc.; and in one i- stem: **vēnī**.

   A few consonant-stems, **agō, capiō, iaciō, frangō,** and the compounds of **pangō (compingō, impingō)** form their perfect with vowel change as well as lengthening. In many of these verbs the perfect was originally reduplicated and the vowel was lengthened after loss of reduplication. The perfects **ēgī, ēdī, ēmī,** of **agō, edō, emō,** are contractions of an old reduplication (**e-ag-, e-ed-, e-em-**).

   > **Note:** A few of the above have long vowel in present as well as perfect : **īcō, cūdō, sīdō, vīsō**.

3. With **unchanged stem-syllable**. This class includes the **u-** stems **acuī, arguī,** etc., and a number of consonant-stems, as **verrī, vertī, scandī,** the compounds of **-cendō, -fendō,** etc., and two **e-** verbs, **prandī** and **strīdī**.

Weak Formation of the Perfect

1. The perfect suffix in **-sī** is joined to the clipped stem of many **e-** and some **i-** verbs; also to a large number of consonant-stems with which it combines according to the laws of consonant change. Thus **gs, cs, hs,** become **x,** as in **rēxī, pīnxī, dūxī, vēxī**. Also **qs** in **coxī**. The guttural drops after **l, r** in **fulsī, mersī,** also in **vīxī** from stem **guigu-** (compare Old English *cwicu*, alive). In **struxī, fluxī,** the perfect preserves the guttural sound which is lost in the present **struō, fluō**. Dental sounds are dropped, **plausī (plaudō), flexī (flectō)**; with lengthening of short vowels, as in **mīsī**. The labial **p** remains unchanged, as in **sculpsī,** but **b** becomes **p, scrīpsī, nūpsī**. After **m, p** is inserted, in **sumpsī, tempsī; s** remains, as in **gessī, ūsī,** where in the present it changes to **r**. It becomes single after a long vowel or diphthong, as **hæsī, hausī**.

2. The weak perfect forms in **-vī** and **-uī** are peculiar to the Latin language. They were probably formed by analogy from the **v-** and **u-** stems like **favī, acuī,** and extended to a very large number of verbs. All the **a-** and **i-** stems which keep their character vowel throughout the tenses as **amāvī, audīvī,** form their perfect tense in **-vī** as well as many consonant-stems. The perfect in **-uī** is joined to the clippped **e-** stems, as **mon-uī,** also to a few clipped stems in **a-** and to a large number of consonant verbs. This form had a tendency to spread in later Latin, and many verbs formed new perfects in **-ui** after the classical period.

151   The Past Participle, Future Participle and Supine

The supine or participial stem ends in **-to**. This suffix is joined to the verb stem or to the clipped stem, either immediately or by the vowel **i**. When it is joined immediately to the vowel stem, as in most of the **a-**, **i-** and **u-** stems, the character vowel is lengthened. When it is joined to a consonant stem, the laws of consonant change again come into force: **g** before **t** becomes **c**; the guttural is dropped after **l** or **r**: *fultum, tortum*; **p** is inserted between **m** and **t**: *emptum*. In a few verbs the stem vowel is changed, as in *lavō*, which has besides *lavātum*, a contracted supine form *lautum*, afterwards becoming *lōtum*; in *satum* (from *serō*), *cultum* (from *colō*). Although different of origin, supines only differ from the masc. sing. of past participles by in ending in **-um**, **-ū** rather than **-us**. The supine in **-sum** was formed in dental stems by a regular change of medial **-dt-, -tt-** to **ss**; thus *ced-to-, mit-to-,* would become *cesso-, misso-,* and the double **s** would become single after a long vowel or diphthong (§ 20).

The future participle only differs from the past participle by ending in **-urus** rather than **-us**.

PRINCIPAL PARTS OF VERBS

152 1st Conjugation, a- stems

PRESENT	INFINITIVE	PERFECT	SUPINE	
		Usual Form		
-ō	-āre	-āvī	-ātum	
amō	amāre	amāvī	amātum	
		Exceptions		
		Perfect in -uī, Supine in -itum		
crepō	-āre	crepuī	crepitum	creak
cubō	-āre	cubuī	cubitum	lie down
domō	-āre	domuī	domitum	tame
plicō	-āre	-plicāvī / -plicuī	-plicātum / -plicitum	fold
sonō	-āre	sonuī	sonitum	sound
tonō	-āre	tonuī	tonitum	thunder
vetō	-āre	vetuī / vetavī	vetitum	forbid
		Perfect in -uī, Supine in -ātum		
micō	-āre	micuī / -micāvī	-micatum	glitter
		Perfect in -uī, Supine in -tum		
ēnecō	-āre	ēnecuī	ēnectum	kill
fricō	-āre	fricuī	frictum / fricatum	rub
secō	-āre	secuī	sectum	cut
		Perfect in -ī, Supine in-tum		
		(a) Reduplicated		
dō	-āre	dedī	datum	give
stō	-āre	stetī, -stitī	statum	stand
		(b) Lengthened Vowel		
iuvō	-āre	iūvī	iūtum	help
lavō	-āre	lāvī	lavātum / lautum / lōtum	wash

Note: For very many supines no authority exists; but the form is inferred from the perfect participle or future participle. Forms printed with a hyphen, as **-plicāvī, -plicātum** are only found in compounds.

153   2nd Conjugation, E- Stems

PRESENT	INFINITIVE	PERFECT	SUPINE	
		Usual Form		
-eō (-ei-o)	-ēre	-uī	-itum	
moneō	monēre	monuī	monitum	
		Exceptions		
		Perfect in -uī, Supine in -tum		
arceō	-ēre	arcuī	—	ward off
doceō	-ēre	docuī	doctum	teach
ferveō	-ēre	ferbuī, fervī	—	be hot
misceō	-ēre	miscuī	mixtum, mistum	mix
teneō	-ēre	tenuī	-tentum	hold
torreō	-ēre	torruī	tostum	scorch
		Perfect in -uī, Supine in -sum		
cēnseō	-ēre	cēnsuī	cēnsum	deem, vote
		Perfect in -vī, Supine in -tum		
aboleō	-ēre	abolēvī	abolitum	destroy
cieō	-ēre	cīvī	cītum	stir up
dēleō	-ēre	dēlēvī	dēlētum	blot out
fleō	-ēre	flēvī	flētum	weep
neō	-ēre	nēvī	notum	spin
-pleō	-ēre	-plēvī	-plētum	fill
		Perfect in -sī, Supine in -tum		
augeō	-ēre	auxī	auctum	increase (tr.)
cōnīveō	-ēre	conīxī	—	wink
frīgeō	-ēre	frīxī	—	freeze
fulgeō	-ēre	fulsī	—	shine
indulgeō	-ēre	indulsī	idultum	indulge
lūgeō	-ēre	lūxī	luctum	mourn
mulgeō	-ēre	mulsī	multum	milk
pollūceō	-ēre	—	pollūctum	make a feast
torqueō	-ēre	torsī	tortum	twist
		Perfect in -sī, Supine in -sum		
algeō	-ēre	alsī	—	be cold
ārdeō	-ēre	ārsī	arsum	burn (intr.)
iubeō	-ēre	iussī	iussum	command
lūceō	-ēre	lūxī	—	shine
maneō	-ēre	mānsī	mānsum	remain
mulceō	-ēre	mulsī	mulsum	soothe
rīdeō	-ēre	rīsī	rīsum	laugh
suādeō	-ēre	suāsī	suāsum	advise
tergeō	-ēre	tersī	-tersum	wipe
turgeō	-ēre	tursī	—	swell
urgeō	-ēre	ursī	—	press

Note: Ārdeō, hæreō have Fut. Part. *ārsūrus, hæsūrus.*

Perfect in -ī, Supine in -sum or -tum

(a) Lengthened Perfect Stem, Supine in -tum

caveō	-ēre	cāvī	cautum	beware
faveō	-ēre	fāvī	fautum	favor
foveō	-ēre	fōvī	fōtum	cherish
moveō	-ēre	mōvī	mōtum	move (tr.)
paveō	-ēre	pāvī	—	quake
voveō	-ēre	vōvī	vōtum	vow

(b) Reduplicated Perfect Stem, Supine in -sum

mordeō	-ēre	momordī	morsum	bite
pendeō	-ēre	pependī	pensum	hang (intr.)
spondeō	-ēre	spopondī	spōnsum	pledge
tondeō	-ēre	totondī	tōnsum	shear

(c) Lengthened Perfect Stem, Supine in -sum

sedeō	-ēre	sēdī	sessum	sit
videō	-ēre	vīdī	vīsum	see

(d) Unchanged Perfect Stem

langueō	-ēre	languī	—	be weary
prandeō	-ēre	prandī	prānsum	lunch, dine
strīdeō	-ēre	strīdī	—	creak

154   3rd Conjugation, Consonant and U-Stems

Consonant Stems

rego	regere	rēxi	rēctum

Perfect in sī, Supine in -tum

adflīgō	-ere	-flīxī	-flīctum	smite down
angō	-ere	—	—	distress
carpō	-ere	carpsī	carptum	pluck
cingō	-ere	cīnxī	cīnctum	surround
clangō	-ere	—	—	clash
cōmō	-ere	cōmpsi	cōmptum	adorn
coquō	-ere	coxī	coctum	cook
dēmō	-ere	dēmpsi	dēmptum	take away
dīcō	-ere	dīxī	dictum	say
dīligō	-ere	dīlēxī	dīlēctum	love
dūcō	-ere	dūxī	ductum	lead
exstinguō	-ere	exstinxī	exstinctum	quench
fingō	-ere	fīnxī	fictum	feign
frīgō	-ere	frīxī	frīctum	roast, fry
gerō	-ere	gessī	gestum	carry on
intellegō	-ere	intellēxī	intellēctum	understand
iungō	-ere	iūnxī	iūnctum	join, attach
neglegō	-ere	neglēxī	neglēctum	neglect

ninguit, ningit	-ere	ninxit	—	it snows
nūbō	-ere	nūpsi	nūptum	marry
pangō	-ere	panxī, pēgī,	pāctum	fasten
pergō	-ere	perrēxī	perrēctum	proceed
pingō	-ere	pīnxī	pictum	paint
prōmō	-ere	prōmpsī	prōmptum	bring out
rēpō	-ere	rēpsī	rēptum	creep
scalpō	-ere	scalpsī	scalptum	scratch
scrībō	-ere	scrīpsī	scriptum	write
sculpō	-ere	sculpsī	sculptum	carve
stringō	-ere	strīnxī	strictum	bind
struō	-ere	struxī	structum	put together
sūgō	-ere	sūxī	sūctum	suck
sūmō	-ere	sūmpsī	sūmptum	take
surgō	-ere	surrēxī	surrēctum	arise
tegō	-ere	tēxī	tēctum	cover
temnō	-ere	-tempsī	-temptum	despise
tingō	-ere	tīnxī	tīnctum	dye
trāhō	-ere	trāxī	tractum	draw
unguō, ungo	-ere	ūnxi	ūnctum	anoint
ūrō	-ere	ūssī	ūstum	burn (tr.)
vehō	-ere	vēxī	vectum	carry
vīvō	-ere	vixī	victum	live

Perfect in -sī, Supine in -sum

cedō	-ere	cessī	cessum	yield
claudō	-ere	clausī	clausum	shut
dīvidō	-ere	dīvīsī	dīvīsum	divide
figō	-ere	fixī	fixum	fix
flectō	-ere	flexī	flexum	bend
fluō	-ere	fluxī	fluxum	flow
lædō	-ere	læsī	læsum	hurt
lūdō	-ere	lūsī	lūsum	play
mergō	-ere	mersī	mersum	drown
mittō	-ere	mīsī	missum	send
nectō	-ere	nexī, nexuī*	nexum	bind
pectō	-ere	pexī	pexum	comb
plaudō	-ere	plausī	plausum	applaud
premō	-ere	pressī	pressum	press (tr.)
rādō	-ere	rāsī	rāsum	scrape
rōdō	-ere	rōsī	rōsum	gnaw
spargō	-ere	sparsī	sparsum	sprinkle
trūdō	-ere	trūsī	trūsum	thrust
vādō	-ere	(in)vāsī	(in)vāsum	go (attack)

* **Nexuī**, the more usual Perf. of **nectō**, is from an obsolete verb, **nexō**.

Perfect in -vī, Supine in -tum

abolēscō	-ere	abolēvī	—	decay
adolēscō*	-ere	adolēvī	adultum	grow up
cernō	-ere	crēvī	crētum	sift, discern
cognōscō	-ere	cognōvī	cognitum	get to know
crēscō	-ere	crēvī	crētum	grow
linō	-ere	lēvī, līvī	litum	smear
nōscō	-ere	nōvī	nōtum	get to know
obsolēscō	-ere	obsolēvī	obsolētum	grow out of use
pāscō	-ere	pāvī	pāstum	feed (tr.)
quiēscō	-ere	quiēvī	quiētum	rest
serō	-ere	sēvī	satum	sow
sinō	-ere	sīvī	situm	allow
spernō	-ere	sprēvī	sprētum	despise
sternō	-ere	strāvī	strātum	strew
suēscō	-ere	suēvī	suētum	grow accustomed

* Adolēscō has adjective adultus.

Perfect in -īvī, Supine in -ītum

arcessō	-ere	arcessīvī	arcessītum	send for
capessō	-ere	capessīvī	capessītum	take in hand
incessō	-ere	incessīvī	—	attack
lacessō	-ere	lacessīvī	lacessītum	provoke
petō	-ere	petīvī	petītum	seek
quærō	-ere	quæsīvī	quæsītum	seek
terō	-ere	trīvī	trītum	rub

Perfect in -uī, Supine in -tum

alō	-ere	aluī	altum	nourish
colō	-ere	coluī	cultum	till, worship
cōnsulō	-ere	cōnsuluī	cōnsultum	consult
occulō	-ere	occuluī	occultum	hide
pīnsō	-ere	pīnsuī, pīnsī	pistum	beat, pound
rapiō	-ere	rapuī	raptum	seize
serō	-ere	seruī	sertum	join
texō	-ere	texuī	textum	weave

Perfect in -uī, Supine in -itum

fremō	-ere	fremuī	fremitum	bellow
gemō	-ere	gemuī	gemitum	groan
gignō	-ere	genuī	genitum	produce
molō	-ere	moluī	molitum	grind
pōnō	-ere	posuī	positum	place
strepō	-ere	strepuī	strepitum	roar
tremō	-ere	tremuī	—	tremble
vomō	-ere	vomuī	vomitum	vomit

Perfect in -uī, Supine in -sum

metō	-ere	messuī	messum	reap
excellō	-ere	excelluī	—	excel

Reduplicated Perfect Stem, Supine in -tum

canō	-ere	cecinī	cantum	sing
discō	-ere	didicī	—	learn
poscō	-ere	poposcī	—	demand
pungō	-ere	pupugī	pūnctum	prick
tangō	-ere	tetigī	tāctum	touch
tendō	-ere,	tetendī	tentum, tēnsum	stretch,

Reduplicated Perfect Stem, Supine in -sum

cadō	-ere	cecidī	cāsum	fall
cædō	-ere	cecīdī	cæsum	beat, kill
currō	-ere	cucurrī	cursum	run
fallō	-ere	fefellī	falsum	deceive
parcō	-ere	pepercī	parsum	spare
pellō	-ere	pepulī	pulsum	drive
pendō	-ere	pependī	pēnsum	hang
tundō	-ere	tutudī	tūsum, tūnsum	bruise

Compounds of dō

abdō	-ere	abdidī	abditum	hide
addō	-ere	addidī	additum	add
condō	-ere	condidī	conditum	found, hide
crēdō	-ere	crēdidī	crēditum	believe
dēdō	·ere	dēdidī	dēditum	give up
ēdō	-ere	ēdidi	ēditum	give out
perdō	-ere	perdidī	perditum	lose
prōdō	-ere	prōdidī	prōditum	betray
reddō	-ere	reddidī	redditum	restore
subdō	-ere	subdidī	subditum	substitute
trādō	-ere	trādidī	trāditum	deliver
vendō	-ere	vendidī	venditum	sell

Note: **Pereō**, perish, **vēneō**, go for sale, are used as passives of **perdo** and **vendo**.

Reduplicated from sto

sistō	-ere	stitī	stātum	make to stand

(b) Lengthened Stem, -tum

agō	-ere	ēgī	āctum	do
emō	-ere	ēmī	ēmptum	buy
frangō	-ere	frēgī	frāctum	break (tr.)
iaciō	-ere	iēcī	iactum	throw
legō	-ere	lēgī	lēctum	choose, read
linquō	-ere	līquī	-lictum	leave

rumpō	-ere	rūpī	ruptum	break
vincō	-ere	vīcī	victum	conquer

Lengthened Stem, Perfect in -ī, Supine in -sum

edō	-ere	ēdī	ēsum	eat
fodiō	-ere	fōdī	fossum	dig
fundō	-ere	fūdī	fūsum	pour
retundō	-ere	retūdī	retūsum	beat back

Perfect in -ī, no Reduplication, Supine in -tum, -sum

bibō	-ere	bibī	bibitum	drink
-cendō	-ere	-cendī	-cēnsum	kindle
cūdō	-ere	cūdī	cūsum	stamp
-fendō	-ere	-fendī	-fēnsum	strike
findō	-ere	fidī	fissum	cleave
īcō, iciō	-ere	īcī	ictum	strike
mandō	-ere	mandī	mānsum	chew
pandō	-ere	pandī	pansum ⎫ passum ⎬	open, spread
percello	-ere	perculī	perculsum	thrill
psallō	-ere	psallī	—	play on strings
prehendō	-ere	prehendī	prehēnsum	grasp
scandō	-ere	scandī	scansum	climb
scindo	-ere	scidī	scissum	tear
sīdō	-ere	sīdī, sēdī	sessum	settle (intr.)
solvō	-ere	solvī	solūtum	loosen
vellō	-ere	vellī, vulsī	vulsum	rend
verrō	-ere	verrī	versum	sweep, drag
vertō	-ere	vertī	versum	turn (tr.)
vīsō	-ere	vīsī	vīsum	visit
volvō	-ere	volvī	volūtum	roll (tr.)

u- Stems, perfect in -ī, Supine in -tum

acuō	-ere	acuī	acūtum	sharpen
adnuō*	-ere	adnuī	adnūtum	nod
arguō	-ere	arguī	argūtum	prove
congruō	-ere	congruī	—	come together
exuō	-ere	exuī	exūtum	put off
imbuō	-ere	imbuī	imbūtum	tinge
induō	-ere	induī	indūtum	put on
luō	-ere	luī	-lūtum	wash, atone
metuō	-ere	metuī	—	fear
minuō	-ere	minuī	minūtum	lessen
pluit	-ere	pluit, pluvit	—	rain
ruō†	-ere	ruī	rutum, ruitum	rush, fall
spuō	-ere	spuī	spūtum	spit out
statuō	-ere	statuī	statūtum	set up
sternuō	-ere	sternuī	—	sneeze
suō	-ere	suī	sūtum	sew
tribuō	-ere	tribuī	tribūtum	assign, render

* Sometimes annuō.   † Future participle ruitūrus.

155   Fourth Conjugation, i- Stems

PRESENT	INFIN.	PERFECT	SUPINE	
			Usual Form	
audiō	audīre	-īvī	audītum	

Exceptions

Perfect in -īvī, Supine in -tum

sepeliō	-īre	sepelīvī	sepultum	bury

Perfect in -uī, Supine in -tum

aperiō	-īre	aperuī	apertum	open
operiō	-īre	operuī	opertum	cover
saliō	-īre	saluī	—	dance

Perfect in -sī, Supine in -tum

amiciō	-īre	amixī amicuī }	amictum	clothe
fulciō	-īre	fulsī	fultum	prop
hauriō	-īre	hausī	haustum	drain
sæpiō	-īre	sæpsī	sæptum	hedge in
sanciō	-īre	sānxī	sānctum	hallow
sarciō	-īre	sarsī	sartum	patch
vinciō	-īre	vīnxī	vīnctum	bind

Perfect in -sī, Supine in sum

sentiō	-īre	sēnsī	sēnsum	feel

Perfect in -ī, Supine in tum

comperiō*	-īre	comperī	compertum	find
reperiō*	-īre	repperī	repertum	discover
veniō	-īre	vēnī	ventum	come

* Originally reduplicating; compounds of **pariō**.

155a   Mixed Conjugation

capiō	-ere	cēpī	captum	take
cūpiō	-ere	cupīvī, cupiī	cupītum	desire
-cutiō	-ere	-cussī	-cussum	shake
faciō	-ere	fēcī	factum	make
fugiō	-ere	fūgī	fugitum	flee
iaciō	-ere	iēcī	iactum	hurl
-liciō	-ere	-lexī	-lectum	entice
pariō	-ere	peperī	partum	bring forth
quatiō	-ere	quassī	quassum	shake (tr.)
rapiō	-ere	rapuī	raptum	snatch
solvō	-ere	solvī	solūtum	loosen, pay
sapiō	-ere	sapīvī, sapuī	—	taste, be wise
-spiciō	-ere	-spexi	-spectum	gaze

156 DEPONENT AND SEMI-DEPONENT VERBS

1st Conjugation, a- Stems (Perfect -ātus sum)
About 160, all regular.

157 2nd Conjugation, ē- Stems (Perfect usually -itus sum)

Present	Infin.	Perfect	
fateor	-ērī	fassus sum	confess
liceor	-ērī	licitus sum	bid in auction.
medeor	-ērī	—	heal
mereor	-ērī	meritus sum	deserve
misereor	-ērī	miseritus ⎫ misertus ⎭ sum	have pity on
reor	-ērī	ratus sum	think
tueor	-ērī	tuitus (tūtus) sum	protect, look at

158 Semi-Deponent Verbs

Present	Infin.	Perfect		
audeō	-ēre	ausus sum	—	dare
gaudeō	-ēre	gāvīsus sum	—	rejoice
soleō	-ēre	solitus sum	—	be wont

159 3rd and Mixed Conjugations, Consonant and u- Stems (Perfect -tus or -sus sum)

adipīscor	-ī	adeptus sum	acquire
amplector	-ī	amplexus sum	embrace
apiscor	-ī	aptus sum	acquire
expergīscor	-ī	experrēctus sum	waken
fatiscor	-ī	fessus sum	grow weary
fruor	-ī	frūctus sum	enjoy
fungor	-ī	fūnctus sum	perform
gradior	-ī	gressus sum	step
īrāscor	-ī	īrātus sum	be angry
lābor	-ī	lāpsus sum	glide
līquor	-ī	—	melt
loquor	-i	locūtus sum	speak
-minīscor	-ī	-mentus sum	have in mind
morior	-ī	mortuus sum	die
nancīscor	-ī	nactus ⎫ nānctus ⎭ sum	obtain

nāscor	-ī	nātus sum	be born
nītor	-ī	nīsus (nīxus) sum	lean on, strive
oblīvīscor	-ī	oblītus sum	forget
pacīscor	-ī	pactus sum	bargain
patior	-ī	passus sum	suffer
proficīscor	-ī	profectus sum	set out
queror	-ī	questus sum	complain
sequor	-ī	secūtus sum	follow
ulcīscor	-ī	ultus sum	avenge
vēscor	-ī	—	feed on
utor	-ī	ūsus sum	use

Note: The form gressus is very rarely found except in compounds. Morior has future participle moritūrus.

160   Semi-Deponent Verbs

| fīdō | -ere | fīsus sum | trust |

161   4th Conjugation, ī- Stems (Perfect -ītus, -tus, or -sus sum)

adsentior } assentior }	-īrī	adsēnsus sum } assēnsus sum }	agree
blandior	-īrī	blandītus sum	coax, carress, flatter
experior	-īrī	expertus sum	try
largior	-īrī	largītus sum	bestow
mētior	-īrī	mēnsus sum	measure
mōlior	-īrī	mōlītus sum	contrive, work
opperior	-īrī	oppertus sum	wait, wait for
ordior	-īrī	ōrsus sum.	begin
orior	-īrī	ortus sum	arise
potior	-īrī	potītus sum	acquire
pūnior	-īrī	pūnītus sum	punish
sortior	-īrī	sortītus sum	cast lots

Note: Orior has some forms like capior (§ 133): oreris, oritur, ortus. Potior has potītur or potitur, potīmur or potimur, potīrer or poterer.

162   PARTICLES

The term **particles** is used as a catch-all expression, grouping together the uninflected parts of speech: adverbs, prepositions, conjunctions and interjections. They are for the most part old cases of nouns or adjectives, which have become limited to special uses. The oldest of these is the adverbial use, which was originally to limit or qualify the action expressed by the verb, but was afterwards extended to qualify adjectives, and sometimes other adverbs.

Latin prepositions are adverbs which have acquired the special use of standing before nouns to express relations of place and time.

Many conjunctions are also adverbs which have come to be used merely as links between words or sentences.

163 ADVERBS (§ 395–8)

Adverbs are formed either from cases of substantives, adjectives or participles, or from pronoun roots. Those which are formed from adjectives or participles generally have comparison (§ 85). Those which are derived from pronoun roots have no comparison.

In regard to meaning, they are divided. chiefly into adverbs of (1) manner; (2) degree; (3) cause; (4) place; (5) time; (6) order.

The following are a few of each class :

164 Adverbs of Manner

lentē, slowly		celeriter, quickly	
facile, easily		sapienter, wisely	
falsō, falsely		vehementer, strongly	
ultrō, spontaneously		adeō, so far	
æquē,		aliter,	otherwise,
perinde,	in like manner, in the same way	secus,	differently
proinde,		ita,	
similiter,		sīc,	so
itidem,		tam,	
quam, how?		adeō, so far	
		ut, as, how	

165 Adverbs of Degree

multum, much	paulum, little
quantum, how much	tantum, so much
satis, enough.	magis, more
nimis, nimium, too much	potius, rather
	potissimum, by preference
valdē, very	parum, too little
fermē, ferē, almost	magnopere, greatly
	vix, ægrē, scarcely

166   Adverbs of Cause

ideō, idcircō, proptereā, on that account

167   Adverbs of Place

Where **ubi**, where?		**hīc**, here
ibi,	} there	**ibidem**, in the same place
illic		**alibi**, elsewhere
ūsquam, anywhere		**nūsquam**, nowhere
Wither **quō**, whither?		**hūc**, hither
eō	} thither	**eōdem**, to the same place
illūc		**ūsque**, so far
Whence **unde**, whence?		**hinc**, hence
inde	} thence	**indidem**, from the same place
illinc		**hāc**, by this way
quā, by what way?		**eā, illāc**, by that way

168   Adverbs of Time

When **quandō, ubi**, when?	**tum, tunc**, then
nunc, modo, now	**iam**, now, already
simul, at the same time	**aliās**, at another time
umquam, ever	**numquam**, never
semper, always	**interdum**, now and then
ōlim } at some time	**mox**, by and by
quondam	**nūper**, lately
ante, before	**post**, after
dēmum, at length	**nōndum**, net yet
How long **quam diū**, how long?	**tam diū**, so long
diū, long	**ūsque**, continuously
iam diū, long since	
How often **quotiēns**, how often?	**totiēns**, so often
semel, once	**iterum**, a second time
sæpe, often	**rārō**, seldom
crēbrō, frequently	**identidem**, repeatedly

169   Adverbs of Order

prīmum, first	**prīmō**, in the beginning
deinde, in the next place	**præfereā,** } moreover
deinceps, afterwards	**īnsuper,**
tertiō, thirdly	**dēnique,** } lastly
	postrēmō,

170   Sometimes an adverb qualifies a sentence or phrase, rather than any particular word.

Adverbs of

Affirmation   **etiam,** also; **quidem, equidem,** indeed; **vērō,** but; **plānē,** quite; **sānē,** certainly; **profectō, omnīnō, certē,** surely, by all means

Limitation   **pariter,** alike; **simul,** together; **plērumque,** usually; **sōlum, tantum, modo,** only; **partim,** partly

Negation   **nōn, haud,** not; **haudquāquam, neutiquam,** by no means

Doubt   **fortasse, forsan, forsitan,** perhaps; **forte,** by chance

Question   **cūr, quārē, quamobrem?** why? **quōmodo, quemadmodum, quam, ut?** how?

171   PREPOSITIONS (§ 284–7)

Prepositions are placed with nouns to show their relation to other words in the sentence. They are also compounded with verbs to modify their meaning.

172   The following prepositions are used with the accusative:

ad, to, at	**iūxtā,** next to, beside
adversus } towards, against,	**ob,** over against, on account of
adversum } opposite to	**penes,** in the power of
ante, before	**per,** through
apud, at, near, among	**pōne,** behind
circum, around	**post,** after, behind
circā, circiter, about	**præter,** beside, past
cis, citrā, on this side of	**prope,** near
clam, unknown to	**propter,** near, on account of
contrā, against	**secundum,** next, along, according to
ergā, towards	**suprā,** above
extrā, outside of, without	**trāns,** across
infrā, below	**ultrā,** beyond
inter, between amidst	**versus, versum,** towards
intrā, within	

173   The following are used with the ablative:

ā, ab, abs, by, from	**palam,** in sight of
absque, without	**præ,** before, in front of
cōram, in the presence of	**prō,** before, for
cum, with	**sine,** without
dē, from, concerning	**tenus,** as far as, reaching to
ex, ē, out of, from	

Note: **Clam** is also used with the ablative; **tenus** is placed after the noun; it is sometimes used with the genitive.

174 The following take the accusative when they denote motion towards and the ablative when they denote rest:

in, into, against, in, on   super over, upon
sub, up to, under   subter, under

175 Prepositions used only in verb compounds are:

ambi, amb-, am-, an-, around   ambiō, go around
dī, dis-,   apart   dissolvō, separate; dīrigō, direct
red-, rē-,   back, again   redeō, go back; referō, bring back
sed-, sē-,   apart   sēcēdō, step apart

176 CONJUNCTIONS

Conjunctions are: (1) co-ordinative (§ 400); (2) subordinative (§ 401, 410 ff.).

177 **1. Co-ordinative conjunctions are:**

Connective: et,
-que,
atque (adque), } and
ac,

neque, } nor
nec,

etiam,
quoque, } also
item,

Separative: aut,
vel, } or, either.
-ve,

sīve, } whether, or
seu,

Adversative: sed,
at (ast), } but

atquī, but, yet
at enim, but it will be said

tamen, { yet, however, nevertheless

autem, { but, now, however

cēterum,
vērum, } but, moreover
vērō,

attamen, { but,
vērumtamen, { nevertheless

Causal: nam, namque,
enim, etenim } for

enimvērō, for indeed

Conclusive: ergō,
itaque, } therefore
igitur,

quārē,
quamobrem, } wherefore
quāpropter,
quōcircā,

Note: For the interrogative particles, see § 405, 406.

178   2. Subordinative conjunctions are:

Consecutive: **ut**, so that
ut nōn, so that not

Final: **ut**, in order that.

nēve, neu { and that not, and lest

quō { whereby, in order that

Causal: **quod**, because
cum, since

quippe { for as much as, seeing that

Temporal: **cum (quum)**, when
ut, when
dum, dōnec, quoad, } while, so long as

antequam, priusquam } before that
simul ac, as soon as

Conditional: **sī**, if
sīve, seu, } whether, or if
sī modo, if only

modo, dummodo, provided that

Concessive: **etsī, etiamsī** } even if, although

quamquam, utut } however, although

cum, whereas, although
ut, licet, granting that, although

Comparative: **ut, utī, velut, veluti, sīcut, sīcuti, ceu** } as

utpote, as being

quasi (quam sī), ut sī (velut sī) } as if

quīn, that not, but that

nē, lest

ut nē, that not, lest

quōminus, { whereby not, in order that not

quia, because
quoniam, quandōquidem, } since

sī quidem, inasmuch as

quandō, when
ubi, when
dum, dōnec, quoad } until

quātenus, how long
postquam, after that

quotiēns, as often as

sīn (sī ne), but if
nisi, nī, unless
sī nōn, if not.
modo, tantum } only

tametsī although

quamvīs } although, however much

quōmodo, quemadmodum } as, how
quam, than, as

ceu, tamquam } as though

179   The following pairs are often used as correlatives

et... et		sīve... sīve	
-que... -que	both... and		whether... or
-que... et		seu... seu	
aut... aut		sīc... ut	so... as
vel... vel	either... or	ut... ita	as... so
neque... neque		ita... ut	so... that
nec... nec	neither... nor	adeō... ut	so far... that
nēve... nēve			

180   Interjections

An interjection is an exclamatory word, used either to draw attention or to express feeling. The most usual are:

ō, O! oh!	prō or prōh, forbid it!
ā or āh, alas!	væ, woe!
ēheu, heu, ei, alas!	ēn, ecce, lo! behold!
ehem, well!	heus, ho there!
iō, euoe, o joy!	

Syntax

THE SIMPLE SENTENCE

INTRODUCTORY OUTLINE

181   **Syntax** describes how sentences are made.

Sentences are **simple, compound** (simple sentences joined by conjunctions – see **co-ordination**, §402, § 403)or **complex** (§ 410 et seq.).

182   A **simple sentence** has two parts:
1. The **subject**: the person or thing spoken about.
2. The **predicate**: that which is said about the subject.

183   The **subject** must be a noun, or some word or words taking the place of a noun:

A **noun**: *lex*, the law;
A **pronoun**: *ego*, I;*
An **adjective, participle,** or **adjectival pronoun**: *Rōmānus*, a Roman; *īrātus*, an angry man; *ille*, that (man);†
A **verb noun infinitive**: *nāvigāre*, to sail, or sailing;
A **phrase**: *satis temporis*, enough time.

---

* Latin nearly always omits pronouns used as subjects; they are *implied* by the verb inflections.

† The word 'man' is understood if a masculine adjective stands without a noun. The word 'woman' is understood if the adjective is feminine: *īrāta*, an angry woman. The word 'thing' is understood in the case of neuter adjectives.

---

184   The **predicate** must either be a verb or contain a verb, because it makes a statement or assertion about the subject; and it is usually a finite verb.

185   Examples of the **Simple Sentence**:

SUBJECT	PREDICATE	SUBJECT	PREDICATE
Lex	**iubet.**	**Nāvigāre**	**dēlectat.**
The law	commands.	Sailing	delights.
[Nōs]	**pārēmus.**	**Satis temporis**	**datur.**
We	obey.	Enough time	is given.

Note: Since the pronoun is usually omitted, a single verb may be a sentence: *Vēnī*, I came.

186 Some verbs cannot by themselves form complete predicates. The verb **sum** is a complete predicate only when it implies mere existence:

Seges	**est**	**ubī**	**Trōia**	**fuit.**	Ovid
Corn	is	where	Troy	was.	

Sum more often links the subject with the **complement**, which completes what is said about it.

187 Verbs which link a subject and **complement** are called **copulative verbs**. Others besides **sum** are:

appāreō, appear	**audiō,** am called	**maneō,** remain
videor, seem	**ēvādō, existō,** turn out	

The passives of verbs of making, saying, thinking, choosing (**factitive verbs***) are also used as copulative verbs (§ 206):

fīō (*faciō*), become *or* am made	**feror,** am reported
appellor, am called	**legor,** am chosen
creor, am created	**putor,** am thought
dēclāror, am declared	**vocor,** am called

---

* So-called from *facere*, to make, because they contain the idea of making.

---

188 **Copulative verbs** have the same case after them as before them. That is to say, the subject and complement are in the same case.

189 The **complement** may be:

1. An adjective or adjectival word.
2. A substantive.

SUBJECT	PREDICATE	
	Copulative Verb	*Complement*
1. **Leō**	**est**	**validus.**
The lion	is	strong.
2. **Illī**	**appellantur**	**philosophī.**
They	are called	philosophers.

190 Many verbs usually require another verb in the infinitive to complete the predicate; such are: **soleō**, am wont; **possum**, am able; **queō**, can; **dēbeō**, ought; **volō**, wish; **cōnor**, endeavor.

| Solet legere. | Possum ire. |
| He is wont to read. | I am able to go. |

These verbs are called **indeterminate**, and the infinitive following them is called **prolative**, because it carries on (*prōfert*) their construction (§ 369, § 370).

191 A simple sentence may be enlarged in many ways.

The **subject** may be qualified by adjectives or pronouns in agreement, or may have words in apposition (§ 194) added to it.

The **verb** may be qualified by adverbs or adverbial phrases; it may have a preposition with a case, or some part of the verb infinite depending on it; if transitive, it has a direct object and may have also an indirect object; if intransitive, it may have an indirect object in the dative.

The **complement** may again be qualified by an adjective or an adverb, or by a case of a noun, or a preposition with a case.

AGREEMENT

Rules of the Four Concords

192 1. A verb agrees with its subject in number and person:

| **Tempus fugit.** | **Librī leguntur.** |
| Time flies. | Books are read. |

193 2. An adjective or participle agrees in gender, number and case with the substantive it qualifies:

Vir bonus bonam uxōrem habet.
The good man has a good wife.

Vērae amīcitiae sempiternae sunt.   Cicero
True friendships are everlasting.

194 3. When a substantive or pronoun is followed by another substantive, so that the second explains or describes the first, and has the same relation to the rest of the sentence, the second noun agrees in case with the first, and is said to be **in apposition**:

Nōs līberī patrem Lollium imitābimur.
We children will imitate our father Lollius.

Procās, rēx Albānōrum, duōs fīliōs,
    Numitōrem et Amūlium, habuit.   Livy
    Procas, king of the Albans, had two sons,
    Numitor and Amulius.

195   4. The relative **quī, quæ, quod,** agrees with its antecedent in gender, number and person; in case it takes its construction from its own clause (§ 330):

    Amō tē, māter, quæ mē amās.
    I love you, mother, who love me.

    Quis hic est homō quem ante ædēs videō?   Plautus
    Who is this man whom I see before the house?

    Arborēs multās serit agricola, quārum frūctūs
    nōn adspiciet.   Cicero
    The farmer plants many trees, of which he
    will not see the fruit.

196   Notes on the Concords

    1. The verb **est, sunt,** is often understood, not expressed:

    Nihil bonum nisi quod honestum.   Cicero
    Nothing is good except what is virtuous.

    2. A **copulative verb** (one which links subject and complement) occasionally agrees with the complement rather than with the subject:

    Amantium īræ amōris integratiō est.   Terence
    The quarrels of lovers are the renewal of love.

197   3. A substantive often agrees in number and gender with the noun to which it is in apposition:

    Stilus, optimus et præstantissimus dīcendī magister.   Cicero
    The pen, best and chief teacher of oratory.

    Philosophia, vītæ magistra.   Cicero
    Philosophy, the mistress of life.

    4. A noun may be in apposition to a personal pronoun understood:

    Hannibal petō pācem.   Livy
    I, Hannibal, sue for peace.

198 Composite Subject

1. When two or more nouns are united as the subject, the verb and adjectives are usually in the plural:

> **Venēnō absūmptī sunt Hannibal et Philopœmēn.**   Livy
> Hannibal and Philopœmen were cut off by poison.

> **Ætās, metus, magister eum cohibēbant.**   Terence
> Age, fear, and a tutor were restraining him.

2. If the persons of a composite subject are different, the verb agrees with the first person rather than the second; with the second rather than the third:

> **Sī tū et Tullia valētis, ego et Cicerō valēmus.**   Cicero
> If you and Tullia are well, I and Cicero are well.

3. When the genders are different, adjectives agree with the masculine rather than with the feminine:

> **Rēx rēgiaque classis ūnā profectī.**   Livy
> The king and the royal fleet set out together.

4. If the things expressed are without life, the adjectives are generally neuter:

> **Rēgna, honōrēs, dīvitiæ, cadūca et incerta sunt.**   Cicero
> Kingdoms, honors, riches, are frail and fickle things.

199 Notes on the Composite Subject

1. When several subjects of the third person are united, the verb is sometimes found in the singular, agreeing with one only:

> **Nunc mihi nihil librī, nihil litteræ,**
> **nihil doctrīna prōdest.**   Cicero
> Now neither do books avail me, nor letters,
> nor does learning.

2. If the union of two subjects forms a single notion, the verb may be singular:

> **Senātus populusque Rōmānus intellegit.**   Cicero
> The Roman senate and people understand.

3. But sometimes when a **collective noun** is the subject, although it is singular in form, the verb and adjectives are plural:

Pars mīlitum captī, pars occīsī sunt.   Livy
Part of the soldiers were taken captive, part were slain.

Observe that the adjectives agree in gender with the individuals of which the collective noun is made up.

THE CASES

The Nominative and Vocative Cases

200 The subject of a finite verb is in the nominative case:

Annī fugiunt.   **Lābitur ætās.**   Ovid
Years flee.   Time glides away.

Note: When an infinitive, called **historic**, is used for the imperfect of a finite verb, the nominative remains as the subject (§ 372):

Tum pius Ænēās umerīs abscindere vestem.   Virgil
Then the pious Æneas began to tear his vest from his shoulders.

201 A substantive joined to the subject by a copulative verb is in the nominative case (§ 187):

Cicerō dēclārātus est cōnsul.   Cicero
Cicero was declared consul.

202 The vocative stands apart from the construction of the sentence, with or without an interjection (§ 404)

Ō sōl pulcher, ō laudande!   Horace
O beauteous sun, worthy of praise!

Pompēī, meōrum prīme sodālium!   Horace
O Pompeius, earliest of my comrades!

Note: The nominative sometimes takes the place of the vocative:

Audī, tū, populus Albānus.   Livy
Hear, thou, people of Alba.

The Accusative Case

203 The accusative case is used to express:
A. The direct object of the verb.
B. Place to which there is motion, and extent in time and place.
C. The idea contained in the verb (**cognate accusative**).
D. Adverbial relations.

A. Accusative of Direct Object

204 The direct object of a transitive verb is in the accusative case:

Agricola colit agrōs; uxor domum tuetur.
The farmer tills the fields; his wife takes care of the house.

Hæc studia adulēscentiam alunt, senectūtem oblēctant.
These studies nurture youth, and delight old age.   Cicero

---

203 **Note 1:** Intransitive verbs when compounded with prepositions are often transitive:

Antōnius oppugnat Brūtum, Mutinam circumsedet.   Cicero
Antonius is making war on Brutus, and besieging Mutina.

Note 2: Some verbs compound with *trāns* take two accusatives:

Cæsar equitēs flūmen trānsiēcit.   Cæsar
Cæsar threw his cavalry across the river.

---

206 Factitive verbs (verbs of making, saying, thinking) have a second accusative in agreement with the object:

Cicerōnem cōnsulem populus dēclārāvit.   Sallust
The people declared Cicero consul.

Sōcratēs tōtīus sē mundī cīvem arbitrābātur.   Cicero
Socrates considered himself a citizen of the whole world.

---

207 **Note:** The accusative is used as the subject of the infinitive to form a **substantival clause** which may be the object of verbs of saying, thinking, and perceiving, or the subject of impersonal verbs (§ 414).

Sōlem fulgēre vidēmus.   We see that the sun shines.

---

208 Some verbs of teaching, asking, concealing (*doceō*, teach; *flāgitō, postulo, posco* demand; *rogō*, ask; *ōrō*, pray; *cēlō*, conceal), take two accusatives, one of the person, the other of the thing:

Racilius prīmum mē sententiam rogāvit.	Cicero
Racilius asked me first my opinion.	
Quid nunc tē litterās doceam?	Cicero
Why should I now teach you letters?	
Antigonus iter omnēs cēlat.	Nepos
Antigonus conceals from all his line of march.	

In the passive they sometimes keep the **accusative of the thing**:

Prīmus ā Raciliō sententiam rogātus sum.
I was asked my opinion first by Racilius.

> **Note 1:** *Quæro, petō,* take ablative of the person with **ā** or **ab**: *hoc ā tē petō,* this I ask of you.

209 **Note 2:** Intransitive verbs which express feeling sometimes take an **accusative of the object** which excites the feeling:

Nōn omnia quæ dolēmus querī possumus.	Cicero
We cannot complain of all things for which we grieve.	
Virgās ac secūrēs dictātōris horrent et tremunt.	Livy
They shudder and tremble at the rods and axes of the dictator.	

Note 3: An accusative is used in exclamations, with or without an interjection

Mē miserum!	**Ō fragilem fortūnam!**
O wretched me!	O fickle fortune!

210 **Note 4:** Some passive verbs in poetry take an accusative, when used reflexively. Such verbs are *induor,* dress oneself, *exuor,* undress oneself, *cingor,* gird oneself:

Inūtile ferrum cingitur.	Virgil	**Exuitur cornua.**	Ovid
He girds on the useless steel.		She puts off her horns.	

Note 5: A similar construction is frequently used with passive participles:

Virginēs longam indūtæ vestem canentēs ībant.	Livy
Virgins marched singing, arrayed, in long robes.	
Nāscuntur flōrēs īnscrīptī nōmina rēgum.	Virgil
Flowers spring up inscribed with names of kings.	

This construction is analogous to that of the **Greek middle voice**.

B. *Accusative Expressing Place Towards*

211 Place to which motion is directed is in the accusative: *eō Rōmam,* I go to Rome (§ 269, 273).

> **Note:** Similar are the phrases: *pessum īre,* to go to the bad; *īnfitiās īre,* to deny; *suppetiās īre,* to march in aid; *vēnum īre,* to be sold.

C. Cognate Accusative

212 Many otherwise intransitive verbs take an accusative containing the same idea as the verb, and often from the same stem:

Fortūna lūdum insolentem lūdit.   Horace
Fortune plays an insolent game.

Modicē et modestē melius est vītam vīvere.   Plautus
It is best to live one's life temperately and modestly.

Itque reditque viam totiēns.   Virgil
He goes and returns the same way as often.

Note: The **cognate accusative** must have some more limited meaning than that which is contained in the verb, either expressed by an adjective or implied in the noun itself: *lūdum īnsolentem lūdere*, to play an insolent game; *dicta dīcere*, to say witty sayings.

D. Adverbial Accusative

213 The **accusative of respect** is joined to verbs and adjectives, especially in poetry:

Tremit artūs.	Virgil	**Nūdæ lacertōs.**	Tacitus
He trembles in his limbs.		Bare as to the arms.	

Omnia Mercuriō similis vōcemque colōremque.   Virgil
In all points like Mercury, both in voice and complexion.

Note 1: Adverbial accusatives with verbs and nouns are very numerous: *multum*, much; *aliquid*, in some degree; *cētera*, in other respects; *id genus*, of that kind; *id temporis*, at that time: *multum amāre*, to love much; *quid rēfert?* what does it matter?

Note 2: Neuter adjectives and pronouns are sometimes used in the accusative by poets in place of adverbs:

Dulce rīdēre.	**Lūcidum fulgēre.**	Horace
To smile sweetly.	To shine brightly.	

Dulce rīdentem Lalagēn amābō, dulce loquentem.   Horace
I will love the sweetly smiling, sweetly speaking Lalage.

(For the accusative of extent see time, § 278, and space, § 281–3.)

The Dative Case

214 The dative is the case of the person or thing for whose interest anything exists or is done. It expresses:

A. The person or thing *to* whom or which something is done: **dative of the indirect object.**

B. The person or thing *for* whom or which something is done: **dative of advantage or reference**.

C. Special uses are: (a) **dative of agent**, (b) **ethic dative**, (c) **dative of possessor**, (d) **dative of result**, (e) **dative of purpose**.

A. Dative of the Indirect Object.

The dative of the indirect object is used:

215   1. With transitive verbs of giving, telling, showing, promising, which take also an accusative of the direct object:

Tibi librum sollicitō damus aut fessō.   Horace
We give you a book when you are anxious or weary.

Sæpe tibi meum somnium nārrāvī.   Cicero
I have often told you my dream.

Nōbīs spondet fortūna salūtem.   Virgil
Fortune guarantees safety to us.

216   2. With intransitive verbs of pleasing, helping, sparing, pardoning, appearing, speaking, believing, obeying, and their opposites. These verbs have the dative as their only object:

Victrīx causa deīs placuit sed victa Catōni.   Lucan
The conquering cause pleased the gods, but the
conquered pleased Cato.

Imperiō parent.   Cæsar   **Parce piō generī.**   Virgil
They obey the command.   Spare a pious race.

Imperat aut servit collēcta pecūnia cuique.   Horace
Money amassed rules or serves every man.

Nōn possum dolōrī tantō resistere.   Cicero
I cannot withstand so great a sorrow.

Note 1: These verbs contain the ideas of being pleasing to, helpful to, obedient to, &c.

217   **Note 2:** *Dēlectō, iuvō,* delight, *lædō,* hurt, *gubernō,* govern, *regō,* rule, *iubeō,* command, take an accusative:

Multōs castra iuvant. Horace   **Animum rege.**   Horace
The camp delights many.   Rule the temper.

Temperō, moderor, govern, restrain, take sometimes the accusative, sometimes the dative:

Hic moderātur equōs quī nōn moderābitur īræ.   Horace
This man controls horses who will not restrain his anger.

218 3. With adjectives implying nearness, fitness, likeness, help, kindness, trust, obedience, or any opposite idea:

Hortus ubi et tēctō vīcīnus iūgis aquæ fōns.   Horace
Where is a garden, and near to the house a fount
of flowing water.

Quis amīcior quam frāter frātrī?   Sallust
Who [is] more friendly than a brother to a brother?

Hominī fidēlissimī sunt equus et canis.   Pliny
The horse and the dog are most faithful to man.

Turba gravis pācī, placidæque inimīca quiētī.   Lucan
The crowd hostile to peace, unfriendly to tranquil rest.

Note: The following take genitive or dative: *commūnis*, common; *proprius*, proper.
Adfinis, akin, *aliēnus*, foreign; *pār*, equal; *sacer*, sacred; *superstes*, surviving, take
usually dative, sometimes genitive. *Similis*, like, takes usually genitive, sometimes
dative. Adjectives of fitness as *aptus*, sometimes take accusative with *ad*.

---

219 4. More rarely with substantives or adverbs:

Nūlla fidēs rēgnī sociīs.   Lucan
No reliance is to be placed on partners in government.

Iūstitia est obtemperātiō lēgibus.   Cicero
Justice is obedience to laws.

Congruenter nātūræ vīvendum est.   Cicero
We must live agreeably to nature.

Note 1: Some verbs, as *crēdō*, believe, entrust, *fīdō*, trust, *suādeō*, persuade, *minor*,
threaten, *grātulor*, congratulate, are used both transitively and intransitively:

Perfidīs sē crēdidit hostibus.   Horace
He trusted himself to treacherous enemies.

Non est, crēdē mihī, sapientis dīcere: vīvam.   Martial
It is not, believe me, the part of a wise man to say, 'I will live.'

Note 2: *Nūbō*, marry (lit. take the veil for), and *vacō*, have leisure for, take the dative:

Hīs duōbus frātribus duæ Tulliæ nūpserant.   Livy
The two Tullias had married these two brothers.

Philosophiæ semper vacō.   Cicero
I have always leisure for philosophy.

Note 3: The verbs *īrāscor*, feel angry, *pugnō*, fight, *certō*, strive, sometimes take a
dative: *sibi īrāscitur*, he is angry with himself.

220 Many verbs, transitive and intransitive, are used with a dative of the
indirect object when compounded with the following prepositions :

ad, ante, ab,	sub, super, ob,
in, inter, dē,	cum (con), post, and præ

Also verbs compounded with **bene, male, satis.**

(a) Transitive:

Gigantēs bellum dīs intulerunt.   Cicero
The giants waged war against the gods.

Præsentia confer præteritīs.   Lucretius
Compare present things with past.

(b) Intransitive:

Hīs negotiīs nōn interfuit sōlum sed præfuit.   Cicero
He not only took part in these affairs, but directed them.

Nūllus in orbe sinus Baiīs prælūcet amœnīs.   Horace
No bay in the world outshines the pleasant Baiæ.

Cēterīs satisfaciō semper, mihi numquam.   Cicero
I always satisfy others, myself never.

B. Dative of Advantage
221 The person or thing for whose advantage or disadvantage something
is done is in the dative case:

Tibi arās, tibi seris, tibi eīdem metis.   Plautus
For yourself you plough, for yourself you sow,
for the same self you reap.

Nōn sōlum nōbīs dīvitēs esse volumus.   Cicero
We do not wish to be rich for ourselves alone.

Sīc vōs nōn vōbīs mellificātis, apēs!   Virgil
Thus you make honey not for yourselves, o bees!

C. Special Uses of the Dative
222 (a) A dative, commonly called the **dative of the agent**, is often used
with the gerundive (§ 381), and occasionally with passive participles
and with adjectives in -bilis:

Ut tibi ambulandum, sīc mihi dormiendum est.   Cicero
As you have to walk, I have to sleep.

Magnus cīvis obīt et formīdātus Othōnī.   Juvenal
A great citizen and one dreaded by Otho has died.

Multīs ille bonīs flēbilis occidit.	Horace
He died a cause of weeping to many good men.	

Note: Rarely, in poetry, a personal passive takes a dative:

Nōn intellegor ūllī.	Ovid
I am intelligible to none.	

223 (b) A dative of a personal pronoun, called the **ethic dative**, is used, in familiar talk or writing, to express interest or call special attention:

Quid mihi Celsus agit?	Horace
Tell me, what is Celsus about?	
Hæc vōbīs per bīduum eōrum mīlitia fuit.	Livy
This, mind you, was their style of fighting for two days.	

224 (c) The **dative of the possessor**, with *esse*, is used when emphasis is laid on the thing possessed, not on the possessor:

Est mihī plēnus Albānī cadus.	Horace
I have a cask full of Alban wine.	
Fōns cui nōmen Arethūsa fuit.	Cicero
A fountain of which the name was Arethusa.	

Note: With such phrases as *cui nomen est* a second dative is sometimes joined by attraction: *Volitāns cui nōmen asīlō Romanum est* (Virgil), an insect of which the Roman name is 'asilus'. A like attraction occurs with other factitive and copulative verbs: *Huic ego diēī nōmen Trinummō faciam* (Plautus), I will give to this day the name Trinummus. Analogous to these are the attractions: *Hoc mihi valentī est, nōn invītō*, this is with my good will, not against it. *Mihi nōn licet esse neglegentī* (Cicero), I must not be negligent.

225 (d) The **predicative dative**, or **dative of purpose and result**, is used in connection with the dative of the person interested (§ 221), to describe what some thing (or person) is or causes:

Exitiō est avidum mare nautīs.	Horace
The greedy sea is a destruction to sailors.	
L. Cassius quærere solēbat, 'cui bonō fuieset.'	Cicero
Lucius Cassius used to ask who had been the gainer.	
(literally 'to whom had it been for a good?')	

Note: The dative of the person interested is often not expressed.

Nimia fidūcia calamitātī solet esse.   Nepos
Too great confidence is wont to be a calamity (to men).

Exemplō est magnī formīca labōris.   Horace
The ant is an example of great industry.

226   (e) The **dative of purpose** expresses the purpose of action:

Equitātum auxiliō Cæsarī mīsērunt.   Cæsar
They sent the cavalry as a help to Cæsar.

Note 1: Observe the phrases, *receptuī canere*, to give the signal for retreat; *alimentō serere*, to sow for food; *laudī vertere alicui*, to turn to the praise of someone; *vitiō vertere alicui*, to impute as a fault to someone.

Note 2: For the dative of the gerundive, see § 380.

227   (f) Sometimes the dative is used in poetry for the place towards which there is motion. This is called the dative of direction:

It clāmor cælō.   Virgil
A shout ascends towards heaven.

The Ablative Case

228   The ablative is the case which defines circumstances; it is rendered in English by many prepositions such as *from, with, by, in.* Its uses may be divided into:

A. Ablative of separation (*from, of*)

B. Ablative of association (*with*)

C. Instrumental ablative (*by, with*)

D. Ablative of place and time (locative, *in, at*)

A. Pure Ablative

229   1. The **ablative of separation** is used with verbs meaning to *remove, release, deprive*; with adjectives such as *līber,* free, *solūtus,* released, and also the adverb *procul,* far from:

Cēdēs coemptīs saltibus et domō.   Horace
You will depart from purchased glades and house.

Populus Athēniēnsis Phōciōnem patriā pepulit.   Nepos
The Athenian people drove Phocion from his country.

> **Vacāre culpā maximum est sōlācium.**   Cicero
> To be free from blame is a very great comfort.
>
> **Procul negōtiis, solūtus omnī fænore.**   Horace
> Far from business, freed from all usury.

230   2. The **ablative of origin** is used with verbs, chiefly participles, implying descent or origin:

> **Atreus, Tantalō prōgnātus, Pelope nātus.**   Cicero
> Atreus, descended from Tantalus, and son of Pelops.

Note: (For 'place from where' see § 270, 274.)

231   3. The **ablative of comparison** (expressing difference) is used with comparative adjectives and adverbs:

> **Nihil est amābilius virtūte.**   Cicero
> Nothing is more amiable than virtue.
>
> **Nēminem Lycurgō ultiōrem Sparta genuit.**   Valerius
> Sparta produced no man more serviceable than Lycurgus.

Note: This construction is equivalent to *quam*, than, with the nominative or accusative. *Virtūte* equals *quam virtus*; *Lycurgō* equals *quam Lycurgum*. With other cases than nom. or accus. *quam* must be used for comparison:

> **Nihilō amīcior est Phædriæ quam Antiphōnī.**   Terence
> He is in no degree more friendly to Phædria than to Antipho.

232   *B. Ablative of Associaton*

Note: This includes the uses of an old case called the **sociative** or **instrumental** case, expressing the circumstances associated with the subject or the action of the sentence (§ 30, note 2).

233   1. The **ablative of association** is used with verbs and adjectives denoting plenty, fulness, possession: *abundō*, abound, *dōnō*, present, *præditus*, endowed with (§ 253):

> **Villa abundat gallīnā, lacte, cāseō, melle.**   Cicero
> The farm abounds in poultry, milk, cheese, honey.
>
> **Iuvenem præstantī mūnere dōnat.**   Virgil
> He presents the youth with a noble gift.
>
> **Legiōnēs pulchrīs armīs præditæ.**   Plautus
> Legions furnished with splendid armor.

Note: *Dōnō* also takes the accusative of the thing with dative of the person: *Cæsar prædam mīlitibus dōnat*, Cæsar gives the booty to the soldiers.

234   2. The **ablative of quality** is used with an adjective in agreement (§ 255):

> **Senex prōmissā barbā, horrentī capillō.**   Pliny
> An old man with long beard and rough hair.
>
> **Habuit frātrem Dumnorigem summā audaciā.**   Cæsar
> He had a brother Dumnorix of supreme audacity.

235   3. **Ablative of respect:**

> **Paucī numerō.**   **Natione Mēdus.**
> Few in number.   By birth a Mede.
>
> **Et corde et genibus tremit.**   Horace
> It trembles both in heart and knees.
>
> **Ennius, ingeniō maximus, arte rudis.**   Ovid
> Ennius, mighty in genius, in art (is) rude.

Note 1: In the phrases *nātū māior*, older, *nātū minor*, younger, *nātū* is an ablative of respect.

Note 2: *Dignus*, worthy, *indignus*, unworthy, *dignor*, deem worthy, are followed by the ablative of respect:

> **Dignum laude virum Mūsa vetat morī.**   Horace
> A man worthy of praise the Muse forbids to die.

236   4. The **ablative of the manner**, in which something happens or is done, has an adjective in agreement with it; or it follows the preposition **cum**, with:

> **Iam veniet tacitō curva senecta pede.**   Ovid
> Presently bent old age will come with silent foot.
>
> **Athēniēnsēs summā vī proelium commisērunt.**   Nepos
> The Athenians began the battle with the greatest vigor.
>
> **Magnā cum cūrā atque dīligentiā scrīpsit.**   Cicero
> He wrote with great care and attention.

Note: *More māiōrum*, in the fashion of our ancestors, *pāce tuā*, with your leave, *iūre*, by right, *iniūriā*, wrongfully, *ratiōne*, on principle, are ablatives of manner which are used without *cum* or an adjective in agreement.

237 5. The **ablative absolute** is a phrase, consisting of a noun in the ablative case and a participle, or another noun or adjective, in agreement with it:

> **Rēgibus exāctīs cōnsulēs creātī sunt.**   Livy
> Kings having been abolished, consuls were elected.
>
> **Pereunte obsequiō imperium intercidit.**   Tacitus
> Obedience failing, government falls to pieces.
>
> **Cæsare ventūrō, Phōsphore, redde diem.**   Martial
> Cæsar being on his way, morning star, restore the day.
>
> **Nīl dēspērandum Teucrō duce et auspice Teucrō.**   Horace
> There must be no despair, Teucer being leader and
> Teucer omen-giver.
>
> **Nātus est Augustus cōnsulibus Cicerōne et Antōniō.**   Suet.
> Augustus was born when Cicero and Antonius
> were consuls.
>
> **Quid dicam hac iuventūtē?**   Cicero
> What can I say when our young men are of this stamp?

Note: The ablative absolute is equivalent to a shortened adverbial clause within the sentence, serving to explain some circumstance which indirectly affects the action of the sentence. It is called absolute because it is independent in construction of the rest of the sentence. A dependent clause joined to the sentence by a conjunction may be used instead of the ablative absolute. In the above example *rēgibus exāctīs* could be replaced by *cum rēgēs exāctī essent*, when kings had been driven out.

C. Instrumental Ablative

238 **Note:** This ablative includes the uses of the old instrumental case (§ 30, note 3).

239 The **agent** by whom something is done is in the ablative case, with the preposition *ā, ab,* after a passive or quasi-passive verb (§ 296, 300, 303).

240 1. The **instrument** by means of which something is done is in the ablative (**the ablative of instrument**) without a preposition:

> **Hī iaculīs, illī certant dēfendere saxīs.**   Virgil
> These strive to defend with javelins, those with stones.
>
> **Dente lupus, cornū taurus petit.**   Horace
> The wolf attacks with his teeth, the bull with his horns.

Opportūna loca armatīs hominibus obsidet.   Sallust
He occupies convenient posts with armed men.

241   2. The **ablative of the cause** is used with adjectives, passive participles, and verbs:

Coeptīs immānibus effera Dīdō.   Virgil
Dido driven wild by her horrible designs.

Ōdērunt peccāre malī formīdine poenæ.   Horace
The bad hate to sin through fear of punishment.

242   3. The deponent verbs **fungor,** perform, **fruor,** enjoy, **vēscor,** feed on,
ūtor, use, **potior,** possess oneself of (§ 253), take an ablative:

Hannibal cum victōriā posset ūtī fruī māluit.   Livy
Hannibal, when he could use his victory, preferred
to enjoy it.

Numidæ ferīnā carne vēscēbantur.   Sallust
The Numidians used to feed on the flesh of wild animals.

Note: *Potior* sometimes takes a genitive (§ 253). *Ūtor, fungor, fruor,* are sometimes
transitive in early Latin and therefore take the accusative.

---

243   4. The adjectives **dignus,** worthy, **indignus,** unworthy, and the transitive verb **dignor,** deem worthy, also **contentus,** contented, and **frētus,**
relying on, take an ablative:

Dignum laude virum Mūsa vetat morī.   Horace
A man worthy of praise the Muse forbids to die.

Haud equidem talī mē dignor honōre.   Virgil
I do not indeed deem myself worthy of such honor.

Note: *Opus est, ūsus est,* there is need of, take the ablative.

Ubī rēs adsunt, quid opus est verbīs?   Sallust
When things are present, what is the need of words?

---

244   5. An **ablative of the measure** of difference is joined as an adverb with
comparatives and superlatives and, rarely, with verbs:

Sōl multīs partibus maior est quam lūna.   Cicero
The sun is many degrees larger than the moon.

Especially the ablatives:

altero, hōc, eō, quō,   **dīmidiō, duplō, quantō, tantō,**
nihilō and **nimiō,**   **paulō, multō, aliquantō**

Quō plūs habent, eō plūs cupiunt.
The more they have, the more they desire.

Hibernia dīmidiō minor est quam Britannia.   Cæsar
Ireland is smaller by half than Britain.

245 6. The **ablative of price** is used with verbs and adjectives of *buying* and *selling*:

Vendidit hic aurō patriam.   Virgil
This man sold his country for gold.

Multōrum sanguine victōria stetit.   Livy
The victory cost (literally stood at) the blood of many.

Note: Ablatives of price are *magnō*, at a high price; *parvō, minimō, vīlī*, at a low price (but see also **genitive of value** § 257):

Parvō famēs cōnstat, magnō fastīdium.   Seneca
Hunger costs little, daintiness much.

D. The Ablative of Place and Time and the Locative Case

246 Originally, Latin had a separate **locative case** to express the place at which something is or happens. Its distinct forms remain in the singular in names of towns and small islands: *Rōmæ*, at Rome; *Corcȳræ*, at Corcyra; and in a few other words, as *domī*, at home. For the most part its uses have passed to the ablative, and it is often difficult to distinguish between the two cases, especially in the plural, where their forms are identical. The locative is sometimes used for a point of time: *diē septimī*, on the seventh day; *Kalendīs*, on the Kalends; *Īdibus*, on the Ides.

Note: The word *animī* in such phrases as *anxius animī*, anxious; *pendēre animī*, to waver in mind, is probably locative.

(For **place where**, see § 268, 272a.)

The Genitive Case

247 The **genitive** is used to define or complete the meaning of another noun on which it depends. It also follows certain verbs.

The uses of the genitive may be divided into:

A. Genitive of definition   D. Partitive genitive
B. Possessive genitive   E. Subjective & objective genitive
C. Genitive of quality   F. Genitives with verbs

A. Genitive of Definition

248   1. The **appositional genitive** follows the noun on which it depends:

Vōx voluptātis.   **Nōmen rēgis.**
The word pleasure.   The name of king.

> **Note:** But the name of a city is always placed in apposition (and therefore shares the same case): *urbs Rōma*, the city of Rome.

249   2. The **attributive** or **descriptive genitive** defines the noun on which it depends like an adjective:

Lūx sōlis   **Annī labor**
The light of the sun   A year's toil.

250   3. The **genitive of the author**:

Ea statua dīcēbātur esse Myrōnis.   Cicero
That statue was said to be Myro's.

Legendī sunt vōbīs Platōnis librī.   Cicero
You should read the works of Plato.

251   4. The **genitive of characteristic** is used in impersonal construction with a copulative verb (§ 187, 188), followed by an infinitive, where in English a word such as nature, part, characteristic, or mark, must be supplied to complete the meaning:

Cuiusvīs hominis est errāre.   Cicero
It is (the nature) of any man to err.

Est adulēscentis maiōrēs nātū verērī.   Cicero
It is a young man's (part) to reverence his elders.

Temporī cēdere habētur sapientis.   Cicero
To yield to occasion is held (the mark) of a wise man.

> **Note:** The word *proprium* is often used:
>
> **Sapientis est proprium nihil quod pænitēre possit facere.**   Cicero
> It is the characteristic of a wise man to do nothing which
> he may repent of.

252   5. Verbs and adjectives of accusing, condemning, convicting, or acquitting take a **genitive of the fault** or **crime**:

Alter latrōciniī reus, alter cædis convictus est.   Cicero
The one was accused of robbery, the other was
   convicted of murder.

Miltiadēs capitis absolūtus pecūniā multātus est.   Nepos
Miltiades, acquitted of a capital crime, was fined.

Note 1: Sometimes the ablatives *nōmine*, on the ground of, *crīmine*, on the charge of, are used:

Themistoclēs crīmine prōditiōnis absēns damnātus est.   Nepos
Themistocles was convicted while absent on the charge of treason.

Note 2: The penalty is expressed by the ablative of instrument (§ 240).

253 6. Verbs and adjectives implying want and fulness, especially *egeō*, *indigeō*, want, *impleō*, fill, *potior*, get possession of (§ 242), *plēnus*, full, often take a genitive (cf. § 233):

Virtūs plūrimæ exercitātiōnis indiget.   Cicero
Virtue needs very much practice.

Hanc iuventūtem speī animōrumque implēvēre.   Livy
They filled these youths with hope and spirit.

Rōmānī signōrum et armōrum potītī sunt.   Sallust
The Romans got possession of standards and arms.

Acerra tūris plēna.   Horace
A pan full of incense.

254 *B. Possessive Genitive*

Rēgis cōpiæ.   Cicero   Contempsī Catilinæ gladiōs   Cicero
The king's forces   I have braved the swords of Catiline.

Singulōrum opēs dīvitiæ sunt cīvitātis.   Cicero
The means of individuals are the state's riches.

Sometimes the genitive depends on a noun understood:

Hectoris Andromachē.   Virgil
Hector's (wife) Andromache.

Ventum erat ad Vestæ.   Horace
We had come to Vesta's (temple).

C. Genitive of Quality

255 1. The **genitive of quality** has an adjective in agreement:

Ingenuī vultūs puer ingenuīque pudōris.   Juvenal
A boy of noble countenance and noble modesty.

Memoriæ fēlīciōris est nōmen Appiī.   Livy
The name of Appius is of happier memory.

256 **2. Number, age and size** are expressed by the genitive:

Classis septuāgintā nāvium. **Puer annōrum novem.**
A fleet of seventy ships. A boy of nine years.

Fossa quīndecim pedum.
A trench fifteen feet deep.

257 **3. Genitives of value**, *magnī, parvī, plūrimī, minimī, nihilī*, are used with verbs of valuing; the genitives *tantī, quantī, plūris, minōris*, are also used with verbs of buying and selling, but not to express definite price.

Voluptātem virtūs minimī facit.
Virtue accounts pleasure of very little value.

Ēmit hortōs tantī, quantī Pȳthius voluit. Cicero
He bought the gardens for as much as Pythius wished.

Quantī id ēmit? Vīlī. Plautus
For how much did he buy it? For a low price.

Note: The genitives *floccī, naucī* were used in the popular speech to express worthlessness, answering to the English expressions, not worth a straw, a nut, &c.

Iūdicēs rempūblicam floccī nōn faciunt. Cicero
The judges consider the republic of no account.

D. Partitive Genitive or Genitive of the Whole

258 The genitive of a noun which is distributed into parts is called a **partitive genitive**.

259 1. Any word denoting a definite part, whether substantive, adjective or pronoun, is used with the genitive of the whole of which it denotes a part.

(a) Substantives:

Sic partem maiōrem cōpiārum Antōnius āmīsit. Cicero
Thus Antony lost the greater part of his forces.

Nēmō mortālium omnibus hōrīs sapit. Pliny
No one of the mortals is wise at all times.

(b) Pronouns or pronominal adjectives:

Incertum est quam longa nostrum cuiusque vīta futūra sit.
It is uncertain how long the life of each one of us will be.

Elephantō bēluārum nūlla est prūdentior. Cicero
Of animals none is more sagacious than the elephant.

(c) Numerals and adjectives of number:

Sulla centum vīgintī suōrum āmīsit.   Eutropius
Sulla lost a hundred and twenty of his men.

Multæ hārum arborum meā manū sunt satæ.   Cicero
Many of these trees were planted by my hand.

(d) Comparatives and Superlatives:

Māior Nerōnum.   Horace
The elder of the Neros.

Hoc ad tē minimē omnium pertinet.   Cicero
This belongs to you least of all men.

Tōtīus Græciæ Platō doctissimus erat.   Cicero
Plato was the most educated man of all Greece.

Note 1: The genitives *gentium*, of nations, *terrārum*, of countries, depend on adverbs of place: *ubī*, where, *ēo*, to there, *quō*, whither, *longē*, far:

Ubīnam gentium sumus?   Cicero
Where in the world are we?

Migrandum aliquō terrārum arbitror.   Cicero
I think we must migrate to some part of the world.

Note 2: A partitive genitive is found in poetry with verbs:

Scrībe tuī gregis hunc.   Horace
Enlist this man in your train.

Fīēs nōbilium tū quoque fontium.   Horace
Thou too shalt become one of famous fountains.

---

260 2. Any word denoting quantity may be used with the **genitive of the whole** in which such quantity is contained.

Aliquid prīstinī rōboris cōnservat.   Cicero
He keeps somewhat of his old strength.

Dīmidium factī quī coepit habet.   Horace
He has half done the work who has begun it.

Catilīnæ erat satis ēloquentiæ, sapientiæ parum.   Sallust
Catiline had plenty of eloquence, of wisdom too little.

E. The Subjective and Objective Genitive

261 The terms **subjective** and **objective genitive** are used to express different relations of the genitive to the noun on which it depends. Thus *amor patris*, the love of a father, may mean either 'the love felt

by a father' (where *patris* is a subjective genitive), or 'the love felt for a
father' (where *patris* is an objective genitive).

262 An **objective genitive** is used with verbal substantives and adjectives,
especially adjectives in **-āx**, and participles which have the meaning
of *love, desire, hope, fear, care, knowledge, ignorance, skill, power.*

(a) With substantives:

Erat īnsitus mentī cognitiōnis amor.   Cicero
Love of knowledge had been implanted in the mind.

Difficilis est cūra rērum aliēnārum.   Cicero
The care of other people's affairs is difficult.

(b) With adjectives:

Avida est perīculī virtūs.   Seneca
Valor is greedy of danger.

Cōnscia mēns rēctī fāmæ mendācia rīsit.   Ovid
The mind conscious of right smiled at the lies of rumor.

Homō multārum rērum perītus.   Cicero
A man skilled in many things.

Vir prōpositī tenāx.   Horace
A man holding to his purpose.

(c) With participles:

Quis famulus amantior dominī quam canis?   Colum.
What servant is fonder of his master than the dog is?

263 **Note:** The genitive of the gerund is an objective genitive: *ars scrībendī*, the art of
writing. An objective genitive also follows the ablatives *causā, grātiā*, by reason of,
by favor of, for the sake of; *honōris causā*, on the ground of honor; *exemplī grātiā*, for
example.

264 *Meī*, of me, *tuī*, of thee, *suī*, of him, her, them, *nostrī*, of us, *vestrī*, of you,
are objective genitives:

Nīciās tuā suī memoriā dēlectātur.   Cicero
Nicias is delighted by your recollection of him.

Sī tibi cūra meī, sit tibi cūra tuī.   Ovid
If you care for me, take care of yourself.

F. Genitive with Verbs

265 Most verbs of remembering, forgetting, reminding, **meminī, reminīscor, oblīvīscor,** usually take the genitive, sometimes the accusative. **Recordor** almost always takes the accusative, rarely the genitive.

Animus meminit præteritōrum.	Cicero
The mind remembers past things.	
Rēs adversæ admonent religiōnum.	Cicero
Adversity reminds of religious duties.	
Nam modo vōs animō dulcēs reminīscor, amīcī.	Ovid
For now I remember you, O friends, dear to my soul.	

The adjectives corresponding to these verbs, **memor, immemor,** always take a genitive.

Omnēs immemorem beneficī ōdērunt.	Cicero
All hate one who is forgetful of a favor.	

266 Verbs of pitying, **misereor, miserēscō,** take a genitive:

Nīl nostrī miserēre.	Virgil
You pity me not at all.	
Arcadiī, quæsō, miserēscite rēgis.	Virgil
Take pity, I entreat, on the Arcadian king.	

Note 1: **Miseror, commiseror** take an accusative.

267 **Note 2:** Verbs of refraining and ceasing and some adjectives are used by poets with a genitive in imitation of the Greek use, especially by Horace:

Abstinētō īrārum.	Horace	**Fessī rērum.**	Vergil
Refrain from angry words.		Weary of toil.	
Integer vītæ, scelerisque pūrus.			Horace
Virtuous in life and pure from wrong.			

PLACE, TIME AND SPACE

Place

268 **Place where** anything is or happens is generally in the ablative case with a preposition; sometimes without a preposition (especially in poetry), when an adjective of place qualifies the substantive:

Castra sunt in Italiā contrā rempūblicam collocāta. Cicero
A camp has been set up in Italy against the republic.

Celsā sedet Æolus arce. Virgil
Æolus is seated on his high citadel.

Mediō sedet insula pontō. Ovid
The island lies in mid ocean.

269 **Place whither** is in the accusative with a preposition; but in poetry the preposition is sometimes omitted:

Cæsar in Ītaliam magnīs itineribus contendit. Cæsar
Cæsar hastened by long marches into Italy.

Ītaliam fātō profugus Lāvīnaque vēnit lītora. Virgil
Driven by fate he came to Italy and the Lavinian shores.

270 **Place whence** is in the ablative with **ā, ab, ex,** or **dē**:

Ex Asiā trānsīs in Eurōpam. Curtius
Out of Asia you cross into Europe.

271 In **names of towns** and **small islands**, also in **domus** and **rūs**, place **where, whither,** or **whence** is expressed by a case without a preposition:

272 (a) **Place where**, by the locative (§ 246):

Quid Rōmæ faciam? Juvenal **Is habitat Mīlētī.** Terence
What am I to do at Rome? He lives at Miletus.

Philippus Neāpolī est, Lentulus Puteolīs. Cicero
Philip is at Naples, Lentulus at Puteoli.

**Sī domī sum, forīs est animus; sīn forīs sum,
animus est domī.** Plautus
If I am at home, my mind is abroad: if I am abroad,
my mind is at home.

Note: The locative *domī* is used with a genitive of the possessor: *domī Cæsaris*, at the house of Cæsar, or with the locative of a possessive adjective, *domī meæ*, at my house.

273 (b) **Place whither** is expressed by the accusative:

> **Rēgulus Carthāginem rediit.**   Cicero
> Regulus returned to Carthage.
>
> **Vōs īte domum; ego rūs ībō.**
> Go home; I will go into the country.

Note: With names of towns, **ad** is used to mean 'to the neighborhood of.'

274 (c) **Place whence**, by the ablative:

> **Videō rūre redeuntem senem.**   Terence
> I see the old man returning from the country.
>
> **Dēmarātus fūgit Tarquiniōs Corinthō.**   Cicero
> Demaratus fled from Corinth to Tarquinii.

Note: With names of towns, **ab** is used to mean 'from the neighborhood of'.

275 The road by which one goes is in the ablative:

> **Ībam forte Viā Sacrā.**   Horace
> I was going by chance along the Sacred Way

Time

276 **Time at which**, in answer to the question when? is expressed by the ablative: *hieme*, in winter; *sōlis occāsū*, at sunset.

> **Ego capuam vēnī eō ipsō diē.**   Cicero
> I came to Capua on that very day.

277 **Time within which**, generally by the ablative:

> **Quicquid est bīduō sciēmus.**   Cicero
> Whatever it is, we shall know in two days.

278 **Time during which**, generally by the accusative:

> **Periclēs quadrāgintā annōs præfuit Athēnis.**   Cicero
> Pericles was leader of Athens for forty years.

Note 1: Often by *per* with the accusative: *per trīduum*, for three days.

Note 2: Age is expressed by the participle *nātus*, born, used with the accusative, sometimes with the ablative:

> **Catō quīnque et octōgintā annōs nātus excessit ē vītā.**   Cicero
> Cato died aged eighty-five years.

Note 3: Occasionally an ablative is used instead of an accusative to express duration of time.

279 **How long ago**, is in the accusative or ablative with **abhinc**:

Hoc factum est fermē abhinc biennium.   Plautus
This was done about two years ago.

Comitia iam abhinc trīgintā diēbus habita.   Cicero
The assembly was held thirty days ago.

280 To express **how long before, how long after,** the worde **ante,** before, **post,** after, are used either with the ablative as adverbs, or with the accusative as prepositions, followed by **quam**:

Numa annīs permultīs ante fuit quam Pȳthagorās.   Cicero
Numa lived very many years before Pythagoras.
(or, **Numa ante permultōs annōs fuit quam Pȳthagorās.**)

Post diem tertium gesta rēs est quam Clōdius dīxerat.   Cicero
The affair took place three days after Clodius had spoken.
(or, **Diē tertiō post gesta rēs est quam Clōdius dīxerat.**)

Space

281 **Space over which motion takes place** is in the accusative:

Mīlia tum prānsī tria rēpimus.   Horace
Then, having had luncheon, we crawl three miles.

282 **Space which lies between**, is in the accusative or in the ablative:

**Marathon abest ab Athēnis circiter mīlia
passuum decem.**   Nepos
Marathon is distant from Athens about ten miles.

**Æsculāpiī templum quīnque mīlibus passuum
ab Epidaurō distat.**   Livy
The temple of Æsculapius is five miles distant
from Epidaurus.

283 **Space of measurement**, answering the questions *how high? how deep? how broad? how long?* is generally in the accusative:

Erant mūrī Babylōnis ducēnōs pedēs altī.   Pliny
The walls of Babylon were two hundred feet high.

PREPOSITIONS

284 Prepositions, like the case-endings, show the relations of nouns to other words, and they are used where these relations cannot be clearly expressed by the case-endings alone. All prepositions except *tenus* take the accusative or the ablative case; they are usually placed before the noun.

285 ## Prepositions with Accusative

Ad, to, towards (with accusative of motion to); at: *ad urbem īre*, to go to the city; *ad summam senectūtem*, to extreme old age; *ad octingentōs cæsī*, there were slain to the number of 800; *pugna ad Alliam*, the battle at the Allia; *ad prīmam lūcem*, at daybreak; *ad hoc*, moreover; *ad tempus*, for a time; *ad verbum*, word for word; *nihil ad Atticum*, nothing to (in comparison with) Atticus; *nihil ad rem*, nothing to the purpose.

Adversus, adversum, towards, against, opposite to: *adversum Antipolim*, opposite to Antipolis; *reverentia adversus senēs*, respect towards the aged.

Ante, before: *ante oculōs*, before one's eyes; *ante merīdiem*, before noon; *ante aliquem esse*, to surpass someone.

Apud, at, near (used chiefly with persons, rarely with places): *apud mē*, at my house; *apud veterēs*, among the ancients; *apud Homērum*, in Homer's works; but *in Īliade Homērī*, in Homer's Iliad.

Circum, circā, around, about (in place): *circum caput*, round the head; *circā forum*, around the forum.

Circā, circiter, about (in time, number): *circā prīmam lūcem*, about daybreak; *circā, circiter trīgintā*, about thirty.

Cis, citrā, on this side of: *cis Alpēs*, on this side of the Alps.

Contrā, against, opposite to: *contrā hostem*, against the enemy; *contrā arcem*, opposite the citadel.

Ergā, towards (not used of place): *ergā aliquem benevolus*, feeling kindly towards someone.

Extrā, outside of, without: *extrā mūrōs*, outside the walls; *extrā culpam*, free from blame.

Infrā, under, beneath: *infrā cælum*, under the sky; *infrā dignitātem*, beneath one's dignity.

Inter, between (in place): during (in time), among: *inter urbem et Tiberim*, between the city and the Tiber; *inter silvās*, among the woods *inter cēnandum*, during dinner; *cōnstat inter omnēs*, all are agreed; *inter nōs*, between ourselves; *inter sē amant*, they love each other.

Intrā, within: *intrā mūrōs*, within the walls; *intrā vīgintī diēs*, within twenty days.

Iūxtā, adjoining to, beside: *iūxtā viam*, adjoining the road; *iūxtā deōs*, next to the gods.

Ob, over against, on account of: *mihi ob oculōs*, before my eyes; *quam ob rem*, wherefore.

Penes, in the power of: *penes mē*, in my power; *penes tē es?* are you in your senses?

Per, through, by: *per viās*, through the streets; *per vim*, by force; *per mē licet*, I give leave; *per tē deōs ōrō*, I pray you by the gods; *per explōrātōrēs certior fīō*, I ascertain through scouts.

Pōne, behind: *pōne nōs*, behind us.

Post, behind, after: *post terga*, behind the back; *post mortem*, after death.

Præter, beside, past, along: *præter rīpam*, along the bank; *præter omnēs*, beyond all others; *præter mē*, except me; *præter opīniōnem*, contrary to expectation.

Prope, near: *prope amnem*, near the river; *prope lūcem*, towards daybreak.

Propter, on account of, (rarely of place) near, close to: *propter aquam*, close to the water's edge; *propter hoc*, on this account.

Secundum, next, along, according to (following): *secundum vōs*, next to (behind) you; *secundum lītus*, along the shore; *secundum lēgem*, in accordance with the law; *secundum nōs*, in our favor.

Suprā, over, above: *suprā terram*, above the ground; *suprā mīlia vīgintī*, more than twenty thousand.

Trāns, across: *trāns Rhēnum dūcere*, to lead across the Rhine; *trāns Alpēs*, on the further side of the Alps.

Ultrā, beyond: *ultrā Euphrātem*, beyond the Euphrates; *ultrā vīrēs*, beyond their powers.

Versus, towards (following the noun): *Italiam versus*, towards Italy.

286   Prepositions with Ablative

Ā, ab, from, by: *ab eō locō*, from that place; *ab ortū ad occāsum*, from East to West; *procul ā patriā*, far from one's country; *prope abesse ab*, to be near; *ā tergō*, in the rear; *ā senātū stetit*, he took the side of the senate; *hoc ā mē est,* this is in my favor; *ab urbe conditā,* from the foundation of Rome; *servus ab epistulīs,* secretary; *nōn ab rē fuerit,* it will not be irrelevant; *ab īrā facere,* to do in anger.

Absque, without (rare): *absque vōbis esset,* if it were not for you.

Cōram, in the presence of: *cōram populō,* in the presence of the people.

Cum, with: *cum aliquō congruere, certare,* to agree, strive with someone, *magnō cum perīculō,* with great danger; with *mē, tē, nōbīs, vōbīs,* often with *quō, quibus, cum* follows the pronoun; *mēcum,* with me.

Dē, from (down from), concerning: *dē monte,* down from the mountain; *dē diē,* in the daytime; *dē diē in diem,* from day to day; *ūnus dē multīs,* one out of many; *dē pāce,* concerning peace; *quid dē nōbīs fiet,* what will become of us? *dē industriā,* on purpose; *dē mōre,* according to custom; *dē integrō,* anew.

Ex, Ē, out of, from: *ex urbe,* out of the city; *ē longinquō,* from far; *ex equīs pugnant,* they fight on horseback; *diem ex die,* from day to day; *ex eō audivī,* I heard it from him; *ūnus ex illīs,* one of those; *ex quō,* from the time when; *ē rēpūblicā,* for the good of the state; *ex sententiā,* satisfactorily; *ex parte,* in part; *ex occultō,* secretly; *ex marmore signum,* a marble bust.

Palam, in sight of: *palam omnibus,* in sight of all.

Præ, before, in front of (for) (place rarely, chiefly used in idioms): *præ sē fert speciem virī bonī,* he wears the semblance of a good man; *præ nōbīs beātus es,* you are happy compared with us; *præ gaudiō ubi sim nescio,* I do not know where I am for joy.

Prō, before, for: *prō foribus,* before the door; *prō patriā mōrī,* to die for one's country (in defence of); *mihi prō parente fuit,* he was in the place of a parent to me; *prō certō hoc habuī,* I held this for certain; *prō ratā parte,* in proportion; *prō rē,* according to circumstances.

Note: **Præ** means in advance of; **prō,** standing for, defending.

Sine, without: *sine rēgibus,* without kings; *sine dubiō,* without doubt.

Tenus, as far as (usually following the noun): *verbō tenus,* so far as the word goes. Sometimes with genitive: *Corcȳræ tenus,* as far as Corcyra; especially with a plural noun: *crūrum tenus,* as far as the legs.

287 Prepositions with Accusative or Ablative

Clam, unknown to: *clam vōbis,* unknown to you; *clam patrem,* unknown to the father.

In, with accusative, into, to, towards, against: *Ībō in Pīrœum*, I will go into the Piræus; *in orbem īre*, to go round; *līberālis in mīlitēs*, liberal towards the troops; *Cicerō in Verrem dīxit*, Cicero spoke against Verres; *in æternum*, for ever; *in vicem*, in turn; *in pœnam dare*, to deliver to punishment; *venīre in cōnspectum*, to come into sight.

In, with ablative, in, among, on: *in urbe Rōmā*, in the city of Rome; *in oculīs esse*, to be before one's eyes; *in tempore*, at the right time; *in dīcendō*, while speaking; *in bonīs habēre*, to count among blessings; *in Ganymēde*, in the case of Ganymede; *in eō reprehendere quod*, to blame on the score that.

Sub, with accusative, up to: *sub montem venīre*, to come close to the foot of the mountain; *sub lūcem*, towards daybreak; *sub noctem*, at nightfall; *sub hæc dicta*, just after these things were said.

Sub, with ablative, under: *sub terrā*, underground; *sub monte esse*, to be beneath the mountain; *sub pœnā*, under penalty of.

Subter, with accusative or ablative, underneath, close to: *subter mūrum venīre*, to come close to the wall; *subter lītore esse*, to be close to the shore.

Super, with accusative, over: *super terram*, over the ground; *super omnia*, above all.

Super, with ablative, upon: *super focō*, on the hearth; *super Hectore*, about Hector.

IMPERSONAL VERBS

CASE CONSTRUCTION

288 The following verbs of feeling take an accusative of the person with a genitive of the cause: **miseret, piget, pænitet, pudet, tædet**:

> **Miseret tē aliōrum; tuī tē nec miseret nec pudet.**   Plautus
> You pity others; for yourself you have neither pity nor shame.

> **Mē cīvitātis mōrum piget tædetque.**   Sallust
> I am sick and weary of the morals of the state.

289 **Decet, dēdecet, iuvat** take an accusative of the person with an infinitive:

> **Ōrātōrem īrāscī minimē decet; simulāre nōn dēdecet.**   Cicero
> It by no means becomes an orator to feel anger;
> it is not unbecoming to feign it.

Si mē gemmantia dextrā scēptrā tenēre decet.   Ovid
If it befits me to hold in my right hand the jewelled sceptre.

290 **Libet, licet, liquet, contingit, convenit, ēvenit, expedit,** take a dative:

Nē libeat tibi quod nōn licet.   Cicero
Let not that please you which is not lawful.

Licet nēminī contrā patriam dūcere exercitum.   Cicero
It is not lawful for anyone to lead an army against his country.

291 **Interest,** it is of importance, it concerns, is used with the **genitive of the person** or thing concerned, but with the feminine ablatives *meā, tuā, suā, nostrā, vestrā* of the possessive pronouns:

Interest omnium rēctē facere.   Cicero
It is for the good of all to do right.

Et tuā et meā interest tē valēre.   Cicero
It is of importance to you and to me that you
should be well.

292 **Rēfert,** it concerns, it matters, is also used with the feminine ablatives of the possessive pronouns:

Quid meā rēfert cui serviam?   Phædrus
What does it matter to me whom I serve?

Note 1: Rarely with a genitive:

quōrum nihil rēfert   Quintilian
whom it does not at all concern

Note 2: The genitives of value, *magnī, parvī, tantī, quantī, pluris,* are often joined with *interest* and *refert:*

Illud meā magnī interest tē ut videam.   Cicero
It is of great importance to me that I should see you.

Hoc nōn pluris rēfert quam sī imbrem in crībrum gerās.   Plautus
This avails no more than if you pour rain-water into a sieve.

---

293 **Pertinet, attinet** take an accusative with ad:

Nihil ad mē attinet.   Terence
It does not concern me at all.

294 **Oportet** is used with the accusative and infinitive clause, or with the subjunctive alone; rarely with the **prolative infinitive** (§ 369):

Lēgem brevem esse oportet.   Cicero
A law should be brief.

Mē ipsum amēs oportet, nōn mea.   Cicero
You ought to love me myself, not my possessions.

Vīvere nātūræ sī convenienter oportet.   Horace
If one ought to live agreeably to nature.

---

295   Note: **Coepit, dēbet, dēsinit, potest, solet** are used impersonally with an impersonal infinitive:

   Pigēre eum factī coepit.   Justinus
   It began to repent him of his deed.

   Pervenīrī ad summa sine industriā nōn potest.   Quintilian
   One cannot reach the highest without industry.

---

296 PASSIVE CONSTRUCTION

When a sentence is changed from the active to the passive form:

(a) The object of a transitive verb becomes the subject; the subject becomes the agent in the ablative with the preposition **ā** or **ab**:

{ **Numa lēgēs dedit.**   Cicero   Numa gave laws.
{ **Ā Numā lēgēs datæ sunt.**   Laws were given by Numa.

297   (b) Factitive verbs and verbs of saying and thinking become copulative (§ 187):

{ **Clōdium plēbs tribūnum**   The common people elected
{   **creāvit.**   Clodius tribune.
{ **Clōdius ā plēbe tribūnus**   Clodius was elected tribune by
{   **creātus est.**   the common people.

298   (c) Transitive verbs which have two objects in the accusative, the person and the thing, keep the accusative of the thing in the passive form:

{ **Mē sententiam rogās.**   You ask me my opinion.
{ **Ā tē sententiam rogor.**   I am asked my opinion by you.

299   Intransitive verbs are only used impersonally in the passive:

300   (a) The subject of an intransitive verb in passive construction becomes the agent in the ablative:

Nōs currimus. }
Ā nōbīs curritur. }   We run.

301   or the agent may be omitted:

Sīc īmus ad astra. }
Sīc ītur ad astra.   Vergil }   Thus we go to the stars.

Ācriter utrimque usque ad vesperum pugnātum est.   Cæsar
There was fierce fighting on both sides until the evening.

302   (b) Intransitive verbs which take the dative keep it in the passive:

Mihi istī nocēre nōn possunt. }
Mihi ab istīs nocēre nōn potest. Cicero }   They cannot hurt me.

Nihil facile persuādētur invītīs.   Quintilian
The unwilling are not easily persuaded of anything.

303   Note: The ablative of the agent is used with quasi-passive verbs (§ 128):

Mālō ā cīve spoliārī quam ab hoste vēnīre.   Quintilian
I would rather be despoiled by a citizen than be sold by a foe.

ADJECTIVES

304   Some adjectives are used as substantives to express persons or things:
sapiēns, a wise man; bonī, the good; Rōmānī, the Romans; omnia, all
things; multa, many things; bona, goods.

Bonōs bonī dīligunt.   Cicero
The good love the good.

Aiunt multum legendum esse, nōn multa.   Cicero
They say that much should be read, not many things.

305   Neuter adjectives are used for abstract substantives: vērum or vēra,
the truth.

Omne tulit pūnctum quī miscuit ūtile dulcī.   Horace
He who has combined the useful with the pleasing
has won every vote.

306 Some adjectives, when used as substantives, can be qualified by other adjectives: *amīcus*, friend; *vīcīnus*, neighbor; *dextra*, right hand; *māiōrēs*, ancestors.

Vetus vīcīnus ac necessārius.   Cicero
An old neighbor and intimate acquaintance.

307 *Medius*, middle, and superlatives of position in place and time, as *summus, īmus, prīmus, ultimus*, are used with a partitive force; *mediō pontō*, in mid ocean; *ad īmam quercum*, at the foot of the oak:

Prīmā lūce summus mōns ā Labiēnō tenēbātur.   Cæsar
At dawn of day the mountain top was held by Labienus.

Note: The singular forms of **cēterī**, the rest (of which the masc. nom. sing. is wanting), are similarly used with collective nouns: *cētera turba*, the rest of the crowd; *ā cēterō exercitū*, by the rest of the army.

---

308 Adjectives are used adverbially when they qualify the verb rather than the substantive:

Sōcratēs lætus venēnum hausit.   Seneca
Socrates drank the poison cheerfully.

Mātūtīnus arā.   Virgil
Plough at morn.

Vespertīnus pete tēctum.   Horace
At eventide go home.

Hannibal prīmus in proelium ībat,
ultimus excēdēbat.   Livy
Hannibal was the first to go into battle,
the last to withdraw.

Comparative and Superlative Adjectives

309 **Superlatives** often express a very high degree, and not the highest:

Ego sum miserior quam tū, quæ es miserrima.   Cicero.
I am more wretched than you, who are very wretched.

310 **Comparatives** may also express a certain degree, without special comparison: *longior*, rather long; *senior*, elderly. After a comparative with *quam*, a second comparative is often used:

Æmiliī cōntiō fuit vērior quam grātior populō.   Livy
The harangue of Æmilius was more truthful than popular.

> **Note:** Comparatives and superlatives are often strengthened by adverbs and adverbial phrases: *multō cārior*, much dearer; *longē cārissimus*, far dearest; *vel minimus*, the very least; *quam maximus*, the greatest possible.

Numeral Adjectives

311 **Cardinals: Ūnus,** apart from other numerals, is used only to give emphasis; it often means the one of all others:

Dēmosthenēs ūnus ēminet inter omnēs ōrātōrēs   Cicero
Demosthenes is pre-eminent among all orators.

Mīlle is used as an indeclinable adjective; sometimes as a substantive taking the genitive after it; **mīlia** is always used as a substantive, followed by a genitive:

Mīlle gregēs illī.	Ovid	**Mīlle annōrum.**	Plautus
He had a thousand flocks.		A thousand years.	

Quattuor mīlia hominum Capitōlium occupāvēre.   Livy
Four thousand men seized the Capitol.

If a smaller number is added to *mīlia*, the compound number becomes adjectival: *tria mīlia et sescentī hominēs*, three thousand six hundred men.

312 **Ordinals** are used in expressing order or time; but in compound numbers *ūnus* is used for *prīmus: ūnō et octōgēnsimō annō*, in the eighty-first year:

Octāvus annus est ex quō Britanniam vīcistis.   Tacitus
It is the eighth year since you conquered Britain.

> **Note:** *Ūnus, alter, tertius*, &c. are used for a first, a second, a third, where the order is of no importance, as distinguished from the regular ordinals, *prīmus, secundus, tertius*, which can only mean the first, the second, &c.

313 **Distributives** express how many each or at a time:

Mīlitibus quīnī et vīcēnī dēnāriī datī sunt.   Livy
Twenty-five denarii were given to each soldier.

> **Note 1:** With a substantive of singular meaning but plural form, distributives are used instead of cardinals, but the plural of *ūnus* is used instead of *singulī*:
>
> **Ūna castra iam facta ex bīnīs vidēbantur.**   Cæsar
> One camp now seemed to have been formed from two.
>
> **Note 2:** *Bīnī* is used for a pair:

Pamphilus bīnōs habēbat scyphōs sigillātōs.   Cicero
Pamphilus had in use a pair of embossed cups.

Note 3: Distributives are also used in expressions of multiplication: *bis bīna sunt quattuor*, twice two is four.

314   **Quam,** is omitted before numerals when they are preceeded by **plūs, amplus** or **minus:**

   Rōmānī paulō plūs sescentī cecidērunt.   Livy
   Rather more than six hundred Romans fell.

PRONOUNS AND PRONOMINAL ADJECTIVES

315   The personal pronoun as subject is usually expressed only by the verb ending, but is sometimes added for emphasis:

   Ego rēgēs ēiēcī; vōs tyrannōs intrōdūcitis.   Cicero
   I expelled kings; you are bringing in tyrants.

   Note: *Nōs* is often used for *ego*, and *noster* for *meus*, but *vōs* is not used for *tū*, nor *vester* for *tuus*.

316   The reflexive pronoun **sē, sēsē, suī, sibi,** refers to the subject in a simple sentence (§ 464):

   Fūr telō sē dēfendit.   Cicero
   The thief defends himself with a weapon.

   Īra suī impotēns est.   Seneca
   Anger is not master of itself.

   Īrātus cum ad sē rediit, sibi tum īrāscitur.   Syrius
   When an angry man has come to himself,
   he is angry with himself.

   Dēforme est dē sē ipse prædicāre.   Cicero
   It is bad taste to boast of oneself.

   Note 1: There is no reciprocal pronoun in Latin; *sē* with *inter* is used reciprocally: *inter sē amant*, they love each other.

   Note 2: In the first and second persons, *mē, tē*, are used reflexively with *ipse; mē ipse cōnsōlor*, I console myself.

317   The possessive adjective **suus,** formed from the reflexive, is used to express *his own, their own*, when emphasis is required, and usually refers to the subject of the verb:

   Nēmō rem suam emit.
   No one buys what is his own.

Sometimes it can refer to other cases if the context shows that it cannot refer to the subject:

Suîs flammîs dēlēte Fīdēnās.   Livy
With its own flames destroy Fidenæ.

Suus is especially used in combination with *quisque:*

Suus cuique erat locus attribūtus.   Cæsar
To each man his own place had been assigned.

318   **Eius** is the possessive used of the third person where no emphasis is required, and never refers to the subject.

Chīlius tē rogat, et ego eius rogātū.   Cicero
Chilius asks you, and I at his request.

> **Note:** The possessive adjectives are often omitted when the meaning is clear without them: *frātrem amat,* he loves his brother.

319   **Hic, ille** are often used in contrast: *hic* usually meaning the latter, *ille* the former:

Quōcumque adspiciō, nihil est nisi pontus et āēr,
flūctibus hic tumidus, nūbibus ille mināx.   Ovid
Wherever I look, there is nothing but sea and sky,
the latter heaped with clouds, the former threatening
with billows.

> **Note: Iste** is sometimes contemptuous: *quid sibi istī miserī volunt?* What do those wretched ones want? **Ille** may imply respect: *philosophus ille,* that famous philosopher. **Is** often is the antecedent to *quī: is cuius,* he whose; *eum cui,* him to whom. **Hic... ille** often mean the latter... the former.

320   **Ipse,** self, is of all the three persons, with or without a personal pronoun: *ipse ībō,* I shall go myself.

> **Note: Ipse** sometimes means of one's own accord: *ipsī veniunt,* they come of their own accord. *Ipse, ipsa,* also stand for the chief person (master, mistress): the scholars of Pythagoras used to say '*Ipse dīxit,*' The master himself said it. Sometimes a superlative is formed: *ipsissima verba,* the very exact words.

321   **Īdem,** the same, is of all the three persons; with *quī* it expresses the same... as. It may often be translated as at the same time; also:

Ego, vir fortis, īdemque philosophus.   Cicero
I, a brave man, and also a philosopher.

322   Of the indefinite pronouns **quis, sīquis, numquis, quispiam, aliquis, quīdam,** the most definite is *quīdam*, the least so *quis*.

Quis, quī, any, cannot begin a sentence; they often follow *sī, num, nē*.

> **Sī mala condiderit in quem quis carmina iūs est.**   Horace
> If anyone has composed malicious verses on another,
> there is a remedy at law.

> **Sī quid tē volam, ubī eris?**   Plautus
> If I want anything of you, where will you be?

Aliquis means someone: *dīcat aliquis*, suppose someone to say; *sī vīs esse aliquis*, if you wish to be somebody.

Quīdam means a certain person (known but not named):

> **Accurrit quīdam, nōtus mihi nōmine tantum.**   Horace
> A certain man runs up, known to me only by name.

Nescio quis, someone or other (I know not who), used as if one word, forms an indefinite pronoun:

> **Nescio quid mihi animus præsāgit malī.**   Terence
> My mind forebodes I know not what evil.

323   **Quisquam** (substantive), **ūllus** (adjective), any at all, are often used after a negative word, or a question expecting a negative answer:

> **Nec amet quemquam nec ametur ab ūllō.**   Juvenal
> Let him not love anyone nor be loved by any.

> **Nōn ūllus arātrō dignus honōs.**   Virgil
> Not any due honor (is given) to the plough.

Note: *Quisquam* and *ūllus* are used after *sī* when negation is implied, or with comparatives:

> **Aut nēmō aut, sī quisquam, Catō sapiēns fuit.**   Cicero
> Either no man was wise, or, if any, Cato was.

---

324   **Quīvīs, quīlibet,** any you like:

> **Quīvīs homō potest quemvīs dē quōlibet rūmōrem prōferre.**   Cicero
> Any man can put forth any report of anybody.

> **Nōn cuivīs hominī contingit adīre Corinthum.**   Horace
> It does not happen to every man to go to Corinth.

325 **Quisque,** each (severally), is often used with *sē, suus:*

> **Sibi quisque habeant quod suum est.**   Plautus
> Let them have each for himself what is his own.

With superlatives it expresses every, all:

> **Epicūrēōs doctissimus quisque contemnit.**   Cicero
> All the most learned men despise the Epicureans.

It also distributes ordinal numbers:

> **Quīntō quōque annō Sicilia tōta cēnsētur.**   Cicero
> A census of all Sicily is taken every fifth year.

326 **Uterque,** each (of two), both, can be used with the genitive of pronouns; but with substantives it agrees in case:

> **Uterque parēns**   Ovid
> Both father and mother.

> **Utrōque vestrum dēlēctor.**   Cicero
> I am delighted with both of you.

327 **Uter,** which? (of two), is interrogative: *uter melior?* which is the better?

> **Uter utrī īnsidiās fēcit?**   Cicero
> Which of the two laid an ambush for which?

Note: *Utrī,* plural, is used for which of two parties?, *utrīque* for both parties. So *alterī... alterī,* one party, the other party.

---

328 **Alter,** the one, the other (of two), the second, is the demonstrative of *uter: alter ego,* a second self.

> **Quicquid negat alter, et alter; affirmant pariter.**   Horace
> Whatever the one denies, so does the other;
> they affirm alike.

329 **Alius,** another (of any number), different:

> **Fortūna nunc mihi, nunc aliī benigna.**   Horace
> Fortune, kind now to me, now to another.

Alius, alius, repeated in two clauses, mean one... another; **aliī, aliī** (plural), some... others:

> **Aliud est maledīcere, aliud accūsāre.**   Cicero
> It is one thing to speak evil, another to accuse.

Alii Dēmosthenem laudant, alii Cicerōnem.
Some praise Demosthenes, others Cicero.

Note 1: Alius repeated in different cases in the same sentence, or with one of its derived adverbs, has an idiomatic use:

Alii alia sentiunt,
Some think one thing, some another.

Illī aliās aliud īsdem dē rēbus iūdicant.   Cicero
They judge differently, at different times, about the same things.

Note 2: Alius expresses comparison and difference: nīl aliud quam, nothing else than; alius Lȳsippō (Horace), other than Lysippus.

330 The relative **quī, quæ, quod,** is of all three persons, and when the antecedent is a noun either expressed or understood, it may be regarded as standing between two cases of the same noun, and agreeing with the second case.

(a) Sometimes both cases are expressed:

Erant itinera duo, quibus itineribus exīre possent.   Cæsar
There were two roads by which they might go forth.

(b) usually the second is omitted:

Animum rege quī, nisi pāret, imperat.   Horace
Rule the temper, which, unless it obeys, commands.

(c) sometimes the first, in poetry:

Sīc tibi dent nymphæ quæ levet unda sitim,   Ovid
So may the nymphs give thee water to assuage thirst.

(d) sometimes both are omitted:

Sunt quibus in satirā videor nimis ācer.   Horace
There are some to whom I seem too keen in satire.

331 The following scheme shows this principle fully:

(1) **vir quem virum vidēs rēx est** (both cases expressed).

(2) **vir quem... vidēs rēx est** (second case omitted) (usual form).

(3) **... quem virum vidēs rēx est** (first case omitted).

(4) **... quem... vidēs rēx est** (both cases omitted).

332 **Note 1:** If the relative is the subject of a copulative verb, it often agrees in gender and number with the complement:

Thēbæ, quod Bœōtiæ caput est.   Livy
Thebes, which is the capital of Bœotia.

Note 2: When an adjective qualifying the antecedent is emphatic, as *ūnus, sōlus*, or is a superlative, it is often attracted to the **clause of the relative,** agreeing with it in case:

Sī veniat Cæsar cum cōpiīs quās habet firmissimās.   Cicero
Should Cæsar come with the very strong forces that he has.

Note 3: If the antecedent consists of two or more nouns, or is a collective noun, the rules for the agreement of the relative are the same as for the agreement of adjectives with the composite subject (see § 198, 199).

Note 4: If the relative refers to a sentence or clause, it is neuter; sometimes *id quod* is used, *id* being in apposition to the clause:

Diem cōnsūmī volēbat, id quod est factum.   Cicero
He wished the day to be wasted, which came to pass.

Note 5: The relative clause sometimes comes first:

Quam quisque nōrit artem, in hāc sē exerceat.   Cicero
Let everyone practice the art which he knows.

(For other uses of the relative see § 403, 450, 451.)

CORRELATION

333 **Pronouns and pronominal adverbs** are said to be **correlatives** when they correspond to one another as antecedent and relative (§ 102).

334 The pronoun antecedent to **quī** is usually the demonstrative **is**; sometimes **hic, ille, īdem**:

Is minimō eget quī minimum cupit.   Publilius Syrus
He wants for least who desires least.

335 **Tālis... quālis** means of such a kind... as; **tantus... quantus**, as much or as great... as; **tot... quot**, as many... as:

Tālis est quālem tū eum esse scrīpsistī.   Cicero
He is such as you wrote word that he was.

Tantō brevius omne, quantō fēlīcius tempus.   Pliny
The happier a time is, so much the shorter is it.

Quot hominēs, tot sententiæ.   Terence
So many men, so many minds.

Tam... quam, so... as, as... as; **ut... ita**, as... so:

Tam ego ante fuī līber quam gnātus tuus.   Plautus
I was formerly as free as your son.

Ut optāstī, ita est.   Cicero
As you wished, so it is.

VERBS

TENSES OF THE INDICATIVE

336   The **present** expresses:

(1) What happens at the present moment: *iaciō*, I throw.

(2) What is going on at the present time: *scrībō*, I am writing.

(3) What is habitually or always: *quod semper movētur æternum est* (Cicero), that which is always in motion is eternal.

337   The **historic present** is used for a past by orators, historians, and poets, to give variety, or call up a vivid picture:

Dīmissō senātū decemvirī prōdeunt in cōntiōnem
abdicantque sē magistrātū.   Livy
When the senate was dismissed, the decemvirs
went forth to the assembled people and resigned office.

338   **Note:** *Dum*, while, is used with the historic present in speaking of past time: *Dum Rōmānī cōnsultant, Saguntum oppugnabātur*, Livy. While the Romans were consulting, Saguntum was being besieged (see § 430). With *iam, iamdiū (dūdum, prīdem)* the present expresses what has long been and still continues: *Iamdūdum videō* (Horace), I have seen it this long time.

339   The **perfect** expresses:

As **primary**, from the point of the present moment what has just been done: *scrīpsī*, I have written. This is called the **present perfect**.
As **historic**, simply a past action, which happened at some indefinite time: *scrīpsī*, I wrote. This is called the **historic perfect**.

Note: The **present perfect** is used in poetry to express past existence which has ceased: *Fuimus Trōes; fuit Īlium*, Virgil. We have been (i.e. are no longer) Trojans; Troy has been (exists no longer).

340   The **imperfect** expresses what was continued or repeated in past time, as opposed to the completed or momentary past:

Æquī sē in oppida recēpērunt mūrīsque sē tenēbant.   Livy
The Æqui retreated into their towns and remained
within their walls.

Carthāgine quotannīs bīnī rēgēs creābantur.   Nepos
At Carthage two rulers were elected annually.

Note: the imperfect is sometimes used to express something attempted or intended:

Hostēs nostrōs prōgredī prohibēbant.   Cæsar
The enemy tried to prevent our men from advancing.

341 The **pluperfect** expresses an action which had already been completed prior to the (past) time of the main narrative:

Massiliēnsēs portās Cæsarī clauserant.   Cæsar
The Marseillais had closed the gates against Cæsar.

Note: The Romans, in writing letters, often talk of the time of writing in a past tense, because it would be in the past when a letter was received:

Rēs, cum haec scrībēbam, erat in extrēmum adducta discrīmen.   Cicero
At the time I write, the affair had been brought to a crisis.

Tenses so used are called **epistolary**. The imperfect and perfect are used for the present; the pluperfect for the perfect; the future participle with *eram* for the future.

342 The **future simple** is used in to express what will happen:

Ut volēs mē esse, ita erō.   Plautus
As you wish me to be, so I shall be.

Note: As might be expected, Latin often uses a future where English uses a present with future meaning.

343 The **future perfect** expresses action to be completed in the future; if two actions are spoken of, one of which will take place before the other, the prior one is in the future perfect:

Ut sēmentem fēceris, ita metēs.   Cicero
As ye sow, so shall ye reap.

Note: Often, as with *fēceris* above, English uses the present where Latin uses the future perfect.

MOODS

344 The **indicative** is the mood which makes a statement or question with regard to a fact, or to something which is dealt with by the speaker as a fact (e.g. something which will be a fact in the future).

---

345 **Note:** Verbs expressing duty, fitness, possibility, as *possum, dēbeō, decet, licet, oportet*, are often used in the indicative tenses of past time, to express that it was proper or possible at that time to do something which in fact was not done. Phrases such as *necesse est, fuit; æquum, longum, melius, satius est, fuit*, are similarly used in the indicative (§ 440 c):

Hic tamen hanc mēcum poterās requiēscere noctem.   Virgil
Yet you might have rested here with me this night.

Et vellem et fuerat melius.   Virgil
I should have wished, and it would have been better.

Longum est ea dīcere: sed hoc breve dīcam.   Cicero
It would be tedious to speak of these things, but this little I will say.

Compare with these:

Nōn Āsiæ nōmen obiciendum Murenæ fuit.   Cicero
Murena should not have been reproached with the mention of Asia.

---

346 The **imperative** is the mood of positive command or direct request:

Ī, sequere Ītaliam.   Virgil   **Pergite, adulēscentēs.**   Cicero
Go, seek Italy.   Proceed, o youths.

347 **Prohibitions** (negative commands) in the second person are expressed by **nōlī, nōlīte** with the infinitive; or, more peremptorily, by **nē** with the perfect subj. (2nd pers.) or pres. subj. (3rd pers.):

Nōlīte id velle quod fierī nōn potest.   Cicero
Do not wish what cannot be.

Nē fēceris quod dubitās.   Pliny
Never do anything about which you are doubtful.

348 but in poetry **nē** is often used with the imperative:

Equō nē crēdite, Teucrī.   Virgil
Do not trust the horse, O Trojans.

349 The imperative forms in **-tō, -tōte** are specially used in laws; but they are also often used for emphasis.

> **Rēgiō imperiō duo suntō, iīque cōnsulēs appellantor.**   Cicero
> Let there be two with royal power, and let them
> be called consuls.

---

350 **Note 1:** The following imperatives are joined with the infinitive or subjunctive of other verbs to form imperatives; **fac, fac ut, cūrā ut**, with the Subjunctive; **mementō** with infinitive or subjunctive. In prohibitions **fac nē, cavē**, take the subjunctive; and in poetry **fuge, mitte, parce**, take the Infinitive:

> **Magnum fac animum habeās.**   Cicero
> Mind you have a lofty spirit.

Note 2 For a courteous imperative the future indicative is often used: *faciēs ut sciam* (Cicero), You will please let me know.

---

351 The **subjunctive mood** makes a statement or asks a question, not so much with regard to a fact as with regard to something thought of or imagined by the speaker, often with some condition expressed or implied. It expresses a modified or conditional command or desire.

The subjunctive has two general uses:

352 **Pure** or **independent**: *velim*, I could wish; *vellem*, I could have wished.

353 **Dependent** on another verb: *cūrā ut faciās*, take care that you do it.

354 The **pure subjunctive** must generally be rendered in English with auxiliaries, may, might, could, would, should.

Note: The subjunctive makes a statement:

355 (a) With a condition expressed or implied (**conditional use**):

> **Ita amicōs parēs.**   Cicero
> Thus you may get friends.

> **Crēderēs victōs.**   Livy
> You would have supposed them conquered
> (from their appearance).

356 (b) Or in a modified tone, to avoid positiveness (**potential use**):

> **Dubitem haud equidem.**   Virgil
> For my part I should not hesitate.

The **perfect subjunctive** is especially so used:

    Forsitan quispiam dīxerit.   Cicero
    Perhaps someone may say.

357   (c) Conveying an admission or supposition (**concessive use**):

    Hæc sint falsa sāne. Cicero   **Fuerit malus cīvis.**   Cicero
    Granting this to be quite untrue.   Suppose he was a bad citizen.

358   It asks a question (**deliberative use**):

    Faveās tū hostī? Cicero   **Quid facerem?**   Virgil
    Would you befriend an enemy?   What was I to do?

    It expresses a desire or command:

359   (a) A wish or prayer (**optative use**): often with *utinam*, Oh that!

    Sīs fēlīx.   Horace   **Utinam potuissem.**
    May you be happy.   Oh that I had been able.

    Doceās iter et sacra ostia pandās.   Virgil
    Pray show me the road and open the sacred doors.

360   (b) An exhortation (**hortative use**) chiefly in the 1st person plural:

    Amēmus patriam, pāreāmus senātuī.   Cicero
    Let us love our country, let us obey the senate.

361   (c) A modified command (**jussive use**) in the 3rd person:

    Sit sermō lēnis.   Cicero
    Let speech be calm.

    Vīlicus nē sit ambulātor.   Cato
    Let not a steward be a loiterer.

362   From the jussive use comes a further use of the subjunctive, by which the expression of a wish is conveyed into past time. This use is chiefly in the second person, but extends also to the others:

    Rem tuam cūrārēs.   Terence
    You should have been minding your own business.

363   The use of the 2nd pers. in the pres. subj. is often indefinite, not addressed to anyone in particular, but expressing a general maxim:

    Agēre decet quod agās consīderāte.   Cicero
    Whatever you do, it is proper to do it with consideration.

THE VERB INFINITE

364 The parts of the verb infinite have some of the uses of verbs, some of the uses of nouns.

THE INFINITIVE

365 The **infinitive** as a verb has voices (active or passive), tenses (present, past, or future), it governs cases and is qualified by adverbs; as a noun it is neuter, indeclinable, used only as nominative or accusative.

366 The **infinitive** in the nominative may be the subject of impersonal verbs, or of verbs used impersonally (§ 289):

Iuvat īre et Dōrica castra vidēre.	Virgil
It is pleasant to go and view the Doric camp.	
Ipsum philosophārī nunc displicet,	Cicero
The very study of philosophy now displeases,	
Dulce et decōrum est prō patriā morī.	Horace
To die for one's country is sweet and seemly.	
Non vīvere bonum est sed bene vīvere.	Seneca
It is not living which is a good, but living well.	

Note: Occasionally the infinitive is the complement:

Homō cui vīvere est cōgitāre.	Cicero
Man to whom to live is to think.	

367 The **infinitive** is often one of the two accusatives depending on an active verb of saying or thinking:

Errāre, nescīre, dēcipī et malum et turpe dūcimus.	Cicero
To err, to be ignorant, to be deceived, we deem both unfortunate and disgraceful,	

368 **Note:** Sometimes, though rarely, it is a simple object:

Hoc rīdēre meum nūllā tibi vēndō Īliade.	Persius
This laughter of mine I won't sell you for an Iliad.	

369 The **prolative infinitive** is used to carry on the construction of indeterminate and some other verbs (§ 190):

Verbs of possibility, duty, habit: *possum, queō, dēbeō*, etc.;

Verbs of wishing, purposing, daring: *volō, nōlō, mālō, optō, statuō, cōnstituō, audeō,* etc.;

Verbs of beginning, ceasing, endeavoring, continuing, hesitating, hastening: *coepī,* begin; *dēsinō,* cease; *cōnor,* try; *pergō,* proceed, etc.;

Verbs of knowing, teaching, learning: *scio, discō, doceō.*

Ego plūs quam fēcī facere nōn possum.	Cicero
I cannot do more than I have done.	
Solent diū cōgitāre quī magna volunt gerere.	Cicero
They are wont to reflect long who wish to do great things.	

Præcēdere coepit.	Horace	**Sapere audē.**	Horace
He begins to walk on.		Dare to be wise.	

Note: The infinitive of a copulative verb (§ 187) used prolatively is followed by a complement in the nominative:

Sōcratēs parēns philosophiæ iūre dīcī potest.	Cicero
Socrates may rightly be called the parent of philosophy.	
Vīs formōsa vidērī.	Horace
You wish to seem beautiful.	

370 The **prolative infinitive** is also used with the passives of verbs of saying and thinking:

Barbara nārrātur vēnisse venēfica tēcum.	Ovid
A barbarian sorceress is said to have come with you.	
Aristīdēs ūnus omnium iūstissimus fuisse trāditur.	Cicero
Aristides is recorded to have been the one man of all most just.	

Note: This construction is called the **nominative with infinitive**, and is used with most passive verbs of saying and thinking. A few, however, *nārror, nūntior, trādor,* are used impersonally – always when in the perfect, and often in the present and imperfect:

Galbam et Āfricānum doctōs fuisse trāditum est.	Cicero
It has been handed down that Galba and Africanus were learned.	

371 With an infinitive perfect passive *esse* is often omitted:

Pōns in Ībērō prope effectus nūntiābātur.	Cæsar
The bridge over the Ebro was announced to be nearly finished.	
Titus Manlius ita locūtus fertur.	Livy
Titus Manlius is reported to have spoken thus.	

372 The **historic infinitive** is the present infinitive used by historians in vivid description for the imperfect indicative:

> **Multī sequī, fugere, occīdī, capī**   Sallust
> Many were following, fleeing, being slain, being captured.

373 An infinitive often follows an adjective prolatively, chiefly in poetry:

> **Audāx omnia perpetī.**   Horace   **Īnsuētus vincī.**   Livy
> Bold to endure all things.   Unused to be conquered.
>
> **Fīgere doctus erat sed tendere doctior arcūs.**   Ovid
> He was skilled in piercing (with a dart), but more
> skilled in bending the bow.

Note: In poetry, the infinitive is sometimes used after a verb of motion to express purpose: *venio vīsere*, I come to look.

GERUND AND GERUNDIVE

374 The **gerund** is a verbal noun with active meaning, the **gerundive** a verbal adjective, passive in meaning. The genitive, dative, and ablative of the gerund, and the accusative with a preposition, are used as cases of the infinitive.

375 The **accusative** of the **gerund** follows some prepositions, especially *ad, ob, inter*:

> **Ad bene vīvendum breve tempus satis est longum.**   Cicero
> For living well a short time is long enough.
>
> **Mōrēs puerōrum sē inter lūdendum dētegunt.**   Quint.
> The characters of boys show themselves in their play.

376 The **genitive** of the **gerund** depends on some abstract substantives, and adjectives which take a genitive:

> **Ars scrībendī discitur.**   **Cupidus tē audiendī sum.**   Cicero
> The art of writing is learnt.   I am desirous of hearing you.

377 The **dative** of the **gerund** is used with a few verbs, adjectives, and substantives implying help, use, fitness:

> **Pār est disserendō.**   Cicero   **Dat operam legendō.**
> He is equal to arguing.   He gives attention to reading.

Note: Observe the phrase: *solvendō nōn est*, he is insolvent.

378 The **ablative** of the **gerund** is of cause or manner, or it follows one of the prepositions *ab, dē, ex, in, cum:*

Fugiendō vincimus.	We conquer by fleeing.
Dē pugnandō dēlīberant.	They deliberate about fighting.

379 If the verb is transitive, the **gerundive** is more often used than the gerund, agreeing with the object as an adjective. It takes the gender and number of the object, but the object is drawn into the case of the gerundive.

The following examples show how the gerundive takes the place of the gerund.

Gerund		Gerundive	
Ad petendum pācem	⎫	ad petendam pācem	in order to seek peace
Petendī pācem	⎪	petendæ pācis	of seeking peace
Petendō pācem	⎪	petendæ pācī	for seeking peace
Petendō pācem	⎬ becomes	petendā pāce	by seeking peace
Ad mutandum lēgēs	⎪	ad mutandās lēgēs	in order to change laws
Mutandī lēgēs	⎪	mutandārum lēgum	of changing laws
Mutandō lēgēs	⎭	mutandīs lēgibus	for or by changing laws

Note 1: *Ad petendam pācem* literally means 'for peace which is to be sought'. In order to seek peace may also be rendered by the genitive of the gerund or gerundive with *causā or grātiā: pācem petendī causā* or *petendæ pācis causā* (see § 423, note 3).

380 **Note 2:** The dative of the gerundive is used with names of office to show the purpose of the office (§ 226):

Comitia rēgī creandō.	Livy
An assembly for electing a king.	
Trēsvirī agrīs dīvidendīs.	Florus
Three commissioners for dividing lands.	

---

381 The gerund is often used to express that something ought or is to be done, the **dative of the agent** being expressed or understood (§ 222).

382 If the verb is **intransitive** the nom. neuter of its gerundive is used with a tense of esse in an impersonal passive construction (§ 299):

Eundum est.
One must go.

Mihi eundum est.
I must go.

> **Suō cuique iūdiciō est ūtendum.**   Cicero
> Each must use his own judgment.

383   If the verb is **transitive** the **gerundive** is used in agreement with the
predicate:

> **Cæsarī omnia ūnō tempore erant agenda.**   Cæsar
> All things had to be done by Cæsar at one time.
>
> **Prīncipiō sēdēs apibus statiōque petenda.**   Virgil
> First of all a site and station must be sought for the bees.

Note 1: If an intransitive verb has an indirect object in the dative, the agent is in the
ablative with the preposition *ā* or *ab: patriæ est ā tē cōnsulendum*, you must consult
for your country.

384   **Note 2** After some verbs, as *dō, trādō, cūrō*, the gerundive is used in agreement with
the object to express that something is caused to be done:

> **Cæsar pontem faciendum cūrat.**   Cæsar
> Cæsar causes a bridge to be made.

SUPINES

385   The supines are also used as cases of the infinitive:

386   The **supine** in **-um** is an accusative after verbs of motion, expressing
the purpose:

> **Lūsum it Mæcēnās, dormītum ego.**   Horace
> Mæcenas goes to play, I to sleep.
>
> **Athēniēnsēs mīserunt Delphōs consultum.**   Nepos
> The Athenians sent to Delphi to consult.

387   With the infinitive **īrī**, used impersonally, the supine forms a future
passive infinitive:

> **Aiunt urbem captum īrī.**
> They say that the city will be taken.

Note: Literally, they say there is a going to take the city.

388 The **supine** in **-ū** (dative and ablative) is used with some adjectives, such as *facilis, dulcis, turpis,* and the Substantives *fās, nefās: turpe factū,* disgraceful to do.

Hoc fās est dictū.
It is lawful to say this.

Lībertās, dulce audītū nōmen.   Livy
Freedom, a name sweet to hear.

Nec vīsū facilis, nec dictū adfābilis ūllī.   Virgil
One not easy for any to gaze on, or to address.

Note: The supine in -ū does not take an accusative.

PARTICIPLES

389 The present and perfect participles of some verbs are used as adjectives:

Homō frūgī ac dīligēns.   Cicero
A thrifty and industrious man.

Odōrāta cedrus.   Virgil
The fragrant cedar.

390 Most participles which can be used as adjectives have comparison: *pietāte prœstantior,* more excellent in piety; *nocentissima victōria,* a very hurtful victory.

391 A participle, agreeing with a noun in any case, often expresses within one sentence what might be expressed by a dependent or a co-ordinate clause:

Sæpe sequēns agnam lupus est a vōce retentus.   Ovid
Often, when following a lamb, the wolf has been
held back by his voice.

Elephantēs, amnem trānsitūrī, minimōs præmittunt.   Pliny
Elephants, intending to cross a river, send forward the
smallest ones.

Timotheus ā patre acceptam glōriam multīs auxit   Nepos
virtūtibus.
Timotheus increased by many virtues the glory which
he had received from his father.

Sacrās iaculātus arcēs terruit urbem.   Horace
He has smitten the sacred towers and terrified the city.

Cæsar mīlitēs hortātus castra mōvit.   Cæsar
Cæsar addressed the soldiers, and moved his camp.

---

392   **Note 1:** Generally speaking, only deponent verbs have an active perfect participle; in other verbs its place is supplied either by a finite active verb with the relative or a particle, or by the **ablative absolute** passive:

The enemy, having thrown away their arms, fled, can be expressed in Latin by

$$\text{Hostēs} \begin{cases} \text{qui arma abiēcerant} \\ \text{cum arma abiēcissent} \\ \text{armīs abiectīs} \end{cases} \text{terga vertērunt.}$$

393   **Note 2:** Sometimes when a substantive has a perfect participle in agreement, the substantive must be rendered in English by a genitive, the participle by a substantive: *ademptus Hector*, Hector's removal (or the removal of Hector); *ante urbem conditam*, before the foundation of the city.

Terra mūtāta nōn mūtat mōrēs.   Livy
Change of country does not change character.

Note on the Verb Infinite

394   The infinitive, the gerund, the supine in *-um* and the participles govern the same cases as the finite verbs to which they belong.

Ingenuās didicisse fidēliter artēs ēmollit mōrēs.   Ovid
To have truly learned the liberal arts refines
the character.

Cupiō satisfacere reīpūblicæ.   Cicero
I desire to do my duty to the republic.

Rōmæ prīvātīs iūs nōn erat vocandī senātum.   Livy
At Rome private persons did not have the right of
summoning the senate.

Ast ego nōn Graiīs servītum mātribus ībō.   Virgil
But I shall not go to be a slave to Greek matrons.

Ausī omnēs immane nefās, ausōque potītī.   Virgil
All having dared monstrous impiety and having
accomplished what they dared.

ADVERBS

395 **Adverbs** show how, when and where the action of the verb takes place; they also qualify adjectives or other adverbs: *rēctē facere*, to do rightly; *hūc nunc venīre*, to come hither now; *facile prīmus*, easily first; *valdē celeriter*, very swiftly.

Many words are both adverbs and prepositions, as *ante*, before, *post*, after:

Adverbs: *multō ante*, long before; *paulō post*, shortly after.

Prepositions: *ante oculōs*, before one's eyes; *post tergum*, behind one's back.

Joined with **quam** they form conjunctions: *antequam*, before that... *postquam*, after that... (see § 428, 431).

396 **Negative adverbs** are **nōn, haud, nē**. **Nōn**, not, is simply negative:

Nivēs in altō marī nōn cadunt.   Pliny
No snow falls on the high seas.

Haud, not, is used with adjectives, with other adverbs, and a few verbs of knowing and thinking: *haud aliter, haud secus*, not otherwise; *rēs haud dubia*, no doubtful matter; *haud scio an vērum sit*, I am inclined to think it is true.

Nē is used with the second person of the perfect subjunctive for prohibitions (§ 347): *nē trānsierīs Hibērum* (Livy), do not cross the Ebro. With the second person of the present subjunctive **nē** often means lest: *nē forte crēdās* (Horace), lest by chance you believe, *or* that you may not by chance believe.

397 Two negatives make an affirmative, as in English: *nōn sum nescius*, I am not unaware, (that is, I am aware). *Nōn nēmō* means, somebody; *nēmō nōn*, everybody; *nōn nihil*, something; *nihil nōn*, everything.

In ipsā cūriā nōn nēmō hostis est.   Cicero
In the very senate-house there is some enemy.

Nēmō Arpīnās nōn Plancīō studuit.   Cicero
Every citizen of Arpinum was zealous for Plancius.

Note 1: **Neque, nec**, nor (conjunction) is used for **et nōn**:

Rapimur in errōrem, neque vēra cernimus.   Cicero
We are hurried into error, and do not perceive truth.

So also are generally rendered:

and no one,	nec quisquam, nec ūllus;
and nothing,	nec quidquam (quicquam);
and never, nowhere,	nec umquam, nec ūsquam.

398   **Note 2:** **Nē** is used with **quidem** to express not even, and the word or words on which emphasis is laid comes between them:

Nē ad Catōnem quidem prōvocābō.   Cicero
Not to Cato even shall I appeal.

'Not only not...', but not even' is *nōn modo nōn...sed nē... quidem* (or *nē... quidem, nōn modo nōn*).

Nōn modo tibi nōn īrāscor, sed nē reprehendō quidem factum tuum.
I am not only not angry with you, but do not even blame your act.   Cicero

If the predicate of both clauses is the same, it is often expressed only in the second clause with *nē... quidem*, and also the negative is omitted in the first clause – i.e. *nōn modo* is used rather than *nōn modo nōn*.

Adsentātiō nōn modo amīcō, sed nē līberō quidem digna est.   Cicero
Flattering is unworthy, not only of a friend, but even of a free man.

CONJUNCTIONS

399   Conjunctions connect words, sentences, and clauses.

400   (1) **Co-ordinative conjunctions** connect two or more nouns in the same case:

Mīrātur portās strepitumque et strāta viārum.   Virgil
He marvels at the gates and the noise and the pavements.

Et nostra rēspūblica et omnia rēgna.   Cicero
Both our own republic and all kingdoms.

Sine imperiō nec domus ūlla nec cīvitās stāre potest,   Cicero
Without government neither any house nor any state can be stable.

Or they join two or more simple sentences (§ 402).

Note 1:   **Aut... aut** are used to mark an emphatic distinction; **vel... vel** where the distinction is of little importance:

Aut Cæsar aut nūllus.
Either Cæsar or nobody.

Vel magna, vel potius maxima.   Cicero
Great, or rather very great.

Note 2: **Sed** distinguishes with more or less opposition, or passes to a fresh point; while **autem** corrects slightly or continues:

Nōn scholæ sed vītæ discimus. Seneca
We learn not from the school but for life.

Note 3: **Autem, enim, quidem, vērō,** never begin a sentence:

Neque enim tū is es quī quid sīs nesciās. Cicero
For you are not the man to be ignorant of your own nature.

401 (2) **Subordinative conjunctions** (§ 178) join dependent clauses to the principal sentence (see **complex sentence**, § 410 ff.).

Co-ordination

402 When two or more sentences are joined together by **co-ordinative conjunctions**, so as to form part of one sentence, they are said to be **co-ordinate sentences**, and each is independent in its construction.

Et mihi sunt vīrēs et mea tēla nocent. Ovid
I too am not powerless, and my weapons hurt.

Gȳgēs ā nūllō vidēbātur, ipse autem omnia vidēbat. Cicero
Gyges was seen by no-one, but he himself saw all things.

403 The **relative pronoun** with a verb in the indicative often forms a co-ordinate sentence:

Rēs loquitur ipsa, quæ semper valet plūrimum. Cicero
The fact itself speaks, and this always avails most.

Constantēs amīcī sunt ēligendī, cuius
generis magna est pēnūria. Cicero
Firm friends are to be chosen, but of such there is great scarcity.

INTERJECTIONS

404 Interjections are apart from the construction of the sentence. *Ō, ah, eheu, heu, prō,* are used with the vocative, nominative, or accusative; *ēn, ecce,* with the nominative or accusative; *ei, væ,* with the dative only:

Ō fōrmōse puer, nimium nē crēde colōrī. Virgil
O beautiful boy, trust not too much to complexion.

Ō fortūnātam Rōmam! Cicero
O fortunate Rome!

Ēn ego vester Ascanius!	Virgil
Lo here am I your Ascanius!	
Ei miserō mihi!	
Alas! wretched me.	
Væ victīs!	Livy
Woe to the vanquished!	

QUESTION AND ANSWER (for indirect questions, § 420)

405 (a) Single questions are asked by:

    nōnne, expecting the answer yes;

    num, expecting the answer no;

    -ne, expecting either answer;

    an, expressing surprise and expecting answer no.

Canis nōnne similis lupō est?	Cicero
Is not a dog like a wolf?	
Num negāre audēs?	Cicero
Do you dare to deny?	
Potēsne dīcere?	Cicero
Can you say?	
An tū mē tristem esse putās?	Platus
Do you think I am sad?	

Note: Questions are also asked by **interrogative pronouns** (§ 98, 100,102, 327) and **adverbs** (§ 167,168,170).

406 (b) Alternative questions are asked by:

    utrum... an (or).

    num... an (or).

    -ne... an (or).

    ... an (anne) (or).

Hæc utrum abundantis an egentis sīgna sunt?	Cicero
Are these the tokens of one who abounds or lacks?	
Num duās habētis patriās an est illa patria commūnis?	Cicero
Have you two countries, or is that your common country?	
Rōmamne veniō, an hīc maneō, an Arpīnum fugiō?	Cicero
Do I come to Rome, or stay here, or flee to Arpinum?	

Note: A single question is sometimes asked without any particle:

Infēlīx est Fabricius quod rūs suum fodit?   Seneca
Is Fabricius unhappy because he digs his land?

407 For **deliberative questions** the present or imperfect subjunctive is
used:

Quid faciam? roger anne rogem?   Ovid
What shall I do? Shall I be asked or ask?

Tibi ego īrāscerer, mī frater? Tibi ego possem īrāscī?   Cicero
Should I be angry with you, my brother? Could I
be angry with you?

408 **Answer in the affirmative** is expressed:
(a) By repeating the emphatic word of the question, sometimes
with **vērō, sānē, inquam:**

Estne?...est.   Livy   **Dasne?... Dō sānē.**   Cicero
Is it? It is.   Do you grant? I grant indeed.

(b) By **ita, ita est, etiam, sānē, sānē quidem...** :

Vīsne potiōra tantum interrogem?... Sānē.   Cicero
Would you have me ask only the principal matters?... Certainly.

409 **Answer in the negative** is expressed:
(a) By repeating the emphatic verb with **nōn.**

Estne frāter intus?... Nōn est.   Terence
Is my brother within?... No.

(b) By **nōn, nōn ita, minimē, minimē vērō:**

Vēnitne?... Nōn.   Plautus
Did he come?... No.

Nōn pudet vānitātis?... Minimē.
Are you not ashamed of your folly?... Not at all.

Note: **Immō,** nay rather, yes even, is used in answers to correct or modify, either by
contradicting, or by strengthening:

Ubī fuit Sulla, num Rōmæ?... Immō longē āfuit.   Cicero
Where was Sulla? at Rome?... Nay, he was far away from it.

Tenāxne est?... Immō pertināx.   Plautus
Is he tenacious?... Yes, even pertinacious.

410 THE COMPLEX SENTENCE

A complex sentence consists of a principal sentence with one or more subordinate clauses.

Subordinate Clauses depend in their construction on the principal sentence. They are divided into:

A. Substantival   B. Adverbial   C. Adjectival

A. A **substantival clause** stands, like a substantive, as subject or object of a verb, or in apposition.

B. An **adverbial clause** qualifies the principal sentence like an adverb, answering the questions *how? why? when?* Adverbial clauses are introduced by subordinative conjunctions, and are (1) consecutive (so that); (2) final (in order that); (3) causal (because, since); (4) temporal (when, while, until); (5) conditional (if, unless); (6) clauses of proviso (provided that); (7) concessive (although, even if); (8) comparative (as if, as though).

C. An **adjectival clause** qualifies the principal sentence like an adjective. It is introduced by the relative **quī** or by a relative particle, as **ubī** (where), **unde** (whence), **quō** (whither).

411 SEQUENCE OF TENSES

The general rule for the sequence of tenses is that a primary tense in the principal sentence is followed by a primary tense in the clause, a historic tense by a historic tense (§ 105).

PRIMARY

Simple Pres.	**rogō**, I ask	Act.	**quid agās**	what you are doing
Pres. Perf.	**rogāvī**, I have asked	Pass.	**quid ā tē agātur**	what you are doing
		Act.	**quid ēgerīs**	what you have done
Simple Fut.	**rogābō**	Pass.	**quid ā tē āctum sit**	what you have done
Fut. Perf.	**rogāvero**	Act.	**quid āctūrus sīs**	what you are going to do

HISTORIC

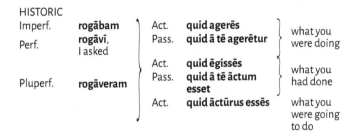

Imperf.	**rogābam**	Act.	**quid agerēs**	what you
Perf.	**rogāvī,** I asked	Pass.	**quid ā tē agerētur**	were doing
Pluperf.	**rogāveram**	Act.	**quid ēgissēs**	what you
		Pass.	**quid ā tē āctum esset**	had done
		Act.	**quid āctūrus essēs**	what you were going to do

Note 1: The historic present (§ 337) and historic infinitive (§ 372) are generally used with historic sequence. The primary perfect indicative has primary sequence in most writers, but Cicero often gives it historic sequence. The perfect subjunctive in its pure use is always primary; in its dependent use, it is generally primary, sometimes historic.

Note 2: For exceptions to the normal sequence of tenses see § 422 note 2, § 433, §467.

---

412 TENSES OF THE INFINITIVE IN INDIRECT SPEECH

If the time of the clause is the same as that of the principal verb, the present infinitive is used.

If the time is before that of the principal verb, the perfect infinitive is used; if the time follows that of the principal verb, the future infinitive.

Dīcō I say	**eum amāre** that he is loving	**amāvisse** has loved	**amātūrum esse** will love
	cōpiās mittī that forces are being sent	**missās esse** have been sent	**missum īrī** will be sent
Dīxī I said	**eum amāre** that he was loving	**amāvisse** had loved	**amātūrum esse** would love
	cōpiās mittī that forces were being sent	**missās esse** had been sent	**missum īrī** would be sent

---

Note: For the supine in -um with **īrī,** may be substituted **fore ut** or **futūrum ut** with the subjunctive: *fore (futūrum esse), ut cōpiæ mittantur, ut cōpiæ mitterentur.*

A. Substantival Clauses

413 Substantival clauses are indirect statements, commands, requests or questions. Their forms correspond to the three direct forms of the simple sentence:

1	DIRECT STATEMENT		1	INDIRECT STATEMENT
	Valeō			**Scis mē valēre**
	I am well			You know that I am well
	Calet ignis			**Sentimus calēre ignem**
	Fire is hot			We feel that fire is hot
2	DIRECT POSITIVE COMMAND OR REQUEST		2	INDIRECT COMMAND OR REQUEST
	Valē			**Curā ut valeās**
	Farewell			Take care that you keep well
	Manē in sententiā			**Ōrō maneās in sententiā**
	Keep firm in your opinion			I beg that you keep firm in your opinion
3	DIRECT QUESTION		3	INDIRECT QUESTION
	Valēsne?			**Quæro an valeās**
	Are you well?			I ask whether you are well
	Quis est?			**Incertum est quis sit**
	Who is he?			It is doubtful who he is

1. Indirect Statement

414 The accusative with infinitive is the most usual form of indirect statement. It may stand:

(a) As the subject of an impersonal verb, or of *est* with an abstract substantive or neuter adjective:

> **Cōnstat lēgēs ad salūtem cīvium inventās esse.**   Cicero
> It is agreed that laws were devised for the safety of citizens.

> **Nūntiātum est Scīpiōnem ad esse.**   Cæsar
> It was announced that Scipio was at hand.

> **Rem tē valdē bene gessisse rūmor erat.**   Cicero
> There was a report that you had conducted the affair very well.

Vērum est amīcitiam nisi inter bonōs esse nōn posse.   Cicero
It is true that friendship cannot exist except between
the good.

(b) As object, after verbs of saying, thinking, feeling, perceiving,
knowing, believing, denying:

Dēmocritus dīcit innumerābīlēs esse mundōs.   Cicero
Democritus says that there are countless worlds.

Pompeiōs dēsēdisse terræ mōtū audīvimus.   Seneca
We have heard that Pompeii has perished in an earthquake.

(c) In apposition:

Illud temerē dictum, sapientēs omnēs esse bonōs.   Cicero
It was rashly said that all wise men are good.

Note: Verbs of hoping, promising, swearing, threatening generally take the accusative with future infinitive:

Spērābam id mē assecūtūrum.   Cicero
I hoped (was hoping) to attain this.

Pollicēbātur pecūniam sē esse redditūrum.   Cicero
He promised that he would return the money.

---

415 A clause formed by **ut** with the subjunctive is used as subject with
impersonal verbs or phrases which express fact or occurrence; it is
also used in apposition, but it seldom stands as object:

Expedit ut cīvitātēs sua iūra habeant.   Livy
That states should have their own laws is expedient.

Mōs erat ut in pāce Ianī templum clauderētur.   Livy.
It was the custom that in time of peace the temple
of Janus was shut.

Extrēmum illud est ut tē obsecrem.   Cicero
The last thing is for me to beseech you.

Note: The accusative with infinitive, or the *ut* clause, used interrogatively, sometimes expresses indignation:

Mēne inceptō dēsistere victam?   Virgil
What! I to be vanquished and abandon my design?

Tē ut ūlla rēs frangat?   Cicero
Can anything break your pride?

416   A clause formed by **quod** with the indicative is used as subject, or in apposition, where a fact is to be dwelt on:

> **Accēdit hūc quod postrīdiē ille vēnit.**   Cicero
> Add to this that he came the next day.

> **Hōc præstāmus maximē ferīs, quod loquimur.**   Cicero
> We excel beasts most in this respect, that we speak.

Rarely as object, after verbs such as *addō, mittō, omittō, prætereō*:

> **Adde quod īdem nōn hōram tēcum esse potes.**   Horace
> Add, moreover, that you cannot keep your own
> company for an hour.

It is also used with verbs of rejoicing and grieving:

> **Dolet mihi quod tū stomachāris.**   Cicero
> It grieves me that you are angry.

> **Gaudē, quod spectant oculī tē mīlle loquentem.**   Horace
> Rejoice, that a thousand eyes behold you speaking.

Note: With verbs of rejoicing and grieving, the accusative with infinitive or the *quod* clause may be used: *Salvum tē advenīre gaudeō* (Plautus). 'I rejoice that you arrive in health' might be, *Gaudeō quod salvus advenīs*.

---

2. Indirect Command, Request or Prohibition

417   A clause depending on a verb of commanding, wishing, exhorting, entreating, is in the subjunctive: if positive, with **ut**; If negative, with **nē**. The clause may stand:

(a) as **subject**;   (b) as **object**;   (c) in **apposition**:

(a)   **Postulātur ab amīcō ut sit sincērus.**   Cicero
      It is required of a friend that he be sincere.

      Nūntiātum est Antōniō nē Brūtum obsideret.   Cicero
      An order was sent to Antony that he should not
      besiege Brutus.

(b)   **Etiam atque etiam tē rogō atque ōrō ut eum iuvēs.**   Cicero
      I urgently beg and pray you to help him.

      Mihi nē abscēdam imperat.   Terence
      He commands me not to go away.

(c)   **Hoc tē rogō, nē dīmittās animum.**   Cicero
      This I beg you, not to lose heart.

Note 1: With *ōrō, rogō, moneō, suādeō, sinō, imperō, cūrō, volō, nōlō, mālō,* and some other verbs, *ut* is often omitted. With *licet, oportet* it is not used. *Idque sinās ōrō;* and I pray that you grant that.

Hæc omnia prætermittās licet.   Cicero
It is allowable to omit all these things.

Note 2: Verbs of willing and desiring, *volō, nōlō, cupiō,* also *iubeō* and many others, frequently take the accusative with infinitive:

Eās rēs iactārī nōlēbat.   Cæsar
He was unwilling to have those things discussed.

Eōs suum adventum exspectāre iussit.   Cæsar
He desired them to await his arrival.

Note 3: Verbs of taking care, effecting, causing, are used with *ut;* verbs of guarding against, with *nē:*

Cūrā et prōvidē ut nē quid eī dēsit.   Cicero
Take care and provide that nothing be wanting to him.

Sōl efficit ut omnia flōreant.   Cicero
The sun causes all things to bloom.

Cavē, beware lest, with *nē* or without a conjunction; *cavē,* take care that, is used with *ut:*

Cavē nē portus occupet alter.   Horace
Beware, lest another forestall you in occupying, the harbor.

Note 4: Verbs of fearing take the subjunctive: with **nē** to express fear that something will happen; with **ut** or **nē nōn** to express fear that something will not happen:

Metuō nē faciat.	**Metuō ut faciat** (*or* **nē nōn faciat**).
I fear he may do it	I fear he may not do it.

418 **Quōminus**, that not (literally 'by which the less'), with the subjunctive, forms a clause depending on a verb or phrase which expresses hindrance or prevention:

Senectūs nōn impedit quōminus litterārum studia teneāmus.   Cicero
Age does not prevent our continuing literary pursuits.

Neque repugnābō quōminus omnia legant.   Cicero
Nor will I oppose their reading all things.

Per Afrānium stetit quōminus proelium dīmicārētur.   Cæsar
It was owing to Afranius that no battle was fought.

419 **Quīn,** that not, with the subjunctive, follows many of the same verbs, and phrases of similar meaning:

Nihil abest quīn sim miserrimus.   Cicero
Nothing is wanting to my being most miserable.

Ægrē sunt retentī quīn oppidum irrrumperent.   Cæsar
They were hardly withheld from bursting into the city.

Note1: The sentence on which *quōminus* depends is generally negative or interrogative, but it may be positive; the sentence on which *quīn* depends is always negative, or virtually negative.

Note 2: Many of these verbs take nē:

Atticus, nē qua sibi statua pōnerētur, restitit.   Nepos
Atticus opposed having any statue raised to him.

Prohibeō takes *quōminus* or *nē*, **vetō** more often *nē*, and both take accusative with infinitive.

3. Indirect Question

420 An indirect question is formed by a dependent interrogative pronoun or particle with a verb in the subjunctive. The clause of the indirect question may be (a) subject or (b) object or (c) in apposition, and the question may be single or alternative:

(a) **Videndum est, quandō, et cui, et quemadmodum,**   Cicero
    et quārē dēmus.
    Care must be taken, when, to whom, how, and why we give.

    Dēmus, necne dēmus, in nostrā potestāte est.   Cicero
    Whether we give or do not give is in our own power.

(b) **Fac mē certiōrem quandō adfutūrus sīs.**   Cicero
    Let me know when you will be here.

    Haud scio an quæ dīxit sint vēra omnia.   Terence
    I am inclined to think that all he has said is the truth.

(c) **Ipse quis sit, utrum sit, an nōn sit, id quoque nescit.**   Catullus
    He knows not even this, who he himself is, whether he is
    or is not.

B. Adverbial Clauses

1. Consecutive Clauses

421a Consecutive clauses define the consequence of what is stated in the principal sentence. They are introduced by **ut**, 'so that,' with a verb in the subjunctive; if negative, by **nōn, ut nōn, ut nihil,** &c.

Ut, in consecutive clauses, usually follows a demonstrative, **adeō, eō, hūc, ita, tam, sīc, tantus, tālis, tot**:

Nōn sum ita hebes ut istud dīcam.	Cicero
I am not so stupid as to say that.	
Quis tam dēmēns est ut suā voluntāte mæreat?	Cicero
Who is so mad as to mourn of his own free will?	
Nēmō adeō ferus est ut nōn mītēscere possit.	Horace
No one is so savage that he cannot soften.	

Note: Sometimes the demonstrative is omitted:

Arboribus cōnsita Ītalia est, ut tōta pōmārium videātur.	Varro
Italy is planted with trees, so as to seem one orchard.	
Clārē et ut audiat hospes.	Persius
Aloud, and so that a bystander may hear.	

421b **Ut** is used in a restrictive sense after **ita**:

Litterārum ita studiōsus erat ut poētās omnīnō neglegeret.	Cicero
He was fond of literature, with the reservation that he cared nothing for poetry.	

421c **Ut consecutive** sometimes follows **quam** with a comparative:

Īsocratēs maiōre ingeniō est quam ut cum Lysiā comparētur.	Cicero
Isocrates is too great genius to be compared with Lysias.	

422 **Quīn,** but that, with the subjunctive, follows phrases and questions such as **nōn**, or **haud dubium est; quīs dubitat?**

Nōn dubium erat quīn tōtius Galliæ plūrimum Helvetiī possent.	Cæsar
There was no doubt that in the whole of Gaul the Helvetii were the most powerful.	
Quis dubitet quīn in virtūte dīvitiæ positæ sint ?	Cicero
Who would doubt that riches consist in virtue?	

Note 1: A consecutive **ut clause** sometimes depends on the phrase *tantum abest* followed by a substantival *ut* clause, the meaning being so far from... that...

**Tantum abest ut nostra mīrēmur, ut nōbīs nōn
satisfaciat ipse Dēmosthenēs.**   Cicero
So far am I from admiring my own productions, that
Demosthenes himself does not satisfy me.

Note 2: In consecutive clauses the sequence of tenses sometimes varies from the general rule. If it is intended to mark the consequence as something exceptional, the primary perfect in the clause may follow the imperfect or historic perfect in the principal sentence.

**Nōn adeō virtūtum sterile erat sæculum ut nōn et
bona exempla prōdiderit.**   Tacitus
The age was not so bare of virtues that it has not furnished
some good examples.

(For consecutive clauses with **quī**, see § 452.)

2. Final Clauses

423 **Final clauses** express the aim or purpose of the action of the principal sentence. They are formed by **ut**, or, if negative, by **nē, ut nē,** with the present or imperfect subjunctive:

Veniō ut videam.   **Abiī nē vidērem.**
I come that I may see.   I went away that I might not see.

Ut iugulent hominēs surgunt dē nocte latrōnēs.   Horace
Robbers rise by night that they may kill men.

Scīpiō rūs abiit nē ad causam dīcendam adesset.   Cicero
Scipio went into the country that he might not be
present to defend his cause.

Ut, with a **final clause**, often corresponds to the demonstratives **eō, ideō, idcircō, proptereā, ob eam rem**:

Lēgum idcircō servī sumus ut līberī esse possīmus.   Cicero
We are the bondmen of the law in order that we may be free.

Note 1: A final clause with **ut** or **nē** is used parenthetically in such phrases as: *ut ita dīcam*, so to say; *nē longus sim*, not to be tedious.

Note 2: **Nēdum**, much less (not to say), may take a verb in the subjunctive:

Mortālia facta peribunt,
Nēdum sermōnum stet honōs et grātia vīvāx.   Horace
Mortal deeds will perish, much less can the honor and
popularity of words be lasting.

Note 3: The purpose of action is expressed in many ways, all equivalent to **ut** with a final clause. He sent ambassadors to seek peace may be rendered:

Lēgātōs mīsit ut pācem peterent.
"   "   quī pācem peterent (§ 453).
"   "   ad petendam pācem (§ 285, § 379).
"   "   petendī pācem causā (§ 254, § 379).
"   "   petītum pācem (§ 386).

Note 4: The sequence of tenses in final clauses always follows the general rule.

(For final clauses with **quī**, see § 453.)

3. Causal Clauses

424 **Causal clauses** assign a reason for the statement made in the principal sentence.

425 When an actual reason for a fact is given, **quod, quia, quoniam, quandō, quandōquidem, quātenus, sīquidem,** are used with the indicative (clauses in **ōrātiō oblīqua,** indirect speech, must be understood to be excepted from this and all following rules for the use of the indicative):

Adsunt proptereā quod officium sequuntur;
tacent quia perīculum metuunt.   Cicero
They are present because they follow duty; they are
silent because they fear danger.

Vōs, Quirītēs, quōniam iam nox est, in vestrā tēctā
discēdite.   Livy
Since it is already night, depart, you, Quirites,
to your tents.

Gerāmus, dīs bene iuvantibus, quandō ita
vidētur, bellum.   Livy
Let us wage war, the gods helping us, since so
it seems good.

Note: Quod, quia, quoniam correspond to **eō, ideō, idcircō, proptereā** in the principal sentence:

Quia nātūra mūtārī nōn potest, idcirco vērae amīctiae   Cicero
sempiternæ sunt.
Because nature cannot be changed, on that account
true friendships are everlasting.

426   **Cum**, since, with a causal clause takes the subjunctive even though the reason is vouched for:

> **Quæ cum ita sint, ab Iove pācem ac veniam petō.**   Cicero
> Since these things are so, I ask of Jupiter peace
> and pardon.

Note 1: After *grātulor, laudō, gaudeō, doleō*, **cum**, for the reason that, takes the indicative, if the verb is in the first person:

> **Grātulor tibi cum tantum valēs apud Dōlabellam.**   Cicero
> I congratulate you that you have so much weight with Dolabella.

Note 2: **Nōn quod, nōn quia** take the indicative when they refer to the actual cause of a fact; if they refer to a cause thought of, not actual, they take the subjunctive, and a following clause, with **sed**, gives the true reason:

> **Nōn quia salvōs vellet, sed quia perīre causā indictā nōlēbat.**   Livy
> Not because he wished them to be saved, but because he did
> not wish them to die without trial.

Note 3: For causal clauses with **quī**, see § 454.

---

4. Temporal Clauses

427   **Temporal clauses** define the time when anything has happened, is happening, or will happen.

    The mood of a temporal clause is indicative if its connection with the principal sentence is one of time only, and if the time of each is independent of the other; but, if the time of the clause is thought of as depending on the time of the principal sentence, the mood of the clause is subjunctive.

428   **Ubī, ut** (when), **postquam** (after), **simulac, cum prīmum** (as soon as), **quandō** (when), **quotiēns** (how often) are generally used with the indicative:

> **Olea ubī mātūra erit quam prīmum cōgī oportet.**   Cato
> When the olive is (shall be) ripe, it must be gathered in
> as soon as possible.

> **Ut Hostus cecidit, cōnfestim Rōmāna inclīnātur aciēs.**   Livy
> When Hostus fell, immediately the Roman line gave way.

> **Eō postquam Cæsar pervēnit, obsidēs,**
> **arma poposcit.**   Cæsar
> After Cæsar had arrived there, he demanded
> hostages and arms.

429   **Dum, dōnec, quoad,** while, as long as, take the indicative:

    Hominēs dum docent discunt.   Seneca
    Men learn while they teach.

    **Dum hæc Veiīs agēbantur, interim Capitōlium
    in ingentī perīculō fuit.**   Livy
    While these things were being done at Veii, the
    Capitol was meanwhile in dire peril.

    Catō, quoad vīxit, virtūtum laude crēvit.   Nepos
    Cato increased in the renown of virtue as long
    as he lived.

430   **Dum**, while, is used with the historic present (§ 337), the verb of the
principal sentence being in a historic tense:

    **Dum hæc in colloquiō geruntur, Cæsarī nūntiātum
    est equitēs accēdere.**   Cæsar
    While this parley was being carried on, it was announced
    to Cæsar that the cavalry were approaching.

431   **Dum, dōnec, quoad,** until, and **antequam, priusquam,** before that,
take the indicative when the only idea conveyed is that of time:

    **Milō in senātū fuit eō diē, quoad senātus
    dīmissus est.**   Cicero
    On that day Milo was in the Senate until the Senate
    was dismissed.

    **Priusquam dē cēterīs rēbus respondeō, dē amīcitiā
    pauca dīcam.**   Cicero
    Before I answer about other matters, I will say a few
    things about friendship.

432   But when the idea of expecting or waiting for something comes in,
they take the subjunctive:

    Exspectāte dum cōnsul aut dictātor fiat Kæso.   Livy
    Wait till Kæso become consul or dictator.

433   **Cum,** if it expresses only the time when something happens,
is used with the indicative:

    Dē tē cum quiēscunt probant; cum tacent clāmant.   Cicero
    Concerning you, when they are quiet they approve;
    when they are silent they cry aloud.

**Cum Cæsar in Galliam vēnit, alterīus factiōnis
prīncipēs erant Hæduī, alterīus Sēquanī.**   Cæsar
When Cæsar came into Gaul, the Hædui were chiefs
of one faction, the Sequani of another.

The addition of the demonstratives **tum, tunc, eō,** marks that the
times of the principal sentence and clause correspond more exactly:

Lituō Rōmulus regiōnēs dīrēxit tum cum urbem condidit.   Cicero
Romulus marked out the districts with a staff at the time
when he founded the city.

**Tum cum in Āsiā rēs āmīserant, scīmus Rōmæ
fidem concidisse.**   Cicero
At the time when they had lost their power in Asia,
we know that credit sank at Rome.

434   If the action of the clause with **cum** takes place while that of the principal clause is continuing, or if it quickly follows it, the clause sometimes contains the main statement, while the principal sentence
defines the time (**inverse cum**):

Iam vēr appetēbat cum Hannibal ex hībernīs mōvit.   Livy
Spring was already approaching when Hannibal moved
out of his winter quarters.

Commodum discesserat Hilarus cum vēnit tabellārius.   Cicero
Hilarus had just departed, when the letter-carrier came.

Note: **Cum** with the indicative sometimes expresses what has long been and still
continues:

Multī annī sunt cum Fabius in ære meō est.   Cicero
For many years past Fabius has been in my debt.

435   **Cum** is used in narrative with the imperfect or pluperfect subjunctive,
the verb of the principal sentence being in the perfect or the historic
present (**historic cum**).

Note: It is used with the imperfect for contemporary time, with the pluperfect for
prior time.

**Cum trīgintā tyrannī oppressās tenērent Athēnās,
Thrasybūlus hīs bellum indīxit.**   Nepos
When the thirty tyrants were oppressing Athens,
Thrasybulus declared war against them.

**Cum Pausaniās dē templō ēlātus esset, cōnfestim
animam efflāvit.**   Nepos
When Pausanias had been carried down from the temple,
he immediately expired.

**Cum hostēs adessent, in urbem prō sē quisque
ex agrīs dēmigrant.**   Livy
On the approach of the enemy, they move, each as he
best can, from the country into the city,

---

436   **Note:** In and after the Augustan age the subjunctive is used in temporal clauses for
repeated action like the Greek optative:

Id fētiālis ubī dīxisset, hastam in fīnēs hostium mittēbat.   Livy
As soon as a fetial (priest) had thus spoken, he used to fling
a spear within the enemies' boundaries.

**Sæpe cum aliquem vidēret minus bene vestītum,
suum amīculum dedit.**   Nepos
Often when he saw someone ill dressed, he gave him
his own cloak.

But **cum is** used down to the time of Cicero and Cæsar (inclusive) with the indicative
for repeated action; in reference to present time with the perfect, in reference to
past time with the pluperfect:

Verrēs cum rosam vīderat, incipere ver arbitrābatur.   Cicero
Whenever Verres saw a rose, he considered that Spring
was comencing.

---

5. Conditional Clauses

437   **Conditional statements** consist of a clause introduced by **sī** (if), **nisī**
(unless), containing the preliminary condition, which is called the
protasis, and a principal clause, containing that which follows from
the condition, which is called the **apodosis**. They have two chief
forms:

(1) where the indicative is used in both protasis and apodosis;
(2) where the subjunctive is used in both.

A primary tense in the protasis is usually followed by a primary in the
apodosis, and a historic by a historic.

438   (1) The indicative is used in the **sī**-clause and in the principal sentence
when the truth of the one statement depends on the truth of the
other; if one is a fact, the other is also a fact:

Sī valēs, bene est.   Cicero
If you are in good health, all is well.

Parvī sunt forīs arma, nisi est cōnsilium domī.   Cicero
Arms are of little avail abroad, unless there is
counsel at home.

Sī fēceris id quod ostendis, magnam habēbō grātiam.   Cicero
If you do what you offer, I shall be very grateful.

Sī quod erat grande vās, lætī adferēbant.   Cicero
If there was any large vessel, they gladly produced it.

Sī licuit, patris pecūniam rēctē abstulit fīlius.   Cicero
If it was lawful, the son rightly took his father's money.

Note 1: A sī-clause with the indicative is often used with the imperative:

Sī mē amās, paullum hīc ades.   Horace
If you love me, stand by me here a short time.

Causam investīgātō, sī poteris.   Cicero
Search out the cause if you can.

Note 2: A sī-clause with the indicative can follow a subjunctive (optative use):

Moriar, sī vēra nōn loquor.   Cicero
May I die if I am not speaking the truth.

---

439   (2) The **subjunctive** is used both in the **sī**-clause and in the principal
sentence when the condition is imaginary:

> (a) The **present subjunctive** is used when the statements are
> thought of as possible, more or less probable:

Sexcenta memorem, sī sit ōtium.   Plautus
I could mention endless things, had I leisure.

Sī ā corōnā relictus sim, nōn queam dīcere.   Cicero
If I were forsaken by my circle of hearers,
I should not be able to speak.

> (b) The **historic subjunctive** is used when the statements are
> purely imaginary; when there is no possibility of their becom-
> ing actual:

Sī foret in terrīs, rīdēret Dēmocritus.   Horace
Democritus would be laughing, if he were upon earth.

Sī id scīssem, numquam hūc tulissem pedem.   Terence
If I had known that, I should never have come hither.

Magis id dicerēs, sī adfuissēs.   Cicero
You would have said so all the more, had you
been present.

440 **Note 1:** The indicative may be used in the principal sentence with a **sī**-clause in the subjunctive,

(a) When the truth of the statement in the principal sentence is less closely dependent on the **sī**-clause:

Tē neque dēbent adiuvāre sī possint, neque possunt sī velint.   Cicero
They neither ought to help you if they could, nor can if they would.

(b) When the principal sentence expresses action begun, but hindered by the condition in the **sī**-clause:

Numerōs meminī sī verba tenērem.   Virgil
I remember the measure if I could recall the words.

(c) With the past tenses of verbs of duty and possibility:

Poterat utrumque præclārē fierī, sī esset fidēs in
hominibus cōnsulāribus.   Cicero
Both might have been done admirably if there had been
honor in men of consular rank.

(d) With the past tenses of *esse*, especially in periphrastic conjugation:

Sī ūnum diem morātī essētis, moriendum omnibus fuit.   Livy
If you had delayed a single day, you must all have died.

Et factūra fuit, pactus nisi Iuppiter esset...   Ovid
And she would have done it, if Jupiter had not agreed...

441 **Note 2:** **Sī** is sometimes omitted:

Ait quis, aiō; negat, negō.   Terence
If anyone affirms, I affirm; if anyone denies, I deny.

Note 3: Nisi **forte**, nisi **vērō** are ironical. **Sī nōn** throws the emphasis of the negative on a single word:

Sī nōn fēceris, ignōscam.
If you have not done it, I will pardon (you).

Note 4: **Sīve... sīve (seu), seu... seu (sīve)**, whether... or, *or* whether... if, are used for alternative conditions:

Sīve retractābis, sīve properābis.
Whether you delay or hasten (it).

442 **Note 5:** The following table shows how to convert conditional sentences into ōrātio oblīqua when the apodosis becomes an infinitive clause, and the protasis is subordinate to it.

after a primary tense

1. Sī peccās (peccāvistī), dolēs		1. sī peccēs (peccāveris), dolēre	
2. Sī peccābis, dolēbis		2. sī peccēs,	dolitūrum
3. Sī peccāveris, dolueris		3. sī peccāverīs,	esse
4. Sī peccēs, doleās	Āiō tē,	4. sī peccātūrus sis,	
5. Sī peccārēs, dolērēs		5. sī peccārēs, dolitūrum esse	
6. Sī peccāvissēs	doluissēs	6. sī peccāvissēs,	dolitūrum
7. Sī peccārēs		7. sī peccārēs,	fuisse
8. Sī peccāvissēs, dolērēs		8. sī pecāvissēs, dolitūrum fore	

after a historic tense

Āiebam tē,
1. sī peccārēs (pecāvissēs), dolēre
2. — peccārēs,
3. sī { peccāvissēs,   } dolitūrum
4. — peccātūrus essēs,   } esse

The other four forms remain unchanged.

Note 6: *Sī pecāvissēs, doluissēs* is equivalent to *sī pecāvissēs, dolitūrus fuistī*; and this may either be converted, as above, into the infinitive clause, or into the subjunctive:

Āiō tē, sī peccāvissēs, dolitūrum fuisse.

Hæc talia sunt ut, sī peccāvissēs, dolitūrus fuerīs.

6. Clauses of Proviso

443 **Dum, dummodo, modo,** if only, provided that, take the subjunctive:

Ōderint dum metuant.   Sueton.
Let them hate provided they fear.

Modo nē laudārent īrācundiam.   Cicero
If only they did not praise wrath.

7. Concessive Clauses

444 **Concessive clauses** are introduced by **etsī, etiamsī, tametsī**, even if, **quamquam, quamvīs, licet**, although.

Note: A concessive clause is so called because it concedes, or allows, an objection to the statement in the principal sentence. The rule for mood is the same as in conditional clauses.

445 **Etsī, etiamsī, tametsī** are used (a) with the indicative, or (b) with the subjunctive:

(a)   **Etiamsī tacent, satis dīcunt.**   Cicero
        Even if they are silent, they say enough.

(b)   **Etiamsī nōn is esset Cæsar quī est, tamen
        ōrnandus vidērētur,**   Cicero
        Even if Cæsar were not what he is, yet he
        would be considered worthy of honor.

446 **Quamquam** is used with the indicative:

Quamquam festīnās, nōn est mora longa.   Horace
Although you are in haste, the delay is not long.

447 Quamvīs, licet are used with the subjunctive:

Quamvīs nōn fuerīs suāsor, approbātor fuistī.   Cicero
Although you did not make the suggestion, you
have given your approval.

Licet vitium sit ambitiō, frequenter tamen
causa virtūtum est.   Quintus
Granted that ambition be a fault, yet often it is a
cause of virtues.

---

448 Note 1: Quamquam is used by later writers with the subjunctive, and quamvīs is
often found in poets with the indicative.

Note 2: Ut, nē, cum are occasionally used in a concessive sense, and take the subjunctive:

Ut dēsint vīrēs, tamen est laudanda voluntās.   Ovid
Though strength be wanting, yet must the will be praised.

Nē sit summum malum dolor, malum certē est.   Cicero
Granted that pain be not the greatest evil, is is surely an evil.

Hīs cum facere nōn possent, loquī tamen et scrībere
honestē et magnificē licēbat.   Cicero
These, though they could not so act, were yet at liberty
to speak and write virtuously and loftily.

Note 3: Concessive clauses are sometimes formed without conjunctions:

Nātūram expellās furcā, tamen ūsque recurret.   Horace
Though you drive out Nature with a pitchfork,
yet she will always come back.

---

449 8. Comparative Clauses

In **comparative clauses** the action or fact of the principal sentence is
compared with a supposed condition. When the condition is asserted
as fact, the indicative is used; when the condition is merely supposed,
the subjunctive is employed.

Assimulābō quasi nunc exeam.   Terence
I will pretend to be just going out.

Tamquam dē rēgnō dīmicārētur ita concurrērunt.   Livy
They joined battle as if it were a struggle for the kingdom..

Tamquam sī claudus sim, cum fūstī est ambulandum.   Plautus
I must walk with a stick as if I were lame.

Eius negōtium sīc velim cūrēs, ut sī esset rēs mea.   Cicero
I would wish you to care for his business just as if
it were my affair.

Note: The demonstratives are ita, sīc, perinde, preinde, æquē, similiter.

C. Adjectival Clauses

450 The **relative quī** in its simple use takes the indicative:

Est in Britanniā flūmen, quod appellātur Tamesis.   Cæsar
There is in Britain a river which is called the Thames.

Quis fuit horrendōs prīmus quī prōtulit ēnsēs?   Tibullus
Who was (the man) who first invented terrible swords?

Note: This rule applies to correlatives, quālis, quantus, quot, and to universals,
quisquis, quīcumque, &c. (§ 102):

Nōn sum quālis eram.   Horace
I am not what I was.

Quidquid erit, tibi erit.   Cicero
Whatever there is will be for you.

---

451 But the relative often introduces a **consecutive clause**, final or causal,
with the subjunctive, corresponding to the adverbial clauses with
similar meaning:

452 **Quī** with the subjunctive forms a **consecutive clause** with the meaning 'of such a kind that':

(a) After a demonstrative:

Nōn sum is quī hīs rēbus dēlēcter.   Cicero
I am not one to delight in these things.

Ea est Rōmāna gēns quæ victa quiēscere nesciat.   Livy
The Roman race is such that it knows not how to rest
quiet under defeat.

Nihil tantī fuit quō vēnderēmus fidem nostram
et libertātem   Cicero
Nothing was of such value that we should sell for it
our faith and freedom.

(b) After indefinite and interrogative pronouns, or negatives,
nēmō, nihil, nūllus, etc.:

Est aliquid quod nōn oporteat, etiamsī licet.   Cicero
There is something which is not fitting, even if it is lawful.

Quis est cui nōn possit malum ēvenīre?   Cicero
Who is there to whom evil may not happen?

Nihil est quod tam deceat quam cōnstantia.   Cicero
Nothing is so becoming as consistency.

Note: Quīn for *quī nōn* is similarly used:
**Nēmō est quīn audierit quemadmodum captæ sint
Syrācūsæ.**   Cicero
There is no one who has not heard how Syracuse was taken.

(c) After **impersonal est**, 'there is,' **sunt**, 'there are':

**Sunt qui duōs tantum in sacrō monte creātōs
tribūnōs esse dīcant.**   Livy
There are who say that only two tribunes were elected
on the sacred mount.

but **est quī, sunt quī** take the indicative if they refer to definite
antecedents:

Sunt item quæ appellantur alcēs   Cæsar
There are also (some animals) which are called elks.

(d) After **comparatives with quam**:

Māiōra dēlīquerant quam quibus ignōsci posset.   Livy
They had committed greater offences than could be pardoned.

(e) After **dignus, indignus**:

Dignus est quī imperet.   Cicero
He is worthy to govern.

453   **Quī** with the subjunctive forms a **final clause**, in order that:

**Clūsīnī lēgātōs Rōmam, quī auxilium ā senātū
peterent, mīsēre.**   Livy
The Clusini sent ambassadors to Rome to seek aid
from the senate.

Quō with a comparative introduces a **final clause**, and takes the subjunctive:

Solōn furere se simulāvit, quō tūtior eius vīta esset. Cicero
Solon pretended to be mad in order that his life might
be the safer.

454 **Quī** introduces a **causal clause**, and usually takes the subjunctive:

Miseret tuī mē quī hunc faciās inimīcum tibi. Terence
I pity you for making this man your enemy.

Note 1: Quī causal is sometimes strengthened by **quippe, ut, utpote.**

Note 2: **Nōn quō** is sometimes used for **nōn quod**:

Nōn quō quemquam plūs amem, eō fēcī. Terence
I have not done it because I love anyone more.

Note 3: Quī with the indicative forms a causal clause as a parenthesis:

Quā es prūdentiā, nihil tē fugiet. Cicero
Such is your prudence, nothing will escape you.

455 The rules for the use of **quī** with indicative or subjunctive apply also
to the relative particles **quō** (whither, to which), **quā** (where, in what
way), **ubī** (where), **unde** (whence).

Locus, quō exercituī aditus nōn erat. Cæsar
A place to which there was no approach for the army.

Collēs, unde erat dēspectus in mare. Cæsar
The hills, from which there was a view over the sea.

Quā dūcitis, adsum. Virgil
Where you lead, I am present.

Nē illī sit cēra, ubī facere possit litterās. Plautus
Let him have no wax on which to write.

A clause introduced by a relative particle may be adverbial, unless
the clause distinctly qualifies a noun in the principal sentence:

Antōnius quō sē verteret nōn habēbat. Cicero
Antony had no place to which he could turn.

456 Note 1: **Quī** with the subjunctive sometimes limits a statement: *quod sciam*, so far
as I know; *omnium quōs quidem cognōverim*, of all those at least whom I have known.

457 Note 2: The **relative** is often used at the beginning of a principal sentence to show
the connection with something which has gone before; *quō factō*, this being done;
quā dē causā, for which reason; *quod dīcis*, as to that which you say.

ŌRĀTIŌ OBLĪQUA

458 Ōrātiō oblīqua (indirect speech) is used in reports, whether short or long, of speeches, letters, &c. Indirect statement, command, and question are often contained in the report of one speech by historians, especially by Cæsar, Livy, and Tacitus.

459 In **indirect statement** the principal verbs are changed from the Indicative to the infinitive in the same tense:

Direct	Indirect
Rōmulus urbem condidit.	**Narrant Rōmulum urbem condidisse.**
Romulus founded the city.	They say that Romulus founded the city.

---

460   **Note:** The subject of the original sentence is put into the accusative in indirect speech

---

461 In **indirect commands**, the subjunctive (usually in the imperfect, but sometimes in the present tense) takes the place of the imperative of direct commands:

Direct	Indirect
Īte, inquit, creāte cōnsulēs ex plēbe.	**Hortātus est: īrent creārent cōnsulēs ex plēbe.**
'Go,' he says, 'and elect consuls from the people.'	He advised them to go and elect consuls from the people.

Note: Prohibitions such as *nōlī abīre* become *nē abeat, nē abīret.*

---

462 In **indirect questions in the second person**, the verbs are in the subjunctive (usually in the imperfect or pluperfect tense, but sometimes in the present or perfect):

Direct	Indirect
Quid agis? inquit. Cūr nōn anteā pugnam commīsistī?	**Quid ageret? Cūr nōn anteā pugnam commīsisset?**
'What are you about?' he says; 'Why have you not joined battle?'	[He asked] what he was about [and] why he had not joined battle.

463 **Rhetorical questions**, typucally in the 1st or 3rd person, are generally expressed by the accusative and infinitive:

Direct	Indirect
Cūr ego prō hominibus ignāvīs sanguinem profūdī? Num semper hostēs ad pugnam cessābunt?	Cūr sē prō hominibus ignāvīs sanguinem profūdisse? Num semper hostēs ad pugnam cessātūrōs?

Why have I shed my blood for cowards? Will the enemy always be slow to fight?

Note: Such questions are really statements put for rhetorical effect in an interrogative form. 'Why have I shed my blood for cowards?' means, 'I have shed my blood for cowards – why?' i.e. 'I have shed my blood for cowards to no purpose.' 'Will the enemy always be slow to fight? means 'The enemy will not always be slow to fight.'

---

464 The pronouns **ego, mē, nōs, meus, noster** of **ōrātiō rēcta** (direct speech) are converted in **ōrātiō oblīqua** into **sē, suus**.

Tu, te, vōs, tuus, vester, are converted into **ille, illum, illī, illōs, illīus, illōrum**:

Direct	Indirect
Ego tē prō hoste habēbō; sociī quoque nostrī amīcitiam tuam exuent.	Dixit sē illum prō hoste habitūrum; sociōs quoque suōs illīus amīcitiam exūtūrōs.

I shall regard you as an enemy; our allies also will throw off your friendship.

465 The reflexive pronoun, **sē, suus,** in complex sentences is often used to refer, not to the subject of the principal sentence (§ 316), but to the subject of the clause in which it stands:

> **Nerviōs hortātur nē suī līberandī occāsiōnem dīmittant.**   Cæsar
> He urges the Nervii that they should not lose the opportunity of freeing themselves.

> **Rēx supplicem monuit ut cōnsuleret sibi.**
> The king warned the supplicant that he should take heed for himself.

466 Sometimes **ipse** is used for the sake of clear distinction.

> [Cæsar asked the soldiers:]
> **Quid tandem verērentur aut cūr dē suā virtūte aut dē ipsīus dīligentiā dēspērārent?**   Cæsar
> What cause had they to fear, or why did they despair either of their own bravery or of his carefulness?

SUBORDINATE CLAUSES IN ŌRĀTIŌ OBLĪQUA

467 **Substantival clauses** (§ 413–420) may have clauses subordinate to them; if the verb in such clauses is finite, it is generally in the subjunctive mood, and the construction is called **suboblique**. This construction is seen in the following examples:

**Cæsar ad mē scrīpsit gratīssimum sibi esse
quod quiēverim.**　　　　　　　　　　　　　　　　　Cicero
Cæsar has written to me that it is very pleasing to him
that I have remained quiet.

**Ais, quōniam sit nātūra mortālis, immortālem
etiam esse oportēre.**　　　　　　　　　　　　　　　Cicero
You say that, since there is a mortal nature, there must
also be an immortal one.

**Quotiēns patriam vidēret, totiēns sē beneficium
meum vidēre dīxit.**　　　　　　　　　　　　　　　Cicero
He said that, as often as he saw his country, so often
did he see my service.

**Sapientissimum esse dīcunt eum, cui, quod opus sit,
ipsī veniat in mentem; proximē accēdere illum,
quī alterīus bene inventīs obtemperet.**　　　　　　Cicero
They say that the wisest man is he to whose mind
whatever is needful occurs; that the next to him is he
who turns to account the useful discoveries of another.

Note 1: A relative clause in *ōrātiō oblīqua*, if added merely by way of explanation, may be in the indicative:

**Xerxem certiōrem fēcī id agī ut pōns, quem in Hellēspontō
fēcerat, dissolverētur,**　　　　　　　　　　　　　Nepos
I sent Xerxes word that a plot was being arranged that the bridge
(which he had made over the Hellespont) might be broken down.

The words 'which he had made over the Hellespont' were not part of the message to Xerxes, but are added by the writer for explanation.

Note 2: Dum, while, is used with the indicative, even in *ōrātiō oblīqua:*

Vident sē, dum lībertātem sectantur, in servitūtem prōlāpsōs.
They see that, while striving for liberty, they have themselves fallen into slavery.

468 A finite verb subordinate to a subjunctive is usually in the subjunctive (**subjunctive by attraction**):

> **Mirāris sī nēmō præstet quem nōn mereāris amōrem?**   Horace
> Are you surprised if no one shows you the love which
> you do not deserve?
>
> **Utinam tunc essem nātus quandō Rōmānī dōna**
> **accipere coepissent.**   Sallust
> Would that I had been born when the Romans began
> to receive gifts.

469 A clause may be virtually oblique, with the verb in the subjunctive (**virtual ōrātiō oblīqua**), when it contains the speaker's statement of another person's words or opinions, for which he does not make himself responsible. If the speaker made the statement his own, as being one of fact, the verb would be in the indicative:

> **Laudat Āfricānum Panætius quod fuerit abstinēns.**   Cicero
> Panætius praises Africanus because (as he says) he was
> temperate.
>
> **Cæsar Hæduōs frūmentum, quod pollicitī essent,**
> **flāgitābat.**   Cæsar
> Cæsar demanded of the Hædui the corn which
> (he reminded them) they had promised.
>
> **Themistoclēs noctū ambulābat, quod somnum**
> **capere nōn posset.**   Cicero
> Themistocles used to walk at night because (as he said)
> he could not sleep.
>
> **Alium rogantēs rēgem misēre ad Iovem,**
> **Inūtilis quōniam esset quī fuerat datus.**   Phædr.
> They (the frogs) sent envoys to Jupiter to ask for another
> king, since (as they complained) the one who had been
> given was useless.

NARRATIVE IN ŌRĀTIŌ OBLĪQUA

470 Direct Statement

Indirect Statement

(1) Ars eārum rērum est quæ sciuntur; ōrātōris autem omnis āctiō opīniōnibus, nōn scientiā, continētur; nam et apud eōs dīcimus quī nesciunt, et ea dīcimus quæ nescīmus ipsī. Cicero

(Antōnius apud Cicerōnem docet:) Artem eārum rērum esse quæ sciantur; ōrātōris autem omnem āctiōnem opīniōnibus, nōn scientiā, continērī; quia et apud eōs dīcant quī nesciant: et ea dīcant quæ ipsī nesciant.

Art belongs to the things which are known; but the whole sphere of an orator is in opinion, not in knowledge; for we both speak in the presence of those who know not, and speak of that which we ourselves know not.

(Antonius teaches in Cicero:) That art belongs to the things which are known; but that the whole sphere of an orator is in opinion, not in knowledge; because they both speak before those who know not; and speak of that which they themselves know not.

(2) Cum Germānīs Ædui semel atque iterum armīs contendērunt; magnam calamitātem pulsī accēpērunt, omnem nōbilitātem, omnem equitātum āmīsērunt. Sed peius victōribus Sēquanīs quam Æduīs victīs accidit; proptereā quod Ariovistus, rēx Germānōrum, in eōrum fīnibus cōnsēdit, tertiamque partēm agrī Sēquanī, quī est optimus tōtīus Galliæ, occupāvit. Ariovistus barbarus, īrācundus, temerārius est, nōn possunt eius imperia diūtius sustinērī.

Locūtus est prō Æduīs Divitiacus: cum Germānīs Æduōs semel atque iterum armīs contendisse; magnam calamitātem pulsōs accēpisse, omnem nōbilitātem, omnem equitātum āmīsisse. Sed peius victōribus Sēquanīs quam Æduīs victīs accidisse; proptereā quod Ariovistus, rēx Germānōrum, in eōrum fīnibus cōnsēdisset, tertiamque partem agrī Sēquanī, quī esset optimus tōtīus Galliæ, occupāvisset. Ariovistum esse barbarum, īrācundum, temerārium, non posse eius imperia diūtius sustinērī.

The Ædui have repeatedly fought with the Germans; they have been defeated and have suffered great misfortune; they have lost all their nobles and all their cavalry. But worse has befallen the conquering Sequani than the conquered Ædui, for Ariovistus, king of the Germans, has settled in their dominions and occupied a third part of their territory, which is the best in all Gaul. Ariovistus is barbarous, passionate and violent; his commands can no longer be endured.

Divitiacus said on behalf of the Ædui that the Ædui had fought repeatedly with the Germans; that, having been defeated, they had suffered great misfortune (and) had lost all their nobles, all their cavalry. But that worse had befallen the conquering Sequani than the conquered Ædui, for Ariovistus, king of the Germans, had settled in their dominions and had occupied a third part of their territory, which was the best in all Gaul. Ariovistus was barbarous, passionate and violent; his commands could no longer be endured.

(3) Cōnsulēs scrīpta ad Cæsarem mandāta remittunt, quōrum hæc erat summa:

'In Galliam revertere, Arīminō excēde, exercitūs dīmitte; quæ sī fēceris, Pompeius in Hispāniās ībit.'

In Galliam reverterētur, Arīminō excēderet, exercitūs dīmitteret; quæ sī fēcisset, Pompeium in Hispāniās itūrum.

The Consuls sent back to Cæsar written instructions, of which this was the sum total: 'Return into Gaul, quit Ariminum, and disband your armies; when you have done these things, Pompey will go into Spain.'

(4) Thrasybūlus, cum exercitus trīgintā tyrannōrum fugeret, magnā vōce exclāmat:

'Cūr mē victōrem fugitis? Cīvium hanc mementōte aciem, nōn hostium esse; trīgintā ego dominīs, nōn cīvitātī, bellum īnferō.'

Cūr sē victōrem fugiant? Cīvium illam meminerint aciem, nōn hostium esse; trīgintā sē dominīs, non cīvitātī, bellum īnferre.

Thrasybulus, when the army of the thirty tyrants was in flight, cried aloud: 'Why do you fly from me as your conqueror? Remember that this is an army of fellow-citizens, not of foreign enemies; I am waging war on the thirty tyrants, not on the community.'

(5) Ōrō vōs, Veientēs (inquit), nē mē extorrem egentem, ex tantō modo rēgnō cum līberīs adolescēntibus ante oculōs vestrōs perīre sinātis. Aliī peregrē in rēgnum Rōmam accītī sunt; ego rēx, augēns bellō Rōmānum imperium, ā proximīs scelerātā coniūrātiōne pulsus sum. Patriam rēgnumque meum repetere, et persequī ingrātōs cīvēs volō. Ferte opem, adiuvāte; vestrās quoque veterēs iniūriās ultum īte, totiēns cæsās legiōnēs, agrum adēmptum.

Ōrat Tarquinius Veientēs nē sē extorrem egentem ex tantō modo rēgnō cum līberīs adolēscentibus ante oculōs suōs perīre sinerent: aliōs peregrē in rēgnum Rōmam accītōs; sē rēgem augentem bellō Rōmānum imperium, ā proximīs scelerātā coniūrātiōne pulsum:... patriam sē rēgnumque suum repetere et persequī ingrātōs cīvēs velle: ferrent opem, adiuvārent; suās quoque veterēs iniūriās ultum īrent, totiēns cæsās legiōnēs, agrum adēmptum.

Livy

I entreat you, men of Veii (said Tarquin), not to let me with my young children die before your eyes, banished in destitution from a kingdom lately so great. Others were fetched to Rome from abroad to reign. I, their king, while enlarging by war the Roman empire, was expelled by a wicked conspiracy of my nearest kinsmen. I wish to reclaim my country and my kingdom, and to punish ungrateful citizens. Give me help, assist me; hasten to avenge also your own old wrongs, your legions so often slaughtered, your land taken from you.

PROSODY

471 Prosody treats of the quantity of syllables and the laws of metre. We shall use the terms **light** and **heavy** for syllables in preference to **short** and **long** to avoid confusion with vowel length.

I. GENERAL RULES OF QUANTITY

1. A syllable is **light** when it contains a short vowel followed by a simple consonant or by another vowel: as *păter, děus.*

2. A syllable is **heavy** when it contains a long vowel or diphthong: *frāter, cǽdēs, nēmō.*

3. A syllable containing a short vowel is **heavy** when it is followed by two consonants, or by **x** or **z**: *cānto, sīmplēx, orȳza.*

> **Exception:** A syllable containing a short vowel before a stop followed by a liquid becomes doubtful: *lugŭbre, tenĕbræ, trĭplex.*

4. A syllable containing a long vowel or diphthong becomes light before another vowel, or before *h* followed by a vowel: *prŏavus, trăho, prǽesse.* But in Greek words the syllable remains heavy: *āēr, Ænēas, Enȳo.*

> **Exceptions:** In *fīō, Gāius, Pompēī, dīus, diēī, Rhēa (Silvia)*, the syllable remains heavy. Also note that *præ* in compounds is the only Latin word in which a diphthong occurs before a vowel.

5. A syllable is called **doubtful** when it is found in poetry to be sometimes heavy, sometimes light: *Diāna, fidĕī, rĕī,* and genitives in *-ius,* as as *illius,* except *alīus, alterĭus.*

6. The quantity of a stem syllable is kept, as a rule, in compounds and derivatives: *cădō occĭdō, rătus irrĭtus, flūmĕn flūmĭneus.* Exceptions to this rule are numerous, *lūceo, lŭcerna.*

472 ## II. RULE FOR MONOSYLLABLES

Most monosyllables are **heavy**: *dā, dēs, mē, vēr, sī, sīs, sōl, nōs, tū, vīs, mūs.* However, there are many exceptions.

Exceptions:

Substantives	*cor, fel, lac, mel, os* (bone), *vas* (surety), *vir*
Pronouns	*is, id, qua* (any), *quis quid, quod, quot, tot* (for *hic*, see § 94)
Verbs	*dat, det, it, scit, sit, stat, stet, fit, fac, fer, es* (from *sum*)
Particles	*ab, ac, ad, an, at, bis, cis, et, in, nec, ob, per, pol, sat, sed, sub, ut, vel* and enclitics *-ne, -que, -ve*

473   III. RULES FOR FINAL SYLLABLES

1. Final a is **short**, and thus the syllable is **light**.

> **Exceptions:** Ablatives of first declension: *mēnsā, bonā*; vocatives of Greek names in **ās**, *Ænēā*; and of some in **-ēs**, *Anchīsā*; indeclinable numerals, *trīgintā*;. imperatives of first conjugation: *amā* (but *pută*); most particles in **-a**; *frūstrā, intereā*. (but *ită, quiă*, short).

2. Final e is short and the syllable is **light**: *legĕ, timētĕ, carērĕ*.

> **Exceptions:** Ablatives of the fifth declension: *rē, diē*, with the derivatives *quārē, hodiē*. Cases of many Greek nouns; also *famē*. Adverbs formed from adjectives: *miserē*; also *ferē, fermē* (but *benĕ, malĕ, facilĕ, impūnĕ, temerĕ*, short). Imperatives of the second conjugation: *monē* (but *cavĕ* is doubtful). Also the interjection *ohē*.

3. Final i is **long** and the syllable is **heavy**: *dīcī, plēbī, dolī*.

> **Exceptions:** Vocatives and datives of Greek nouns; *Chlōrĭ, Thyrsidĭ*; but datives sometimes long: *Paridī*. Particles; *sīcubī, nēcubī, nisī, quasī. Mihĭ, tibĭ, sibĭ, ubĭ*, and *ibĭ* are doubtful.

4. Final o is **long** and the syllable is **heavy**: *virgō, multō, iuvō*.

> **Exceptions:** *Duŏ, egŏ, modŏ, citŏ*, and a few verbs: *putŏ, sciŏ, nesciŏ*. In the Silver Age (approximately the first and second centuries of the Christian era) final **ō** was often shortened in verbs and nouns.

5. Final u is **long** and the syllable is **heavy**: *cantū, dictū, diū*.

6. **Finals in c** are **long** and the syllable is **heavy**: *illĭc;* except *nĕc* and *dōnĕc.*

7. **Finals in l, d, t** are **short**, the syllables **light**: *Hannibăl, illŭd, amāvĭt.*

8. **Finals in n** are **short** and the syllables are **light**: *Īliŏn, agmĕn.*

   Exceptions: Many Greek words: *Hymēn, Ammōn.*

9. **Finals in r** are **short**, the syllables **light**: *calcăr, amābitŭr, Hectŏr.*

   Exceptions: Many Greek words: *āēr, crātēr;* and compounds of *pār: dispār, impār.*

10. **Finals in -as** are **long**, the syllables **heavy**: *terrās, Menalcās.*

   Exceptions: Greek nouns of third declension: *Arcăs* (gen. *-ădis*) and accusative plural *lampadăs; anăs,* a duck.

11. **Finals in -es** are **long**, syllables **heavy**: *nūbēs, pariēs, vidērēs.*

   Exceptions: Cases of Greek nouns: *Arcadĕs, Nāiadĕs.* Nominatives of a few substantives and adjectives with dental stems in **-ĕt, -ĭt,** or **-ĭd**: *segĕs, pedĕs, obsĕs, dīvĕs;* also *penĕs.* Compounds of *es: adĕs, potĕs.*

12. **Finals in -is** are **short**, the syllables **light**: *dīcerĭs, ūtilĭs, ēnsĭs.*

   Exceptions: Datives and ablatives in **īs**, including *grātīs, forīs.* Accusatives in **īs**: *navīs;* some Greek nouns in **īs**: *Salamīs. Sanguīs, pulvīs,* are doubtful. 2nd Pers. sing. pres. ind. 4th conj. *audīs;* compounds of *vīs, sīs;* also *velīs, mālīs, nōlīs.* In 2nd pers. sing. fut. perf. the ending is doubtful: *dixerĭs.*

13. **Finals in -os** are **long**, syllables **heavy**: *ventōs, custōs, sacerdōs.*

   Exceptions: Greek words in **-os** (ος): *Dēlŏs, Arcadŏs;* also *compŏs, impŏs, exŏs.*

14. **Finals in -us** are **short**, the syllables **light**: *holŭs, intŭs, amāmŭs.*

   Exceptions: Nominatives from long stems of third declension are long: *virtūs, tellūs, incūs, iuventūs;* the contracted cases of the fourth declension: *artūs, gradūs;* and a few Greek words: *Dīdūs, Sapphūs* (genitive).

15. The Greek words *chelys, Tiphys, Erīnys* have the final syllable **light** and the vocative ending **-y**.

474   IV. ON THE LAWS OF METRE

A **verse** (*versus*, line) is composed of a certain number of feet. A **foot** consists of two or more syllables, of which one has the **ictus** or principal accent, said to be in **arsis** (rise); the other syllable or syllables are said to be in **thēsis** (fall). The principal feet in Latin poetry are the following:

Iambus, one light and one heavy syllable ($\smile$ fall, $-$ rise), *cărō*.

Trochee, one heavy and one light syllable ($- \smile$), *ārmă*.

Dactyl, 1 heavy and 2 light syllables ($- \smile \smile$), *lītŏră*.

Anapæst, 2 light and 1 heavy syllable ($\smile \smile -$), *pătŭlæ*.

Spondee, 2 heavy syllables ($- -$), *fātō*.

Tribrach, 3 light syllables ($\smile \smile \smile$), *tĕmĕrĕ*.

The **spondee** often takes the place of the dactyl in dactylic verse. It may also take the place of the iambus or trochee in certain parts of an iambic or trochaic verse.

The **tribrach** can take the place of the iambus or the trochee in any place but the last, but is more rarely used than the spondee (see § 479).

A light syllable in versification constitutes one **mora** or 'time.' A heavy syllable (= two light) constitutes two moræ, or 'times.'

The **iambus, trochee, tribrach** are feet of three moræ; **dactyl, anapæst, spondee**, are feet of four moræ.

If a word ends in a vowel and the next word begins with one, the two vowels merge: *Phyllid' am' ant' aliās*, for *Phyllida amō ante aliās*; this is called **elision** (*synalœpha*). A vowel and **m** are at the end of a word are treated similarly: *Ō cūrās homin' Ō quant' est in rēbus ināne*, for *Ō cūrās hominum Ō quantum est in rēbus ināne* This is called **ecthlipsis**.

A vowel unelided in such a position is said to be in **hiatus**:

Ter sunt | cōnā ˈtī ĭm ˈpōnere | Pēlio | Ossam.

475   V. METRE AND RHYTHM

(a) Metre

Metre (*metrum*, measure) is used in two different senses:

1. It means any system of versification: which may take its name
   (a) from the foot which prevails in it: dactylic, iambic, trochaic,
   anapæstic, metre; or (b) from the subjects of which it treats: heroic
   (elegiac) metre; or (c) from the musical instrument to which it
   was sung: lyric metres; or (d) from the poet who is said to have
   invented or chiefly used it: Alcaic metre (from Alcæus), Sapphic
   (from Sappho), etc.

2. Some part of a verse is called 'a metre'. In dactylic and some other
   verses each foot constitutes a metre. In iambic, trochaic, and
   anapæstic verses, two feet constitute a metre.

Note: A verse often gains a name from the number of such metres, hence the
terms dimeter, trimeter, tetrameter, pentameter, hexameter. A verse which has its
metres complete is said to be **acatalectic** (unclipped). If its metres are incomplete, it
is **catalectic** (clipped).

---

476   (b) Rhythm

Harmonious order of words is called **rhythm**. Prose has rhythm as
well as verse; but that of verse is called **poetic rhythm**. The dividing
of a verse according to rhythm is called **scanning** or **scansion**. The
method of scansion may be shown by two dactylic hexameters of
Virgil :

1	2	3	4	5	6

(a) Tītyre | tū || patu | læ || recu | bāns || sub | tegmine | fāgī

(b) Fōrmō | sam || reso | nāre || do | cēs || Ama | ryllida | silvās.

Note: The numerals and single strokes show the six feet or metres of the hexameter. The short double strokes mark **cæsuras** (see below). Remember that a short
vowel does not necessarily mean a light syllable. For instance, *sub* in (a) above is
heavy because the the short vowel **u** is followed by two consonants, **b** and **t**.

Cæsura means the division of a word before the ending of a foot. There are three cæsuras in each of the verses (a), (b), marked by a short double stroke. A verse without cæsura is unrhythmical and inadmissible. Cæsura after a long syllable is called strong, and is most frequent. Cæsura after a short syllable is called weak, as that in the third foot of (b) after -*nāre* (see dactylic hexameter § 477 below). The ending of word and foot together is called **diæresis**, as in *Tityre* and *tegmine* in line (a) above.

VI. DACTYLIC, IAMBIC AND SOME LYRIC SYSTEMS OF VERSE

477   (a) Dactylic Hexameter:

This metre has six feet. The first four may be dactyls or spondees. The fifth must be a dactyl (or rarely a spondee). The sixth a spondee or trochee, for the last syllable in a verse may be heavy or light.

Scheme

1	2	3	4	5	6
$- \smile \smile$	$- \smile \smile$	$- \smile \smile$	$- \smile \smile$	$- \smile \smile$	$- \smile$
$- -$	$- -$	$- -$	$- -$	$- \smile \smile$	$- -$

(See the examples, a, b, § 476)

Note: A verse called **hypermeter** (a syllable over-measure) is occasionally found, the syllable in excess being elided before the initial vowel of the next line:

Ærea | cui gradi|bus sur|gēbant | līmina nēxæ|qu[e]
Ære tra|bēs...

The cæsura by far most common in dactylic hexameters is that in the third foot (called **penthemimeral**), which is generally strong, as in (a) after *patulæ*, but occasionally weak, as in (b) after *resonāre*.

Next in importance is that in the fourth foot (called **hephthemimeral**) which is sometimes the chief cæsura of the verse, as here:

(c) clāmōr|ēs || simul | horren|dōs || ad | sīdera | tollit.

The **trihemimeral cæsura** in the second foot often contributes to the rhythm usefully, as after *clāmōrēs* (c).

Note: *Hemimeris* means 'a half.' Hence, *Trihemimeral* means 'after three half-feet': clā-mōr-ēs; *Penthemimeral* means 'after five half-feet': *hīc il-lum vī-dī*; *Hephthemimeral* means 'after seven half-feet': *quam lūnō fertur terrīs*. This notation counts two short syllables as one half-foot: *Tītyre tū patu-læ recu-bāns.*

The **heroic measure** of epic poets, Virgil, Lucan, &c., consists of dactylic hexameters only.

478 **(b) Dactylic Pentameter**

This verse consists of two parts, called **penthemimers**, which are kept distinct. The first penthemimer contains two feet (dactyls or spondees) and a long syllable. The second contains also two feet (both dactyls) and a long syllable.

Scheme

Example: **tū domi|nus tū | vir‖tū mihi | frāter e|rās.**

This verse is not used alone, but follows a hexameter in the **elegiac distich** (couplet):

Dōnec eris fēlix, mūltōs numerābis amīcōs,
Tempora sī fuerint nūbila, sōlus eris.

The chief Elegiac poets are Ovid, Tibullus, and Propertius.

479 **(c) Iambic Trimeter (as Written by Horace)**

This verse has three 'metres', each of two feet. Each foot may be an iambus:

Suīs | et ip|sa Rō|ma vī | ribus | ruit.

But a spondee may stand in the first, third, and fifth foot; and (rarely) a dactyl or anapæst in the first. A tribrach sometimes takes the place of an iambus, except in the two last feet.

Scheme

1	2	3	4	5	6
⌣ —	⌣ —	⌣ —	⌣ —	⌣ —	⌣ —
— —		— —		— —	
⌣ ⌣ ⌣	⌣ ⌣ ⌣	⌣ ⌣ ⌣	⌣ ⌣ ⌣		
— ⌣ ⌣					
⌣ ⌣ —					

Examples

(a) lābun|tur al|tīs ǀǀ in|terim | rīpīs | aquæ.
(b) Cānid|a brevi|bus ǀǀ im|plicā|ta vī|perīs.
(c) positōs|que ver|nās ǀǀ dī|tis ex|āmen | domūs.

The usual cæsura is after the first syllable of the third foot. Another less usual, is after the first syllable of the fourth foot, as:

Ibē|ricīs | perus|te ǀǀ fū|nibus | latus.

Horace sometimes uses this meter throughout a poem.

Note: The iambic line of six feet called the **sēnārius** is less strict than Horace's trimeter.

480   (d) Iambic Dimeter

This verse leaves out the third and fourth feet of the trimeter, with which it is used to form an iambic distich:

pater|na rū|ra bō|bus ex|ercet | suis,
solū|tus om|nī fæ|nore.

Horace uses this distich more often in his Epodes than any other measure.

481   (e) Lyric Metres

The lyric poets Horace and Catullus used more than twenty metres. But we shall notice here only the **Sapphic** and **Alcaic** stanzas, each of four lines.

> **Note:** Anacrusis is a short or long syllable, which introduces the scansion of a verse. **Base** is a foot of two syllables (spondee, iambus or trochee) which introduces the scansion. These may be represented in English:
>
> Anacrusis   1   2   3
>   O | Mari|on's a | bonnie | lass
>
> Base   1   2   3
>   O my | Mari|on's a | bonnie | lass
>
> A double base means two feet, each of two syllables, introducing the scansion.

482   1. The Sapphic Stanza

The stanza, which takes its name from Sappho, the Greek poetess, is scientifically scanned in Latin by three verses of this form:

Double Base	Dactyl	Trochee	Trochee or spondee

followed by a verse called **Adonius**,

Dactyl	Trochee or spondee

1. Terruit gen|tēs grave | nē re|dīret
2. Sæculum Pyr|rhæ nova | mōnstra | questæ
3. Omne cum Prō|teus pecus | ēgit | altōs
4. Vīsere | montēs.

Sappho often uses a trochee as the second foot of the double base; but Horace always uses a spondee.

The strong cæsura after the fifth syllable is most frequent, but the weak cæsura after the sixth is occasionally used for variety.

Nōn semel dīcēmus ‖ Iō triumphe.

The Adonian verse is so closely united with the third line that hiatus at the close of this line is unusual, and words are sometimes divided between the two:

Thrāciō bacchante magis sub inter-
lūnia ventō.

Note: A hypermeter also occurs (§ 477, note):

Dissidēns plēbī numerō beātō | r(um)
Eximit virtūs.

---

483 **2. The Alcaic Stanza**

	Anacrusis	Double Base	Dactyl	Trochee	
1					
2	⏑̱	— ⏑ — —	— ⏑ ⏑	— ⏑	⏑̱

	Anacrusis	Trochee	Spondee	Trochee	Trochee or Spondee
3	⏑̆	— ⏑	— —	— ⏑	— ⏑̱

	Dactyl	Dactyl	Trochee	Trochee or Spondee
4	— ⏑ ⏑	— ⏑ ⏑	— ⏑	— ⏑̱

1. Quī | rōre pūrō | Castali|æ la|vit.
2. Crī|nēs so|lūtōs | quī Lyci|æ te|net
S. Dū|mēta | nātā|lemque | silvam
4. Dēlius | et Pata|reus A|pollō.

Rules for the Rhythm of the Alcaic Stanza

(a) First and Second Lines

(1) The anacrusis is rarely short.

(2) The fifth syllable generally ends a word; but an elision often occurs after it, as:

Quō Styx et invīs|(ī) horrida Tænarī.

(3) The fifth and the last syllables are rarely monosyllables.

(b) Third Line

(1) The anacrusis is rarely short.

(2) The line rarely begins with a word of four syllables, and only when elision follows, as:

Fūnāli(a) et vectēs et arcūs.

It never begins with two dissyllables.

(3) The line should not end with a word of four syllables and rarely ends with two dissyllables.

(4) No monosyllable should end the line except (rarely) *et* or *in*, with an elision:

    (a)   **Cum flōre Mæcēnās rosār(um), et**
    (b)   **Incūde diffingās retūs(um) in**

(c) Fourth Line.

(1) If the first dactyl ends a word, the second should end in the middle of a word.

(2) A weak cæsura in the second dactyl should be avoided, but is sometimes justified by the sense of the passage:

    (a)   **Iuppiter ipse ruēns tumultū.**
    (b)   **Stēsichorīque gravēs Camēnæ.**

Note: Hypermeters occur only twice in Horace:

    (a)   **Sors exitūra, et nōs in æter|n(um)**
            Exsili(um) impositūra cymbæ.
    (b)   **Cum pāce dēlābentis Etrus|c(um)**
            In mare.

But in his third and fourth books of Odes he avoids ending a verse with a vowel or **m** before a verse in the same stanza beginning with a vowel.

DERIVED AND COMPOUNDED WORDS

Many **substantives** are derived from verbs, adjectives and other substantives. The chief classes of substantives derived from verbs are the following:

484 SUBSTANTIVES FROM THE VERB STEM

-a, denoting the agent: *scrība*, notary (*scrībō*) ; *advena*, newcomer (*adveniō*) ; *convīva*, guest (*convīvō*).

-or, abstract words denoting action or feeling: *amor*, love (*amō*); *timor*, fear (*timeō*); *clāmor*, outcry (*clāmō*); *terror*, terror (*terreō*).

-ium, denoting action or effect: *gaudium*, joy (*gaudeō*); *ingenium*, mind (*ingignō*); *iūdicium*, judgment (*iudicō*, for *iūs-dicō*); *naufragium*, shipwreck (*naufragiō*, formed from the stems of *nāvis*, ship, and *frangō*, break).

-**iēs**, denoting a thing formed: *aciēs*, line of battle (*aceō*); *faciēs*, face, form (*faciō*); *effigiēs*, likeness (*effingō*); speciēs, appearance (*speciō*); *seriēs*, order (*serō*).

-**es**: *sēdēs*, seat (*sedeō*); *nubēs*, cloud (*nūbō*).

-**iō**, denoting the thing acted on: *regiō*, region (*regō*); *legiō*, legion (*legō*); *opīniō*, opinion (*opīnor*).

-**men**, denoting the instrument or the thing done: *agmen*, column (*agō*); *tegmen*, covering (*tegō*).

-**mentum**: *documentum*, document (*doceō*); *īnstrūmentum*, instrument (*īnstruō*).

-**bulum**, -**brum**, denoting the instrument or object: *vocābulum*, name (*vocō*); *vēnābulum*, hunting-spear (*vēnor*); *flābrum*, blast (*flō*, stem *flā-*).

-**culum**, -**crum**: *curriculum*, course (*currō*); *spectāculum*, spectacle (*spectō*); *sepulcrum*, tomb (*sepeliō*).

-**īle**, denoting the instrument: *sedīle*, seat (*sedeō*); *cubīle*, couch (*cubō*).

485 SUBSTANTIVES FROM THE SUPINE STEM

-**tor, -sor**, denoting the agent: *arātor*, ploughman (*arō*); *auctor*, author (*augeō*); *victor*, victor (*vincō*) ; *auditor*, hearer (*audiō*); *dictātor*, dictator (*dictō*); *spōnsor*, surety (*spondeō*); *cursor*, runner (*currō*). A few nouns in -**tor** form a feminine in -**trīx**, as *victrīx*.

-**tus, -sus**, denoting action: *ēventus*, event (*ē-veniō*); *mōtus*, motion, (*moveō*); *sonitus*, sound (*sonō*); *cursus*, running (*currō*); *plausus*, clapping (*plaudō*) ; *lūsus*, game (*lūdō*).

-**tūra, -sūra**, denoting function or result of action: *dictātūra*, dictatorship (*dictō*); *cultūra*, culture (*colō*); *pictūra*, picture (*pingō*); *tōnsūra*, tonsure (*tondeō*); *cæsūra*, dividing (*cædō*).

-**tiō, -siō**, abstract: *āctio*, action (*agō*); *cōgitātiō*, thought (*cōgitō*); *relātiō*, relation (*referō*); *vīsiō*, sight (*video*); *pēnsiō*, payment (*pendō*).

486 SUBSTANTIVES DERIVED FROM ADJECTIVES

-**ia**: *memoria*, memory (*memor*); *concordia*, peace (*concors*); *sapientia*, wisdom (*sapiēns*); *dīvitiæ*, pl., riches (*dīves*).

-**itia**: *lætitia*, joyfulness (*lætus*); *amīcitia*, friendship (*amīcus*); *mollitia*, also *mollitiēs*, softness (*mollis*).

-tās: *lībertās,* freedom *(līber); vēritās,* truth *(vērus); fēlīcitās,* happiness *(fēlīx).*

-tūdō: *fortitūdō,* valor *(fortis); multitūdō,* multitude *(multus).*

-mōnia: *ācrimōnia,* sharpness *(ācer); sānctimōnia,* sanctity *(sānctus); parcimōnia,* parsimony *(parcus).*

487 SUBSTANTIVES DERIVED FROM SUBSTANTIVES

-tor: *viātor,* traveller *(via); iānitor,* doorkeeper *(iānua); balneātor,* bathkeeper *(balneum).* The feminines *iānitrix, balneātrix* are used.

-ātus: *senātus,* senate *(senex); magistrātus,* magistracy *(magister); cōnsulātus,* consulship *(cōnsul).*

-iō, -ō: *lūdiō,* player *(lūdus); pelliō,* furrier *(pellis); centuriō,* captain of a hundred *(centum, centuria); prædō,* robber *(præda).*

-ārius: *aquārius,* water-carrier *(aqua); tabulārius,* registrary *(tabula).* A secondary derivative is *tabellārius,* letter-carrier *(tabella).*

-ārium: *grānārium,* granary *(grānum); tabulārium,* archives *(tabula).*

-ētum, -tum: *olīvētum,* olive-grove *(olīva); rosētum,* rose-garden *(rosa); pīnētum,* a pine-wood *(pīnus); arbustum,* shrubbery; also the later form *arborētum* (stem *arbos-, arbor-); salictum,* willow-ground *(salix).*

-īna, -īnum: *textrīna,* weaver's shop *(textor); pistrīnum,* bakehouse *(pistor).*

-ulus -olus, (-a, -um): *ānulus,* little ring *(annus); gladiolus,* little sword *(gladius); fōrmula,* little form *(fōrma); līneola,* little line *(līnea); scūtulum,* little shield *(scūtum); palliolum,* little cloak *(pallium).*

-ellus, (-a, -um): *agellus,* small field *(ager); fābella,* short story *(fābula); flagellum,* little whip *(flagrum); corōlla,* chaplet *(corōna).*

-culus, (-a, um): *versiculus,* little verse *(versus); mātercula,* little mother *(māter); rēticulum,* little net *(rēte).*

488 ADJECTIVES DERIVED FROM VERBS

-āx: *audāx,* daring *(audeō); rapāx,* grasping *(rapiō); tenāx,* tenacious *(teneō); ferāx,* fruitful *(ferō).*

-bundus, -cundus: *furibundus,* raging *(furō); moribundus,* dying *(morior); iūcundus,* pleasant *(iuvō).*

-uus: *continuus*, continuous (*con-tineō*) ; *vacuus*, empty (*vacō*); *assiduus*, persevering (*assideō*).

-ulus: *tremulus*, trembling (*tremō*); *querulus*, complaining (*queror*); *crēdulus*, trustful (*crēdō*).

-idus, -idis: *calidus*, hot (*caleō*); *pavidus*, timid (*paveō*); *viridis*, green (*vireō*).

-ilis: *ūtilis*, useful (*ūtor*) ; *facilis*, easy (*faciō*); *docilis*, teachable (*doceō*).

-bilis: *penetrābilis*, penetrable (*penetrō*); but sometimes active: *penetrābile frīgus*, penetrating cold; *flēbilis*, lamentable (*fleō*).

-īvus, joined to the supine stem: *captīvus*, captive (*capiō*); *natīvus*, native (*nāscor*); *fugitīvus*, fugitive (*fugiō*).

489 ADJECTIVES DERIVED FROM NOUNS OR ADJECTIVES

-ius: *rēgius*, royal (*rēx*); *plēbēius*, plebeian (*plēbs*); *ēgregius*, out of the common (*grex*).

-icus: *bellicus*, warlike (*bellum*); *barbaricus*, barbarous (*barbarus*); *Gallicus*, Gaulish (*Gallia*); *cīvicus*, civic (*cīvis*).

-ticus: *rūsticus*, belonging to the country (*rūs*); *domesticus*, domestic (*domus*).

-ānus, -iānus: *hūmānus*, human (*homō*); *urbānus*, urban (*urbs*); *Rōmānus*, Roman (*Rōma*); *Āfricānus*, African (*Āfer*); *prætōriānus*, prætorian (*prætor*).

-nus: *frāternus*, fraternal (*frāter*); *æternus*, eternal (*ætās*); *externus*, external (*exter*); *alternus*, alternate (*alter*).

-īnus: *marīnus*, marine (*mare*); *Latīnus*, Latin (*Latium*); *palātīnus*, belonging to the palace (*palātium*).

-estis: *cælestis*, heavenly (*cælum*); *agrestis*, rural (*ager*).

-ēnsis: *forēnsis*, belonging to the forum; *castrēnsis*, belonging to the camp (*castra*).

-ālis, -āris (see § 20): *nātūrālis*, natural (*nātūra*); *generālis*, general (*genus*); *rēgālis*, kingly (*rēx*); *vulgāris*, common (*vulgus*); *salūtāris*, healthful (*salūs*).

-ōsus: *fōrmōsus*, beautiful (*fōrma*); *glōriōsus*, glorious (*glōria*).

-lentus: *fraudulentus*, deceitful (*fraus*); *turbulentus*, noisy (*turba*).

-bris, -cris: *fūnebris*, funereal (*fūnus*), *mediocris*, middling (*medius*).

-eus: *aureus*, golden (*aurum*); *ferreus*, iron (*ferrum*).

-ulus: *parvulus* very small (*parvus*).

-ellus: *misellus* poor (*miser*).

-tus: *modestus*, moderate (*modus*); *rōbustus*, strong (*rōbur*); *vetustus*, aged (*vetus*).

-tinus: *crāstinus*, of tomorrow (*crās*); *diūtinus*, lasting (*dīu*).

490   VERBS DERIVED FROM NOUNS, ADJECTIVES

ā-stems: *cūrō*, take care (*cūra*); *onerō*, burden (*onus*); *pācō*, pacify (*pāx*).
Deponents: *moror*, delay (*mora*); *dignor*, deem worthy (*dignus*); *miseror*, pity (*miser*).
ē-stems: *flōreō*, bloom (*flōs*); *lūceō*, shine (*lūx*); *flāveō*, am yellow (*flāvus*).
u-stems: *metuō*, fear (*metus*); *minuō*, diminish (*minus*).
ī-stems: *fīniō*, limit (*fīnis*); *serviō*, am a slave (*servus*); *largior*, bestow (*largus*).

491   VERBS COMPOUNDED WITH PREPOSITIONS

ā, ab, abs: *āvertō*, turn away; *absum*, am absent; *absterreō*, frighten away.
ad: *adeō*, go to; *adspiciō*, look at; *accipiō*, accept; *adferō* or *afferō*, carry to; *adloquor*, address; *appōnō*, place near; *arripiō*, seize; *adsentior* (or *assentior*), agree; *attrahō*, attract.
ambi-: *ambiō*, go around.
con: *contrahō*, contract; *compōnō*, compose; *committō*, commit; *colligō*, collect; *corripiō*, seize violently; *cōnfīdō*, rely on.
dē: *dēcēdō*, depart; *dēcipiō*, deceive; *dēscendō*, come down.
ē, ex: *ēdūcō*, lead forth; *ēloquor*, utter; *ēvocō*, evoke; *effundō*, pour out; *exeō*, go forth; *expellō*, expel.
in: *īnferō*, bring into; *imperō*, command; *immineō*, overhang; *inligō* or *illigō*, bind on; *irrigō*, water; *indūrō*, make hard.
inter: *intersum*, am among; *interrogō*, question; *intellegō*, understand.
ob: *obtineō*, maintain; *offerō*, offer; *oppōnō*, oppose; *occurrō*, meet, occur.
per: *permittō*, let go, permit; *pereō*, perish; *pellūceō*, shine through, am transparent; *perterreō*, frighten greatly.
post: *postpōnō*, put after.

præ: *præcēdō*, go before; *præferō*, prefer; *præstō*, excel.

præter: *prætereō*, pass by.

prō, prōd-: *prōdeō*, go or come forth; *prōcēdō*, proceed; *prōpōnō*, propose; *prōmō*, produce.

red, re: *redeō*, return; *recordor*, remember; *referō*, refer; *restituō*, restore.

sē: *sēcernō*, separate; *sēparō*, separate; *sēclūdō*, shut up, seclude.

sub: *subdō*, subdue; *submergō*, submerge; *subcurrō or succurrō*, succour; *sufferō*, suffer; *suggerō*, suggest; *supplicō*, supplicate; *surripiō*, steal; *suspiciō*, look up at, suspect.

trāns, trā: *trānsmittō*, transmit; *trānsportō*, transport; *trādūcō*, lead across; *trāiciō*, throw across.

Note: A few verbs are compounded with adverbs, as: *benedīcō*, commend (*bene dīcō*); *benefaciō*, benefit (*bene faciō*) *maledīcō*, speak ill (of) (*male dīcō*); *malefaciō*, do evil (to) (*male faciō*); *satisfaciō*, satisfy (*satis faciō*) ; *satisdō*, give bail (*satis dō*).

---

492 SPECIMENS OF COMPOUND WORDS: NOUN + VERB

auceps, birdcatcher (*avis, avi-capiō*).

agricola, husbandman (*ager, agro-colō*).

fidicen, lute-player (*fidēs-canō*)

tībīcen, flute-player (*tibia, tibi-canō*)

tubicen, trumpeter (*tuba, tubi-canō*)

artifex, artisan (*ars, arti-faciō*).

Lūcifer, morning star (*lūx, lūci-ferō*),

frūgifer, -a, -um, fruit-bearing (*frūx, frūgi-ferō*).

Graiugena, Greek by birth (*Graius, Graio-gignō*).

armiger, armor-bearer (*arma, armo-gerō*).

iūsiūrandum, oath (*iūs-iūrō*).

senātūscōnsultum, decree of the senate (*senātūs-cōnsultum*, from *cōnsulō*).

---

493 TWO SUBSTANTIVES, OR SUBSTANTIVE + ADJECTIVE

paterfamiliās, father of a family (*pater, familiās*, an old genitive).

rēspūblica, state, republic (*rēs-pūblicus*).

bipēs, two-footed (*bis-pēs*).

tridēns, three-pronged, trident (*trēs-dēns*).

ROMAN MONEY, WEIGHTS, MEASURES, AND TIME

494 MONEY

(a) The **ās** (primary unit) of money was the **lībra**, or pound of 12 ounces (**ūnciæ**), and was thus divided:

ūncia = 1 oz. or $\frac{1}{12}$ of the **ās**.	**septūnx** = 7 oz. or $\frac{7}{12}$ of the **ās**.
sextāns = 2 oz. or $\frac{1}{6}$ of the **ās**.	**bēs** = 8 oz. or $\frac{2}{3}$ of the **ās**.
quadrāns = 3 oz. or $\frac{1}{4}$ of the **ās**.	**dōdrāns** = 9 oz. or $\frac{3}{4}$ of the **ās**.
triēns = 4 oz. or $\frac{1}{3}$ of the **ās**.	**dēxtāns** = 10 oz. or $\frac{5}{6}$ of the **ās**.
quīncūnx = 5 oz. or $\frac{5}{12}$ of the **ās**.	**deūnx** = 11 oz. or $\frac{11}{12}$ of the **ās**.
sēmissis = 6 oz. or $\frac{1}{2}$ of the **ās**.	

(b) Interest rates were expressed in **ūnciæ ūsūræ** = $\frac{1}{12}$ % per month = 1% per annum. **Sextantēs ūsūræ** = $\frac{1}{6}$ % per month, etc.

Assēs ūsūræ = 1 % per month = 12 % per annum. **Assēs ūsūræ** were also called **centēnsimæ: bīnæ centēnsimæ** = 2 % per month = 24 % per year. **Ūnciārium fænus** was 1 *ūncia* yearly per *ās*.

(c) **Hērēs ex asse**   means heir to the whole estate
  Hērēs ex sēmisse, or ⎱
  Hērēs ex dīmidiā parte ⎰ means heir to half the estate
  etc.   etc.

(d) The **sēstertius, sesterce** (= *sēmis tertius*, the third half, i.e. 2½) or **nummus**, was a silver coin equal to 2½ *assēs*, being ¼ of the **dēnārius** (coin of 10 *assēs*). Its symbol is **HS** (for **IIS**, *duo et sēmis*, 2½ *assēs*).

The **sēstertium** (= 1,000 *sēstertiī*) was not a coin, but a sum, and is only used in the plural number, *sēstertia*.

Sēstertia (also represented by **HS**) joined with the cardinal or distributive numbers, denotes so many 1,000 sēstertiī.

The numeral adverbs, joined with (or understanding) *sēstertiī* (gen. sing.), *sēstertium*, or *HS*, denote so many 100,000 *sēstertiī*:

Thus   **HS.X** = *sēstertiī decem*, 10 sesterces

    HS.X̄ = *sēstertia dēna*, 10,000 sesterces

    H̄S.X̄ = *sēstertium deciēns*, 1,000,000 sesterces

(e) Fractions might also be expressed by the ordinals as denominators and the cardinals for numerators (above 1). Thus, ½ is *dīmidia pars*; ⅓ *tertia pars*, etc.; ⅙ *sexta* or *dīmidia tertia* (½ × ⅓); ⅛ *octāva pars* or *dīmidia quārta* (½ × ¼), etc. So ¹⁄₂₁ was *tertia septima* (⅓ × ½). Again, ⅔ was *duæ tertiæ*, or *duæ partēs*, or *dīmidia et sexta* (½ + ⅙ = ⁴⁄₆ = ⅔). And ¾ is *trēs quārtæ*, or *trēs partēs*, or *dīmidia et quārta* (½ + ¼ = ¾).

495 WEIGHT

The unit or *ās* of weight was the **lībra**, or Roman pound (the supposed weight which a man could support on his hand horizontally extended). It was divided duodecimally, the **ūncia** (ounce) being its 12th part; the **scrīpulum** (scruple) the 24th part of an *ūncia*. The *ūncia* was approximately 96% of the modern ounce, at about 27.3 g, the *lībra* at 328 g, only about 72% of the modern pound (which, of course, has 16 ounces).

496 LENGTH

The unit or *ās* of length was the **pēs** (foot), also divided duodecimally, the **ūncia** (inch) being its 12th part.

The **cubitum** (cubit) was 1½ *pedēs*. The **ulna** (ell) was variously measured; sometimes = cubit. Land was measured out by the *decempeda* (rod of 10 feet). In roads the unit was the *passus*, pace or double step (5 *pedēs*). *Mille passūs* (5,000 feet) were the Roman mile, ⅛ of which was called a **stadium** (furlong). The exact measure of the *pēs* is a difficult point, but it seems to have been about ³⁄₁₀ inch shorter than an English foot (≈ 0.3m).

497 SURFACE

The *ās* of surface was the **iūgerum** (the Roman acre), about ⅝ of a US or English acre (approx. 0.25 hectares). The **scrīpulum**, or **decempeda quadrāta** (ten square feet) was the most important subdivision of the *iūgerum*.

498   CAPACITY

1. Liquid measure

The *ās* was the **sextārius** (less than a pint), divided into 12 **cyathī** (wine ladles), one of which (its *ūncia*) was only about 45 ml (~3 tbsp). 24 *sextāriī* were 1 **urna** (water jar), and 2 *urnæ* were an **amphora**, a vessel of 10 cubic Roman feet.

2. Dry measure

Here too the *ās* was the **sextārius** and the **cyathus** its *ūncia*; 16 *sextariī* made the **modius**, which was about 2.4 US gallons (approx. 2 gallons avoirdupois, 9 litres).

499   TIME: THE ROMAN CALENDAR

Every Roman month had three chief days: **Kalendæ** (Calends) **Nōnæ** (Nones), **Īdūs** (Ides). The Calends were always the 1st day of the month; the Nones were usually on the 5th; the Ides on the 13th; but in four months the Nones were on the 7th, the Ides on the 15th:

> March, May, July, October; these are they
> Make Nones the 7th, Ides the 15th day.

These three days, the Calends, Nones, and Ides, were taken as points, from which the other days were counted backwards. That is, the Romans did not say, such and such a day after, etc., but such and such a day before the Calends, or Nones, or Ides. They reckoned inclusively, counting in the days at both ends; therefore the rules are: (1) For days before the Calends subtract the day of the month from the number of days in the month increased by two; (2) for days before the Nones or Ides subtract from the day on which they fall, increased by one.

Examples:	May 31	**Prīdiē Kalendās Iūniās.**
	May 30	**Ante diem tertium (a.d. III) Kal. Iūn**
	May 11	**Ante diem quīntum (a.d. V) Īd. Māi.**
	May 2	**Ante diem sextum (a.d. VI) Nōn. Māi.**

THE JULIAN CALENDAR

day of month	MĀRTIUS, MĀIUS, IŪLIUS, OCTŌBER. 31 days	IĀNUĀRIUS, AUGUSTUS, DECEMBER, 31 days	APRĪLIS, IŪNIUS, SEPTEMBER, NOVEMBER, 30 days	FEBRUĀRIUS, 28 days, 29 days in every fourth year
1	Kalendīs	Kalendīs	Kalendīs	Kalendīs
2	a.d. VI	a.d. IV	a.d. IV	a.d. IV
3	a.d. V	a.d. III	a.d. III	a.d. III
4	a.d. IV	Prīdiē	Prīdiē	Prīdiē
5	a.d. III	Nōnīs	Nōnīs	Nōnīs
6	Prīdiē	a.d. VIII	a.d. VIII	a.d. VIII
7	Nōnīs	a.d. VII	a.d. VII	a.d. VII
8	a.d. VIII	a.d. VI	a.d. VI	a.d. VI
9	a.d. VII	a.d. V	a.d. V	a.d. V
10	a.d. VI	a.d. IV	a.d. IV	a.d. IV
11	a.d. V	a.d. III	a.d. III	a.d. III
12	a.d. IV	Prīdiē	Prīdiē	Prīdiē
13	a.d. III	Īdibus	Īdibus	Īdibus
14	Prīdiē	a.d. XIX	a.d. XVIII	a.d. XVI
15	Īdibus	a.d. XVIII	a.d. XVII	a.d. XV
16	a.d. XVII	a.d. XVII	a.d. XVI	a.d. XIV
17	a.d. XVI	a.d. XVI	a.d. XV	a.d. XIII
18	a.d. XV	a.d. XV	a.d. XIV	a.d. XII
19	a.d. XIV	a.d. XIV	a.d. XIII	a.d. XI
20	a.d. XIII	a.d. XIII	a.d. XII	a.d. X
21	a.d. XII	a.d. XII	a.d. XI	a.d. IX
22	a.d. XI	a.d. XI	a.d. X	a.d. VIII
23	a.d. X	a.d. X	a.d. IX	a.d. VII
24	a.d. IX	a.d. IX	a.d. VIII	a.d. VI
25	a.d. VIII	a.d. VIII	a.d. VII	a.d. V
26	a.d. VII	a.d. VII	a.d. VI	a.d. IV
27	a.d. VI	a.d. VI	a.d. V	a.d. III
28	a.d. V	a.d. V	a.d. IV	Prīdiē
29	a.d. IV	a.d. IV	a.d. III	
30	a.d. III	a.d. III	Prīdiē	
31	Prīdiē	Prīdiē		

Column annotations (braces): Nōnās, Īdūs, Kalendās, with month abbreviations Mārt., Māi., Iūl., Oct., Nov.; Iān., Aug., Dec.; Apr., Iūn., Sept., Nov.; Feb., Mārt.

In leap-years, February 24 (a.d. VI Kal. Mārt.) was reckoned twice – hence this day was called **diēs bissextus**, and the leap-year itself **annus bissextus**.

Note 1: *Ante diem tertium (a.d. III) Kal. Iūn.*, means 'on the third day before the Kalends of June,' or 'before the Kalends of June by three days.' *Diem tertium*, being placed between *ante* and *Kalendās*, instead of being an ablative of measure (§ 244, 280), is attracted to the accusative case. This mode of expression became so purely idiomatic that it was used with prepositions: *ex ante diem tertium, ex ante diem sextum*, &c. *Prīdiē*, the day before, takes an accusative.

Note 2: The names of the months are adjectives used in agreement with *mēnsis, m.* expressed or understood, *Iānuārius, Aprīlis, September*, &c. The old names of July and

August were *Quintīlis, Sextīlis* (see next note), but later they were called *Iulius* and *Augustus* after the two Cæsars.

Note 3: The Roman calendar originally contained only ten months: *Mārtius* (31 days), *Aprīlis* (30 days), *Māius* (31 days), *Iūnius* (30 days), *Quintīlis* (31 days), *Sextīlis* (30 days), *September* (30 days), *October* (31 days), *November* (30 days) and *December* (30 days). This meant that there were only 304 calendar days in the year, leaving sixty-odd winter days 'off-calendar'. In about 713 BC. the introduction (attributed to Numa Pompilius) of *Iānuārius* and *Februārius* brought the tally up to 355 days. The Julian Calendar, introduced by Julius Cæsar in 45 BC, consisted of 365 days and a leap-day every fourth year. It was not until AD 1582 that Pope Gregory introduced a minor revision to the Julian Calendar. Great Britain and its colonies (including those in North America) did not adopt the Gregorian Calendar until 1752.

Note 4: The Romans usually distinguished the year by the two consuls holding office, and sometimes by the regnal year of the emperor. The year was also expressed *ab urbe conditā*, from the founding of the city of Rome (traditionally identified as 753 BC).

500 ABBREVIATIONS

(1) Praenomina or forenames

A. Aulus	**M.** Mārcus	**Ser.** Servius
C. Gaius	**M'.** Mānius	**Sp.** Spurius
Cn. Gnæus	**Mam.** Māmercus	**T.** Titus
D. Decimus	**P.** Pūblius	**Ti.** (Tib.) Tiberius
K. Kæsō	**Q.** Quīntus	
L. Lūcius	**S.** (Sex.) Sextus	

Note: A Roman of distinction had at least three names: the **praenōmen**, individual name; the **nōmen**, name showing the **gēns** or clan; and the **cognōmen**, surname showing the **familia** or family. Thus, *Lūcius Iūnius Brūtus* expressed Lūcius of the *gēns* Iūnia and *Familia* Brūtōrum. To these were sometimes added one or more **agnōmina**, titles either of honor (as *Āfricānus, Macedonicus, Magnus*, etc.), or expressing that a person had been adopted from another *gēns*: as *Æmiliānus*, applied to the younger Scīpiō Āfricānus, who was the son of L. Paulus Æmilius, but adopted by a Scīpiō. The full name of the emperor Augustus (originally an Octāvius) after he had been adopted by his uncle's will and adorned by the Senate with a title of honor, was Gaius Iūlius Cæsar Octāviānus Augustus.

(2) Varia

A. D. Ante diem
A. U. C. Annō urbis
  conditæ *or* ab urbe conditā
Æd. Ædīlis
Cal. (Kal.) Calendæ
Cos. Cōnsul
Coss. Cōnsulēs
D. Dīvus
Des. Dēsignātus
Eq. Rom. Eques Rōmānus
F. Fīlius
HS. Sēstertius,
  Sēstertium
Id. Īdūs
Imp. Imperātor
Kal. (Cal.) Kalendæ

L. Lībra
LL. Dupondius
Non. Nōnæ
O. M. Optimus Maximus
P. C. Patrēs Cōnscrīptī
P. M. Pontifex Maximus
P. R. Populus Rōmānus
Pl. Plēbis
Proc. Prōcōnsul
S. Senātus
S. P. Q. R. Senātus
  Populusque Rōmānus
S. C. Senātūscōnsultum
S. D. P. Salūtem dīcit
  plūrimam
Tr. Tribūnus

FIGURES OF SPEECH

501   FIGURES OF SYNTAX

Asyndeton: omission of conjunctions: *Abiit, excessit, ēvāsit, ērūpit.*
Cicero.

Attraction: words are drawn by the influence of others to take
irregular constructions: (1) attraction of copulative verb (§ 196);
(2) attraction of relative and of adjective to relative clause (§ 332).
Attraction of case happens after copulative verbs, especially the
dative (§ 224), and especially with *licet esse*: *Vōbīs licet esse beātis.*
Horace. *Licuit esse ōtiōsō Themistoclī.* Cicero.

Ellipsis (omission): words are left out which can be supplied from the
sense. Thus are used:
  (1) An adjective without its substantive: *gelida, calida* (*aqua*); *dextra,*
  sinistra (*manus*).

(2) A genitive without the word on which it depends: *Cæcilia Metellī (fīlia), Faustus Sullæ (fīlius)*.

(3) A verb without its object: *obīre (mortem); movēre (castra)*.

(4) A sentence without its verb: *Suus cuique mōs. Quid multa? (dīcam)*.

Enallage: use of one word for another:
(1) One part of speech for another: *aliud crās (alius diēs crāstinus)*.
(2) One case for another: *Mātūtīne pater, seu Iāne libentius audīs*. Horace (for *Iānus*.)
(3) One number for another: *nōs* for *ego; mīles* for *mīlitēs*.

Hendiadys: use of two substantives coupled by a conjunction for a substantive and adjective: *Paterīs lībāmus et aurō*, 'we drink from cups and gold' (for *paterīs aureīs*, from 'golden cups'). Virgil.

Hypallage: interchange of cases: *Dare classibus Austrōs*, 'give the winds to the fleets' Virgil. (for *dare classēs Austrīs*, 'give the fleets to the winds') Also attraction of adjectives to substantives to which they do not properly belong: *Fontium gelidæ perennitātēs* – Cicero (for *fontium gelidōrum perennitātēs*).

Hyperbaton: alteration of natural order of words: *Per tē deōs ōrō* (for *per deōs tē ōrō*). The four following figures belong to hyperbaton:

(1) **Anacoluthon**: passing from one construction to another before the former is completed: *Si, ut Græcī dīcunt, omnēs aut Graiōs esse aut barbarōs, vereor nē Rōmulus barbarōrum rēx fuerit*. Cicero (for *Graī sunt aut barbarī*).

(2) **Hysteron-proteron**: when, of two things, that which naturally comes first is placed last: *Moriāmur et in media arma ruāmus*. Virgil.

(3) **Anastrophe**: placing a preposition after its case: *quōs inter* for *inter quōs*. Horace.

(4) **Parenthesis**: interpolation of one sentence within another: *At tū (nam dīvum servat tūtēla poētās), præmoneō, vātī parce, puella, sacrō*. Tibullus.

Pleonasmus (redundance): use of needless words: *Sīc ōre locūta est*. Virgil

Polysyndeton: redundance of conjunctions: *Ūnā Eurusque Notusque ruunt crēberque procellīs Āfricus*. Virgil.

Syllepsis: Connection of a verb or adjective with a composite subject.

Synesis: Agreement with meaning not with form:
1 Gender: *Capita coniūrātiōnis virgīs cæsī sunt.* Livy. *Capita*, though neuter in form, is masculine in meaning, therefore *cæsī*.
2. Number: A collective noun or a phrase implying more than one, though singular in form, may take a plural verb: *Cētera classis... fūgērunt.* Livy. *Optimus quisque iussīs pāruēre.* Tacitus.

Tmesis: separation of the parts of a compound word: *Quæ mē cumque vocant terræ.* Virgil. (for *quæcumque*).

Zeugma: connection of a verb or adjective with two words or clauses to both of which it does not equally belong; therefore zeugma is a sort of ellipsis: *Ex spoliīs et torquem et cognōmen induit;* 'put on the necklace and (assumed) the surname'. Agreement with one only of two or more subjects is also called zeugma.

502 FIGURES OF RHETORIC

Allegoria: a chain of metaphors:

Claudite iam rīvōs, puerī, sat prāta bibērunt.   Virgil
Cease to sing, shepherds, recreation enough has been taken.

Antithesis: contrast of opposites:

Urbis amātōrem Fuscum salvēre iubēmus rūris amātōrēs   Horace
To Fuscus, a lover of the city, I, a lover of the countryside, send greetings.'

Aposiopesis: the conclusion of a thought is suppressed:

Quōs ego – sed mōtōs præstat compōnere flūctūs.   Virgil
Which I – but it is better to quell the raging waves.

Apostrophe: an appeal to some person or thing:

Quid nōn mortālia pectora cōgis, aurī sacra famēs?   Virgil
What don't you force mortal hearts [to do], accursed lust for gold?

Climax: a high point of effect led up to gradually:

Quod libet iīs, licet; quod licet, possunt; quod possunt, audent. Cicero.
If those men may do as they please, if they can do as they may,
if they dare do what they can...

Hyperbole: exaggeration.

Ironia: one thing is said while the contrary is meant, but so that the
real meaning may be understood:

Ēgregiam vērō laudem et spolia ampla   Virgil.
Ignoble praise and paltry spoils

Note: *Vērō* is often used to signal irony.

Litotes: less is said than is meant: *nōn laudō* for *culpō*.

Metaphora: one expression put for another which has some resem-
blance to it in a different kind, generally a concrete for an abstract;
portus for *refugium*; *sentīna* (dregs) *reīpūblicæ* for *turpissimī cīvēs*;
exsultō for *gaudeō*. A strong metaphor is often qualified by *quasi*,
tamquam, *quīdam*, or *ut ita dīcam*: *In ūnā philosophiā quasi taber-
nāculum vītæ suæ allocārunt*. Cicero. *Scōpās, ut ita dīcam, mihi videntur
dissolvere* Cicero (*scōpās disolvere*, literally 'to untie the broom,' here
means 'to throw into confusion').

Metonymia: a related word to *metaphora* meaning that one idea is
put for another. *Mārs* for *bellum*; *cēdant arma togæ* (for *cēdat bellum
pācī*) Cicero; *iuventūs* for *iuvenēs*; *Græcia* for *Græcī*; *aurum* for *vāsa
aurea*.

Oxymoron: union of seeming contraries: *Temporis angustī mānsit concordia discors*. Lucan.

Paronomasia: a play upon the sound of words: *Tibi parāta sunt verba,
huic verbera*. Terence.

Periphrasis: description of a simple fact by various attending circumstances. Instead of 'Now night is approaching,' Virgil says *Et
iam summa procul vīllārum culmina fūmant, māiōrēsque cadunt altīs
dē montibus umbræ*. See the beautiful periphrases of old age and
death in *Ecclesiastes*, ch. xii.

Polyptoton: cases of the same noun are brought together: *Iam clipeus clipeīs, umbōne repellitur umbō; ēnse mināx ēnsis, pede pēs et cuspide cuspis.* Statius.

Prosopopœia: personification. An abstract idea, as faith, hope, youth, memory, fortune, is addressed or spoken of as a person: *Tē Spēs et albō rāra Fidēs colit vēlāta pannō.* Horace.

Simile: illustration of a statement by an apt comparison, as: *Per urbēs Hannibal Ītalās ceu flamma per tædās vel Eurus per Siculās equitāvit undās.* Horace.

Synecdoche: the part stands for the whole: *caput* for *homō*; *tēctum* for *domus*; *carīna* for *nāvis.*

Subject Index

[Note: reference is to sections, not page numbers]

Index of Latin Words

[Note: reference is to sections, not page numbers]

TIGER OF THE STRIPE

Typeset in the United Kingdom
of Great Britain & Northern Ireland
by Tiger of the Stripe,
Richmond, Surrey.

The main typeface is
Alegreya Sans
designed by
Juan Pablo del Peral

CPSIA information can be obtained
at www.ICGtesting.com
Printed in the USA
BVHW070109240221
600901BV00006B/307